W. Brad Johnson, PhD
William L. Johnson, PhD

W9-CKB-724

The Pastor's Guide to Psychological Disorders and Treatments

Pre-publication
REVIEWS,
COMMENTARIES,
EVALUATIONS . . .

"**T**his book is the most comprehensive and clinically sound attempt that I have encountered to help bridge the slippery area between pastoral care and psychological intervention. In this day and age, pastors must be informed and skillful in dealing with a broad range of issues and personalities within their congregations. Due to cutbacks in mental health coverage, pastors will more and more have the responsibility of providing triage for those in mental and emotional distress. This book is a must not merely as a reference on every pastor's shelf, but as a textbook to be studied carefully, whether in seminary or out. Besides extensive and useful descriptions of psychiatric disorders, the authors provide essential guidance for pastors on how, when, and whom to refer parishioners who are in distress. The section on evaluating self-help books alone is worth the price of this book for the tools it provides pastors in navigating through the morass of unscientific, self-promoting, and potentially destructive publications."

Rev. K. Casey Longwood, MDiv
Rector,
Christ Episcopal Church,
Puyallup, Washington

"**S**ome resources belong in a pastor's library. This book is one of them. Good shepherding requires being able to identify parishioners who have mental health issues. Brad and William Johnson have written an excellent handbook for pastors to guide them in assessing psychological concerns that require special care. This work presents complex psychiatric information clearly, systematically, and succinctly in language pastors understand. Each of the major psychiatric disorders is well illustrated by vignettes of parishioners in distress and charts that list symptoms for quick reference. Guidelines and suggestions are also given for appropriate pastoral care for each disorder. This is a 'user-friendly' book for pastors.

Pastors will find the chapter on 'Maladaptive Personalities' worth the price of the book. They will quickly identify folks in their ministry who they thought were simply troubling people, but are in fact troubled people—many of whom may need mental health care along with pastoral care.

Teachers of pastoral care and counseling will find this a useful text. Pastors with little training in pastoral care and counseling will find the chapters on various kinds of psychological disorders helpful, as well as how to select a mental health professional and what to expect from professionals. Even well-trained chaplains, pastoral counselors, and ministers who work in the mental health field will find this a good resource."

David W. Sharrard, ThD
*Professor of Pastoral Care
and Counseling,
Lexington Theological Seminary,
Lexington, Kentucky*

"**J**ust what every pastor needs! Written in understandable language and geared to the particular interests of pastors, this book is a rich resource covering the range of emotional and psychiatric disorders every pastor is likely to encounter. But more than this, it also covers the wide range of therapies used to treat these disorders in such a way that pastors can be better informed about how to make referrals to mental health professionals. I intend to include it in my courses for pastors as required reading."

Archibald D. Hart, PhD, FPPR
*Professor of Psychology
and Former Dean
of the Graduate School of Psychology,
Fuller Theological Seminary*

The Haworth Pastoral Press®
An Imprint of The Haworth Press, Inc.

The Pastor's Guide
to Psychological Disorders
and Treatments

THE HAWORTH PASTORAL PRESS
Religion and Mental Health
Harold G. Koenig, MD
Senior Editor

New, Recent, and Forthcoming Titles:

A Gospel for the Mature Years: Finding Fulfillment by Knowing and Using Your Gifts by Harold Koenig, Tracy Lamar, and Betty Lamar

Is Religion Good for Your Health?: The Effects of Religion on Physical and Mental Health by Harold G. Koenig

Adventures in Senior Living: Learning How to Make Retirement Meaningful and Enjoyable by J. Lawrence Driskill

Dying, Grieving, Faith, and Family: A Pastoral Care Approach by George W. Bowman

The Pastoral Care of Depression: A Guidebook by Binford W. Gilbert

Understanding Clergy Misconduct in Religious Systems: Scapegoating, Family Secrets, and the Abuse of Power by Candace R. Benyei

What the Dying Teach Us: Lessons on Living by Samuel Lee Oliver

The Pastor's Family: The Challenges of Family Life and Pastoral Responsibilities by Daniel L. Langford

Somebody's Knocking at Your Door: AIDS and the African-American Church by Ronald Jeffrey Weatherford and Carole Boston Weatherford

Grief Education for Caregivers of the Elderly by Junietta Baker McCall

The Obsessive-Compulsive Disorder: Pastoral Care for the Road to Change by Robert M. Collie

The Pastoral Care of Children by David H. Grossoehme

Ways of the Desert: Becoming Holy Through Difficult Times by William F. Kraft

Caring for a Loved One with Alzheimer's Disease: A Christian Perspective by Elizabeth T. Hall

"Martha, Martha": How Christians Worry by Elaine Leong Eng

Spiritual Care for Children Living in Specialized Settings: Breathing Underwater by Michael F. Friesen

Broken Bodies, Healing Hearts: Reflections of a Hospital Chaplain by Gretchen W. TenBrook

Shared Grace: Therapists and Clergy Working Together by Marion Bilich, Susan Bonfiglio, and Steven Carlson

The Pastor's Guide to Psychological Disorders and Treatments by W. Brad Johnson and William W. Johnson

Faith, Spirituality, and Medicine: Toward the Making of the Healing Practitioner by Dana E. King

The Pastor's Guide
to Psychological Disorders
and Treatments

W. Brad Johnson, PhD
William L. Johnson, PhD

The Haworth Pastoral Press®
An Imprint of The Haworth Press, Inc.
New York • London • Oxford

Published by

The Haworth Pastoral Press®, an imprint of The Haworth Press, Inc., 10 Alice Street, Binghamton, NY 13904-1580

Cover design by Jennifer M. Gaska.

Library of Congress Cataloging-in-Publication Data

Johnson, W. Brad.
    The pastor's guide to psychological disorders and treatments / W. Brad Johnson, William L. Johnson.
        p. cm.
    Includes bibliographical references and index.
    ISBN 0-7890-0712-6 (hardcover : alk. paper) — ISBN 0-7890-1111-5 (pbk. : alk. paper)
1. Pastoral psychology. 2. Psychiatry and religion. I. Title: Guide to psychological disorders and treatments. II. Johnson, William L., Ph. D. III. Title.
BV4012 .J64 2000
253.5′2—dc21
                                                                                    99-462148

Lovingly dedicated to Rachel H. Johnson,
an extraordinary woman

ABOUT THE AUTHORS

W. Brad Johnson is Assistant Professor of Psychology in the Department of Leadership, Ethics, and Law, United States Naval Academy. He is also Adjunct Professor at the Naval Post-Graduate School, Monterey, California. He earned an MA in theology and a PhD in clinical psychology from the Graduate School of Psychology, Fuller Theological Seminary. A former Navy psychologist, he served at Bethesda Naval Hospital and Pearl Harbor Naval Medical Clinic. He has authored over thirty journal articles and book chapters, and specializes in psychotherapy with religious clients.

William L. Johnson is Professor Emeritus of the Department of Psychology, Whitworth College. He earned his MA and PhD in experimental psychology from the University of Oregon. He is a licensed psychologist and enjoys an active clinical practice. He has written several scholarly articles on self-help materials for Christians and psychotherapy for men. He is an Elder at Whitworth Presbyterian Church in Spokane, Washington.

CONTENTS

Foreword   xi
Jim Singleton

Chapter 1. Why a Pastor's Guide?   1

Chapter 2. The Parishioner in Distress: Major Psychological Disorders, Part I   7

Anxiety Disorders   8
Mood Disorders   17
Psychotic Disorders   25
Brain-Injury/Disease Disorders   32

Chapter 3. The Parishioner in Distress: Major Psychological Disorders, Part II   41

Trauma-Related Disorders   41
Substance Abuse Disorders   48
Sleep Disorders   57
Sexual Disorders   64

Chapter 4. Causing Distress in Others: Maladaptive Personalities   73

Paranoid Personality Disorder   77
Schizoid Personality Disorder   79
Schizotypal Personality Disorder   81
Histrionic Personality Disorder   84
Narcissistic Personality Disorder   87
Borderline Personality Disorder   90
Antisocial Personality Disorder   93
Avoidant Personality Disorder   96
Dependent Personality Disorder   99
Obsessive-Compulsive Personality Disorder   102

Chapter 5. The Family in Distress: Childhood and Relationship Problems   107

Attention Deficit Hyperactivity Disorder   108
Oppositional Defiant Disorder   111

Conduct Disorder   114
Separation Anxiety Disorder   116
Eating Disorders   119
Child and Spouse Abuse   124

Chapter 6. Selecting a Mental Health Professional   **131**

Types of Mental Health Professionals   131
Values and Faith Commitment   134
Experience and Specialties   135
Personal Traits   136
Other Details   136

Chapter 7. Types of Mental Health Treatment   **139**

What Are Counseling and Psychotherapy?   139
Does Psychotherapy Really Work?   141
Should Therapy (and the Therapist) Be Christian?   143
Psychological Assessment and Testing   144
Individual Psychotherapy   151
Marital Therapy   158
Family Therapy   160
Group Therapy   161
Psychiatric Medications   163
Inpatient Hospitalization   174
Alcohol and Drug Treatment Programs   176
Eating Disorder Treatment Programs   178
Hypnosis   179
Electroconvulsive Therapy   181
Fads in Mental Health Treatment   182

Chapter 8. Self-Help Books   **183**

What Is Self-Help?   183
The Value of Self-Help Books   184
Problems with Self-Help Books   185
Books Recommended by Christian Psychologists   188
Summaries of Top-Rated Self-Help Books   191
Guidelines for Evaluating Self-Help Books   199

Chapter 9. Ethical Guidelines: What to Expect from Professionals   **203**

An Ethics Primer   204
Ethical Standards   206
A Strategy for Responding to Unethical Behavior   219

Notes   **223**

Index   **229**

Foreword

People enter the pastoral ministry for a host of reasons and with many different interests. Some focus on communicating the gospel, with preaching as their passion. Others love to teach the faith and find their greatest joy in Christian education. Some are gifted in managing the administrative machinery of a local church and find this their area of interest. Every pastor, however, regularly encounters pastoral care issues that require counseling intervention. Yet only a fraction of ministers feel fully prepared for this significant role in the initial encounter with troubled parishioners. Sometimes the presenting issues seem simple and perhaps routine. Others are complex and difficult to discern. Today's field of psychology is vast and specialized. The knowledge many of us received in a course or two in seminary is rudimentary, and oftentimes we feel ill-equipped to triage people in crisis.

This book is a tremendous resource for pastors who have no extensive specialized training in pastoral counseling. It contains clear explanations of mental disorders and case studies of what our parishioners may experience. It is a rare and rich combination of psychological information placed uniquely in the context of the pastor's role in shepherding a church body. The authors offer guidelines for assessing when a referral to another mental health professional is necessary. The different types of mental health therapists are clearly described, with suggestions for building a referral network that enhances the pastoral work done in the church setting. Through their years of clinical practice and academic teaching, the Johnsons responsibly integrate faith and psychological therapy. In my years in the ministry I have never discovered such a comprehensive resource for pastoral care as this one.

I have had the joy of knowing Bill Johnson for many years, both in the context of a local church and a Christian college. I regularly referred people to his counseling practice and watched these parishioners grow in psychological healing and faith. Bill is one of my most significant spiritual mentors. His son Brad is a recognized leader in psychiatric research, teaching first at George Fox University and now at the United States Naval Academy. Both Bill and Brad bring with them reservoirs of knowledge gleaned from many years of combined teaching. Together they offer pastors a timeless resource, which should be a part of every seminary curriculum and should reside on every pastor's shelf.

Jim Singleton, ThD
Senior Pastor
Covenant Presbyterian Church
Austin, Texas

Chapter 1

Why a Pastor's Guide?

Pastoring may be one of the most difficult jobs in the world. Pastors are called to be active and wise shepherds to a wide range of flawed and fallen human beings. To make matters worse, pastors are also mortal, imperfect, and naturally limited in their capacity to understand and help with every problem and situation presented by their flocks. In addition to preaching, teaching, evangelizing, and generally administering the local church, pastors are likely to spend a great deal of time counseling men and women who come to them with the widest possible array of problem situations and personal concerns. Although some may find themselves particularly gifted when it comes to counseling, and may even find counseling to be the component of pastoring they most enjoy, many others may not feel at all called to this task and some may fear or even loathe the demands of counseling parishioners.

Regardless of how much a pastor does or does not enjoy helping church members with personal problems, survey data suggest that when people experience distress and decide to seek assistance, 40 percent go to their pastor first.[1] As a result, the average pastor reports spending between 10 percent and 46 percent of his or her time counseling. Though many pastors report having comparatively little formal training in assessing and treating emotional and behavioral problems, and often report feeling unprepared to handle some of the problems presented by parishioners, nearly one-half of parishioners will consult with their pastors when distressed.

More than 50 million American adults suffer from mental or addictive disorders at any given time, yet fewer than one-third of them ever receive professional help. This would suggest that pastors and family physicians will be called upon to help individuals and families with a wide range of sometimes quite serious problems. These may include

1

difficult psychiatric syndromes such as depression, anxiety, panic, phobias, drug or alcohol dependence, psychotic disorders, or chronic personality disorders, as well as comparatively less serious concerns such
as marital or sexual problems, low moods, problems with children,
job-related difficulties, grief, and stress-related ailments. Although
many pastors might be undaunted by this list and may have specialized
training in pastoral counseling, most are unlikely to feel qualified to
treat serious emotional or psychiatric problems. In our experience,
there is often a wide range of skill level and confidence among pastors
when it comes to determining which problems to address in counseling
and which to refer to a mental health professional. Consider the
following three case vignettes:

> Marlyce, a thirty-two-year-old divorced mother of two, pres-
> ents for her first pastoral counseling appointment. Marlyce is
> new to your church and you know very little about her or her
> background. In this first counseling session, Marlyce is dressed
> quite provocatively and insists on sitting close to you during the
> session. She then begins to describe a lengthy history of sexual
> abuse and chronic symptoms of depression and suicidal think-
> ing. She has been treated with antidepressant medication for
> several years and episodes of suicidal behavior have resulted in
> at least four psychiatric hospitalizations. In your office she is
> tearful and has frequent outbursts of angry screaming when
> describing her abuse and "all the men" who have "used" her
> over the course of her life. Marlyce ends the session by stating
> that you'll probably turn out like "all the rest" and that she
> feels like hurting herself. She abruptly leaves without schedul-
> ing another appointment to see you.

*   *   *

> Steven is a fifty-one-year-old married construction worker. He
> has been a solid member of the church for three decades and has
> always been a stable family man. Steven began coming to you
> six months ago for "guidance" about feelings of despair and
> hopelessness, which he had never before experienced. He has
> worked diligently in sessions with you on exploring the root of

his depressed mood. He has had no major life changes and appears to have much to look forward to. A recent physical exam showed him to be healthy. He has become even more active in scripture study, prayer, and fellowship opportunities through the church. In spite of this, he begins to appear increasingly disheveled, he sleeps only three to four hours per night, and his wife complains to you that Steven is "barely eating." For the first time in his life, Steven is completely disinterested in sex.

*   *   *

Anthony Jones and his parents call and request an "emergency" appointment with you on Saturday afternoon. Anthony is a sixteen-year-old and the youngest of three Jones children. When the Joneses arrive, it is apparent that a significant crisis has occurred. Anthony sits as far away from his parents as possible and glares at the ground. He has a swollen lower lip. His mother appears horrified and shaken while his father is obviously quite angry. You immediately hear that Anthony's parents discovered a significant amount of methamphetamine in Anthony's bedroom earlier that day. They note that their son had been increasingly secretive and withdrawn during the past year. His grades had slipped and he had begun affiliating with a group of friends with whom his parents are quite uncomfortable. Anthony admits grudgingly that the amphetamine is his, that he "needs it," and that he "will never live with them again," pointing at his parents. At this, Mrs. Jones becomes hysterical. You then learn that Mr. Jones became so enraged with his son that he punched him in the mouth after discovering the drugs in his room.

How would you proceed with these parishioners? What are the primary concerns in each case? Do they suffer from formal psychological disorders? Would it be wise to engage any of them in an ongoing pastoral counseling relationship? Do their presenting symptoms suggest the need for referral to a mental health specialist? What type of professional is indicated? What treatments are likely to be offered? Due to widely varied seminary and postseminary experiences with mental health services and counseling skills, responses to these questions may be remarkably varied among pastors. Rest assured, however, that each of these cases would prove quite challenging to most mental health professionals as well!

Why a *Pastor's Guide to Psychological Disorders and Treatments?* Over the course of our careers, each of us has had the pleasure of working closely with a number of excellent pastors in several different denominations. As psychologists and active church members, we often found ourselves called on by our own pastors, and others in the community, to help with difficult personal problems among church members. Most often, these pastors were providing excellent ministerial care in the sense of tremendous caring, steadfast support, and facilitation of referrals for problems that appeared more serious. However, there were often questions about how to refer parishioners, what signs and symptoms indicated significant pathology, which problems were manageable via counseling, prayer, and pastoral support, and which problems might necessitate more intensive mental health treatment. Pastors wondered about the type of psychiatric disorder indicated by certain symptoms and to which type of professional various members should be referred. They had excellent questions about the type of training indicated by specific degrees and which psychological treatments were most likely to be effective for certain problems. They also experienced ethical and legal quandaries about referring church members and what to do when parishioners had bad experiences with mental health professionals. Finally, there were "crisis" calls regarding how to proceed and who to contact when a member was suicidal or involved in an episode of domestic violence.

We decided to write this guide for our friends. It is for pastors who work hard at meeting their flocks where they are, in the midst of human frailty and an often insane world, and for pastors who have a range of training in mental health care, but seldom an expertise in psychology or psychiatry. This book is designed to be a quick and easy reference source for pastors interested in the essential concerns posed by common psychological (psychiatric) disorders (we use the terms "psychiatric" and "psychological" interchangeably). Four chapters are devoted to a careful summary of the major psychological disorders. We discuss how to select a mental health professional and what kinds of expertise may be indicated by certain degrees and credentials. The most common forms of psychological and psychiatric treatment are highlighted and we emphasize those treatments which are considered most effective. We also describe commonly used psychological tests and the most common psychiatric medications. The most important ethical guidelines and practice standards for mental health professionals are outlined. Finally, an entire chapter is devoted to self-help books, especially those which are recommended by Christian practitioners.

We have written this guide in hope of offering pastors a useful and fruitful resource as they attempt to help children, adults, and families in their churches. We hope it comes to be a tattered and much-referenced guidebook for those who counsel as part of their ministries. Most of all, we hope this guide will serve God's kingdom as pastors find the right services for parishioners in need.

Chapter 2

The Parishioner in Distress: Major Psychological Disorders, Part I

In this chapter, we briefly describe the most prevalent psychiatric disorders that the pastor may encounter in the congregation. We include the following disorder categories: anxiety disorders, mood disorders, psychotic disorders, and brain-injury/disease disorders. In Chapter 3, we describe several additional disorders that are somewhat less prevalent, yet still reasonably common. Although other psychiatric disorders may be found in the American Psychiatric Association's *Diagnostic and Statistical Manual of Mental Disorders,* Fourth Edition, (DSM-IV),[1] we believe our list is fairly comprehensive and that most of the serious mental health problems among parishioners can be located in these two chapters.

For each of the major disorder categories, we offer a *presenting complaints* section, which provides several examples of how this class of disorders might look in everyday life. In other words, we describe how the pastor might first become aware that a parishioner is suffering from a disorder of this type. Next, we summarize the *common features and symptoms* of this class of disorder. We then offer short descriptions of the different *subtypes* of the disorder, including the main symptoms and indicated treatments. For each disorder subtype, we have included a *key indicators* box, which highlights the most important diagnostic criteria. Although many of these key indicators are similar to those in the DSM-IV, we have modified them to enhance readability and reduce technical jargon. For the official diagnostic criteria for each psychiatric disorder, pastors should directly consult the DSM-IV. We conclude our discussion of each disorder with a *summary and guidelines* section, which briefly highlights the major characteristics of the disorder category and recommends specific things for the pastor to consider in caring for the parishioner who may suffer from a particular disorder.

ANXIETY DISORDERS

Presenting Complaints

Mary is a single forty-eight-year-old who has not attended church services for several years. In a conversation with Mary's daughter, you learn Mary has not been out of her house for nearly three years and that her daughter is growing weary of having to take her mother groceries and other goods. She notes that her mother would love to return to church but that "leaving the house makes her fall apart."

*   *   *

Todd is a twenty-one-year-old college senior with excellent grades and tremendous people skills. He has expressed strong interest in becoming a pastor but now seems to avoid the topic altogether. When you bring this change to Todd's attention, he tearfully describes an inability to speak in front of others without trembling, forgetting his speech, and feeling nauseated. He claims to have tried everything to reduce his anxiety but nothing has seemed to help.

*   *   *

Arthur is thirty-five years old and is known in the church as "Mr. Clean." He has never had a serious relationship and has been deemed by his fellow church board members as "impossible to work with." It seems that Arthur becomes obsessed with the minute details of any decision the board must address. He checks and rechecks all figures, will sometimes seek up to twenty bids for minor repair jobs and cannot delegate work to others. At home, Arthur adheres to rigid rituals for eating and cleaning. He becomes very distressed when things are out of place.

Common Features and Symptoms

Anxiety is a universal human emotion. It is a general feeling of apprehension about possible danger. Nearly all human beings experience anxiety from time to time and research indicates that some anxiety may be optimal for many kinds of tasks and performances. It is only when anxiety becomes overwhelming or chronic that it may be classified as an *anxiety disorder*. Each of the major disorders in this category share as a common element an unrealistic, irrational fear or anxiety of disabling intensity. Some of the anxiety disorders are characterized by extreme fear or *panic*. Panic is a basic and primitive emotional state that involves activation of the "fight or flight" response of the sympathetic nervous system.

Like all human emotions, anxiety has three primary components: physiological, subjective (cognitive), and behavioral. The physiological symptoms are those nervous system responses that are normally triggered in all of us when exposed to sudden threat (e.g., sudden air turbulence while flying or the sound of someone approaching rapidly from behind when walking down a darkened street). These symptoms include sweating, rapid heart rate, shortness of breath, nausea, dizziness, hot or cold flashes, trembling, dry mouth, and difficulty swallowing.

Subjective or cognitive components of anxiety are less directly observable from the outside, and we must often rely on the person's direct report of these experiences. Such internal experiences of anxiety include worrying, dread, fear of dying or being humiliated, feeling tense, feeling that things are not real, and the ongoing fear that something awful is about to happen.

The behavioral components of anxiety are more easily observed from the outside. These behaviors may include: pacing; increased speed, volume, and intensity in speech; being easily startled; and a variety of avoidance behaviors. Avoidance behaviors are attempts by the person to avoid those situations viewed as threatening as a means of reducing anxiety. Unfortunately, avoidance usually has some negative consequences. For example, the agoraphobic is fearful of wide open spaces and crowds and therefore avoids the possibility of being in an open or crowded place by staying at home. Obviously, refusing to leave one's home is likely to have adverse occupational and social consequences.

Large-scale population studies of psychiatric disorders in the United States have shown that one type of anxiety disorder, phobias, is the most common category of psychiatric disturbance among women and the second most common among men. The probability that anyone will develop an anxiety disorder at some point in his or her lifetime is about 15 percent.[2] Anxiety problems and reports of various fears were tied with addictions as the third most frequent counseling problem reported by pastors.[3]

As a pastor, it is likely that many of the parishioners you see will suffer from anxiety at one time or another. In addition, anxiety is a common symptom of other types of psychiatric disorder and anxiety symptoms should be a signal that the person is suffering and may need further assistance. A calm and reassuring demeanor is always indicated when exploring the experience of anxiety with a parishioner.

Subtypes

Phobias

A phobia is a persistent and disproportionate fear of some specific object or situation that presents little or no actual danger. There are three major types of phobias: *specific phobia, social phobia,* and *agoraphobia*. We will describe specific and social phobia here and cover agoraphobia in a separate section.

Specific Phobia: Key Indicators

- Marked, excessive, unreasonable, and persistent fear of a specific object or situation (e.g., animals, storms, sight of blood, heights)
- Exposure to the object or situation provokes an immediate anxiety response, which can be as severe as a panic attack.
- The person knows that his or her fear is excessive and unreasonable.
- The person avoids the feared object or situation if at all possible or else endures it with intense distress.
- Avoiding the anxiety significantly disrupts the person's normal activities (e.g., work, school, social activities, and relationships), or the person is quite distressed about having the fear.

Parishioners with any of the specific phobias will usually demonstrate intense, and sometimes incapacitating, anxiety in the presence of the feared object or situation. Interestingly, the person understands the irrational nature of the fear, yet can do little on his or her own to overcome it. Although people can develop phobias to nearly anything, there are some commonalities. For example, nearly half of all Americans are fearful of snakes. Other common forms of specific phobia include *acrophobia* (fear of heights), *claustrophobia* (fear of enclosed places), *mysophobia* (fear of contamination or germs), and *nyctophobia* (fear of darkness).

Treatment for specific phobias generally involves referral to a practitioner with expertise in the use of behavioral and cognitive techniques for anxiety disorders. Systematic desensitization is the most common behavioral technique for treating phobias. It is relatively short term and very often successful. Psychiatrists and other physicians may also prescribe minor tranquilizers for use when the parishioner must face the feared object or situation. However, because phobias are highly treatable with psychotherapy, medication should not generally be the first approach to treatment.

Social Phobia: Key Indicators

- A marked and ongoing fear of one or more social- or performance-focused situations in which the person believes he or she will be evaluated or observed by others.
- The person fears that he or she will act in a way that will be humiliating or embarrassing.
- When exposed to the feared social situation, the person experiences intense anxiety, which may be as severe as a panic attack.
- The person understands the fear is excessive and unreasonable.
- The person attempts to avoid the feared social situation at all costs or endures it only with great discomfort.
- Avoiding the anxiety significantly disrupts the person's normal activities (e.g., work, school, social activities, and relationships), or the person is quite distressed about having the fear.

Socially phobic individuals are extremely anxious about being exposed to the scrutiny of others. They fear they will act in an embarrassing or humiliating manner in front of others. For example, persons with social phobia may be intensely frightened about speaking in front of others, urinating in a public bathroom, or eating or writing in public. Obviously, social phobia could pose a major problem for individuals who desire to serve actively in church leadership. These individuals are likely to avoid social events, opportunities to speak, and even any situation involving public eating or drinking. Although they may appear disinterested in social interaction, they are actually quite fearful.

Treatment of social phobia can be very successful with cognitive-behavioral therapies. Most often, these treatments involve a mixture of exposure to social situations (in vivo training) and cognitive challenges to the person's extreme thinking (e.g., "If people saw me trembling, it would be absolutely awful!"). In severe cases, antianxiety medications can be used to reduce anxiety symptoms during performances. For example, many entertainers use Inderal before major performances or speeches to control the symptoms of speaking anxiety.

Panic Disorder and Agoraphobia

Although panic disorder and agoraphobia are distinct psychiatric disorders, they often coexist and are therefore highly linked in most diagnostic systems. We will discuss them both here and explain why they are so closely connected.

Panic Disorder: Key Indicators

- Unexpected and reoccurring panic attacks. Panic attacks typically last ten minutes or less and involve intense fear or discomfort in which at least four of the following symptoms of panic are present: (1) palpitations, pounding heart, or accelerated heart rate; (2) sweating; (3) trembling or shaking; (4) sensations of shortness of breath or smothering; (5) feeling of choking; (6) chest pain or discomfort; (7) nausea or abdominal pain; (8) feeling dizzy, lightheaded, or faint; (9) feelings of unreality or feeling detached from oneself; (10) fear of losing control or going crazy; (11) fear of dying; (12) numbness or tingling sensations; (13) chills or hot flashes.
- Following the initial panic attack, the person may have persistent concerns about additional attacks, concern about the health implications of the attack, or a seriously restricted lifestyle in anticipation of further attacks.
- The attacks cannot be explained by substance abuse or other medical problems.

Persons with panic disorder live in perpetual fear of experiencing a panic attack. The attacks seem to come "out of the blue" with no apparent warning or trigger. As you can discern from the list of physical symptoms in the key indicators, the panic attack experience can be quite distressing and individuals often report that they believed they were going to die or that they were surely "going crazy." Following their first attack, sufferers will often consult many different doctors searching for explanations. When nothing physical is discovered, the person often lives in constant fear of the next episode, which makes panic disorder particularly debilitating.

Agoraphobia: Key Indicators

- The person is extremely anxious about being in situations in which escape might be difficult or embarrassing, or situations in which help may not be immediately available should symptoms of panic occur.
- The most commonly feared situations include being outside the home alone, being in a crowd or standing in a line, being on a bridge, or traveling in a plane, bus, etc.
- The person can endure these situations only with great difficulty and usually requires a great deal of reassurance.

Agoraphobia and panic disorder often occur together. In fact, agoraphobic avoidance of situations and places is often triggered by experiences of panic as well as the ongoing and increasing anxiety that the person will panic again in a crowded or inescapable situation. As the person avoids more and more anxiety-provoking situations, his or her life can become extremely restricted. In the worst cases, a person may be literally "self-imprisoned" at home. Agoraphobia can also occur without panic attacks. In these cases, the pattern is one of gradually increasing fearfulness of environments outside the home. Lifetime prevalence rates for panic disorder and agoraphobia are between 2 and 5 percent.[4]

As with most psychiatric disorders, the exact causes of panic disorder and agoraphobia are not clear. However, there is strong evidence that both genetic and situational factors play a role. It has been estimated that as many as 80 percent of persons who experience a panic attack have had a stressful life event in the period immediately preceding the attack. Parishioners who suffer from these disorders are bound to be experiencing a great deal of distress. Treatment is more extensive than for phobias and may require a combination of cognitive-behavioral therapy and medication to alleviate the panic symptoms initially. Referrals to both a physician and a practitioner with expertise in treating anxiety disorders is indicated.

Generalized Anxiety Disorder

People with generalized anxiety disorder (GAD) have persistent, uncomfortable, uncontrollable anxiety, the source of which cannot be identified. Freud originally called GAD "free-floating" anxiety because the anxiety did not seem to be connected to a specific object or situation as with specific or social phobias. Generalized anxiety disorder is characterized by chronic, excessive worry about a number of events or activities. These parishioners will be continually tense, worried, and physically upset or anxious. They often worry about bad things that might happen (e.g., loss of a job, financial failure, injury or death of children, etc.). In general, these parishioners live with constant suffering from tension, worry, and vague uneasiness.

Generalized Anxiety Disorder: Key Indicators

- Excessive anxiety and apprehension about a range of events or activities.
- The person finds it difficult to control the worry.
- The anxiety or worry is usually associated with symptoms such as restlessness, fatigue, poor concentration, irritability, muscle tension, and sleep disturbance.
- The anxiety is usually severe enough to interfere with the person's work or relationships.

Parishioners with GAD will truly be suffering. The various symptoms of tension and apprehension associated with this disorder are nearly always unpleasant and, cumulatively, they can fatigue and overwhelm a sufferer. In one study, the most frequently reported experiences of persons with GAD included inability to relax, tension, poor concentration, agitation, feeling frightened, fear of losing control, fear of being rejected, unsteady movement, weakness, and an inability to control one's thoughts.[5] It is likely that effective treatment will require a cognitive-behavioral or interpersonal approach. Referral to a physician is also indicated to rule out a physical explanation for these symptoms.

Obsessive-Compulsive Disorder

Persons with obsessive-compulsive disorder (OCD) are caught in a vicious cycle of obsessions and compulsions. *Obsessions* are persistent, intrusive, unwanted, and inappropriate thoughts that cause the person significant anxiety and distress. The person views these thoughts as beyond his or her control and the thoughts appear quite at odds with things the person might normally think about. Common obsessions include repeated thoughts about becoming contaminated by dirt, germs, or toxins, fearful thoughts that something terrible is about to happen, aggressive or horrible impulses (killing a spouse, parent, or child; shouting blasphemies in church), and sexual thoughts (pornographic images). The obsessive thoughts are usually extremely distressing to the person and may be in obvious conflict with religious values.

Compulsions are either repetitive behaviors or mental activities, the goal of which is to reduce or avoid anxiety and distress—often produced by obsessions. Compulsive acts are not pleasurable for the person, but feel absolutely necessary in order to ward off intense anxiety. Examples of repetitive behaviors include hand washing, placing things in order, counting, and checking. Mental acts may include compulsive praying, counting, or repeating words or phrases.

Obsessive-Compulsive Disorder: Key Indicators

- The person has recurrent obsessions or compulsions.
- At some point, the person has been able to recognize that the obsessions or compulsions are excessive or unreasonable.
- In most cases, the obsessions or compulsions cause substantial distress, take a great deal of the person's time, and seriously interfere with the person's normal routine and relationships.
- During the episodes, the person may or may not have insight about the excessive or unreasonable nature of the obsessions or compulsions.

A connection often exists between a particular obsession and its accompanying compulsion. For example, a person obsessed with dirt and germs may wash his or her hands until the skin is raw. Another person may avoid persistent obsessive thoughts about pornography only by chanting several scriptures in a specific order many times.

These compulsions may cause extreme disruption in the person's life and relationships. It is likely that OCD has several contributing causes, some of which are biological and genetic. Very often, psychiatric medication is required for the person to experience full relief from OCD symptoms. Behavioral approaches, involving exposure to the feared thoughts while preventing the usual compulsions, can also be effective with many sufferers.

Summary and Guidelines

Although the anxiety disorders include a range of specific and distinct syndromes, they are united by the underlying presence of fear or panic as the core emotional state. While panic involves activation of the autonomic nervous system and a number of very primitive self-protective bodily responses, anxiety is a more diffuse emotional state characterized by worry, unrest, and a less specific sense of danger. Parishioners with anxiety disorders may be fearful of specific situations and objects, and each of the disorders is characterized by irrational and excessive evaluation of the danger these situations present.

In nearly every case, we recommend referral of parishioners with extreme and unrelenting anxiety to a physician. Certain cardiologic, neurologic, and endocrine-based illnesses may produce anxiety symptoms that mimic these psychiatric problems. Once these potential problems are ruled out, referral to a mental health service provider with expertise in treating anxiety disorders is recommended. Certain anxiety disorders (e.g., panic disorder and obsessive-compulsive disorder) have been shown to respond best to a combination of drug and psychological therapies. For example, minor tranquilizers (anxiolytics) such as Valium or Xanax have been helpful in creating initial reductions in severe anxiety so that persons can respond to other interventions. Also, antidepressant medications have been used successfully with panic disorder, and Anafranil has shown marked promise in reducing the intensity of OCD symptoms. Of course, certain antianxiety medications can be quite addictive and their use should be closely supervised by a psychiatrist.

Cognitive-behavioral therapies are perhaps the best researched and most often practiced approaches to treating anxiety disorders. Psychologists, psychiatrists, social workers, and others with expertise in this area will help parishioners to reduce maladaptive behaviors, reduce the thoughts that tend to produce anxiety, learn and sharpen adaptive skills (e.g., relaxation, assertiveness, etc.), and approach objects and situations that they have previously avoided. As a pastor, it is critical to communicate to the parishioner that these disorders are highly treatable and that effective treatment is often quite brief. Helping the person to realize that the experience of anxiety is neither abnormal nor catastrophic is an important starting place.

MOOD DISORDERS

Presenting Complaints

Frank, a twenty-eight-year-old parishioner who is relatively new to the congregation, calls you in the middle of the night and excitedly begins to tell you about a wonderful plan he has developed to make the church and the entire denomination completely financially secure by the end of the year. His speech is rapid and pressured and you find it nearly impossible to interrupt his wildly rambling discussion. Frank acknowledges that he has not slept for two days and states that God has given him the "energy of a million men." Frank mentions some annoyance at having received three speeding tickets earlier in the day. He insists that nothing must be allowed to thwart his master plan for the church.

*   *   *

Emma is a single thirty-four-year-old who is feeling "down" and "blah." In your meeting with Emma, you learn she has nearly always felt this way. She denies despair or suicidal thinking and insists her low mood has never caused her to miss work or any other significant event. She appears matter-of-fact in describing her mood as "always on the down side."

*   *   *

Robert is a fifty-eight-year-old insurance broker who has been extremely healthy all his life. Following a significant demotion at work, he begins to feel increasingly depressed. Eventually, Robert's appetite and ability to sleep are so diminished, his wife becomes alarmed. Robert describes a constant depressed mood, a sense of hopelessness about the future, significant guilt about his inability to correct his mood, and loss of interest in all the activities he once enjoyed. He has begun to perform poorly at work and spends most of his waking hours in bed. For the first time, Robert admits thinking about suicide.

Common Features and Symptoms

Mood disorders are among the most common of all mental health problems in the United States.[1,2] The most prominent symptom is a disturbance of mood that is intense and persistent enough to be clearly maladaptive. In each of the major mood disorder types, the parishioner will suffer extremes of emotion (also called *affect*) that dominate his or her appearance and behavior. These emotional extremes may range from soaring elation, or *mania,* to deep *depression.* Depression refers to feelings of extreme sadness and dejection, and mania refers to the experience of intense and unrealistic excitement and euphoria. Most people suffering from a mood disorder have a *unipolar* disorder, which means they experience only depressive feelings. Others will experience both manic and depressive episodes and are considered to suffer from a *bipolar* disorder.

Most parishioners (and pastors!) will experience periods of depressed mood during their lifetime. So-called "normal depression" is quite common and is most often associated with some sort of life stress. Following episodes of loss (e.g., death of a loved one, divorce, retirement, job loss, separation from a friend), depressed mood related to grief and normal adjustment is quite common and would not be considered indicative of a psychiatric problem. In this section, we will discuss the major mood disorders with an emphasis on their defining symptoms.

Lifetime prevalence rates for unipolar (depressive) disorders average about 13 percent—indicating that about 13 percent of your parishioners can be expected to suffer a depressive disorder at some time during their lives.[4] It is not surprising that depression was the second most common counseling problem reported by pastors.[3] Mood disorders may also be present in parishioners who present to the pastor with other problems such as substance abuse, chronic illness, marital conflict, and marital dissolution. Women have a higher probability of developing a severe depression (21 percent) than men (8 percent). The rates are reversed for alcoholism—leading some to speculate that males are more inclined to self-medicate depressive symptoms while women are more willing to express these symptoms and seek help. Rates for bipolar mood disorders are considerably lower (between 1 and 2 percent). Parishioners of all ages can become depressed. Even infants may experience a form of depression if separated for a prolonged period from their parents.[6]

Mental health professionals with the necessary expertise in treating mood disorders recognize that they are caused by a variety of factors and, often, an interaction of these factors. These causative agents include genetics, biochemistry, past experience, faulty thinking patterns, and situational stressors (especially losses). If a therapist suggests that depression is "always" caused by any single factor, be very cautious. Research has convincingly demonstrated that mood disorders run in families and that having parents with either unipolar or bipolar mood problems significantly increases the probability that a person will suffer from a similar disturbance. It is also clear that an imbalance in brain neurotransmitters (e.g., serotonin and norepinephrine) will produce depressed or manic symptoms. Each of the antidepressant medications, which can be so effective in treating severe depression, work to correct neurotransmitter imbalances in the depressed person's brain. Finally, research from cognitive psychology has demonstrated that depressed persons make excessively negative evaluations of themselves, their environments, and their futures. The point here is that mood disorders have multiple causes. A pastor, like any professional, should avoid assumptions regarding "why" a parishioner is depressed.

Subtypes

Dysthymia

Dysthymia is basically "mild depression." The forlorn character Eeyore in *Winnie the Pooh* is a classic example of the dysthymic character. Poor Eeyore is rarely happy, hangs his head frequently, and generally expects things to go poorly for him. Yet, Eeyore is not severely depressed or suicidal. Dysthymia is a milder but more chronic problem than major depression. The dysthymic person often reports a lengthy history of low mood with accompanying thoughts of guilt, worthlessness, and pessimism about the future. More severe indicators of depression are usually not present and the person often maintains a reasonable level of functioning, even though his or her poor mood interferes with relationships or work performance. Parishioners with dysthymia will have intermittent periods of normal mood (those with severe depression usually do not). They will report a long-standing history of mood problems, and they must have suffered with the problem for at least two years to be diagnosed with the disorder.

Dysthymia: Key Indicators

- Person has depressed mood for most of the day, most of the time, as indicated by his or her own report or that of others.
- This low mood pattern has persisted for at least two years.
- While feeling depressed, the person reports at least two of the following: (1) poor appetite or overeating; (2) insomnia or hypersomnia; (3) low energy or fatigue; (4) low self-esteem; (5) poor concentration; (6) feelings of hopelessness.
- The person is not without the symptoms for more than two months.

Of course, the pastor must be cautious not to assume that all who describe themselves as sometimes "down in the dumps" have a depressive disorder. As we noted previously, nearly all of us will feel depressed now and then. The difference is that this becomes a way of life for the dysthymic person. Various kinds of therapy (primarily cognitive, behavioral, or interpersonal) are likely to be helpful and antidepressant medication may also help. Such parishioners are unlikely to present in "crisis," but are more likely to come to the pastor's attention due to the adverse social and occupational effects of dysthymia.

Adjustment Disorder with Depressed Mood

Adjustment disorders involve the development of a significant emotional and/or behavioral syndrome that is clearly in response to an *identifiable stressor*. The parishioner who has lost a loved one, begun divorce proceedings, or been seriously injured may suffer an understandable and even predictable adjustment reaction to that stressful event.

Someone suffering from an adjustment disorder with depressed mood may appear to have dysthymia—that is, the symptoms of the two syndromes are remarkably similar. The critical difference is that the person with an adjustment disorder is responding to an identifiable stressor. Also, the adjustment problem must have begun within three months of the stressful event and, after termination of the stressful event, the problem should resolve within six months, or it may be something more serious.

Adjustment Disorder with Depressed Mood: Key Indicators

- The person has developed depressive symptoms (see Dysthymia Key Indicators) within three months from the start of the stressor(s).
- These depressive symptoms and behaviors are either in excess of what could be expected following the stressor, or their presence impairs social relationships or occupational functioning.
- Once the stressor ceases, the symptoms do not persist for more than six months.
- The symptoms do not represent bereavement (which should not be diagnosed or considered pathologic).

Helping the person suffering an adjustment disorder to view depressive symptoms more tolerantly may be the most important therapeutic task for pastors and therapists. Although determining which stressors qualify as likely to induce an adjustment disorder is somewhat subjective, many life events may be stressful enough to cause adjustment problems—particularly in parishioners with few resources and low resilience. If the person's symptoms are quite severe or seem not to resolve quickly, a referral for the same types of services noted for dysthymia is indicated.

Major Depression

The criteria for diagnosing major depression require that individuals have more numerous and severe depressive symptoms, and that they suffer with them more consistently than individuals with dysthymia. These parishioners will have very depressed moods and/or loss of interest in pleasurable activities nearly all of the time. Major depression is a potentially fatal problem and should be taken quite seriously by those who know the depressed person. Up to 15 percent of persons with major depressive disorder die by suicide.[4] Major depression may strike parishioners in any age, gender, or racial group, but it is particularly notable in those over the age of fifty. Those with a history of milder (dysthymic) depression are at greater risk for developing the disorder.

Although rare, some people with major depression can become so severely depressed that they begin to have psychotic symptoms such as delusions (fixed beliefs that are incongruent with reality). The themes of these delusions would usually be *mood congruent* and include personal inadequacy, guilt, deserved punishment, death, and disease. A parishioner may be suffering his or her first episode of major depression—in which case it is described as a *single episode*. Major depression may also be *recurrent* and occur episodically. In either case, most major depressive episodes are time-limited. With appropriate assistance, the parishioner may be expected to return to a more normal mood state.

Major Depression: Key Indicators

- Person reports either seriously depressed mood or loss of interest or plea-sure in usual activities for at least a two-week period.
- At least five of the following specific symptoms are present: (1) depressed mood most of the day, nearly every day; (2) markedly diminished interest in all or almost all activities most of the day; (3) significant weight loss, weight gain, or either decrease or increase in appetite every day; (4) insomnia or hypersomnia nearly every day; (5) obvious agitation or slowing in physical movements; (6) fatigue or loss of energy nearly every day; (7) feelings of worthlessness or excessive or inappropriate guilt nearly every day; (8) poor concentration or increased indecisiveness; (9) recurrent thoughts of death or committing suicide.
- These symptoms significantly interfere with the person's social well-being and his or her performance at work or school.

The severely depressed parishioner may or may not be a self-refer-ral to the pastor. Very often, a family member may be the first one to contact the pastor about the person's deteriorated mood and poor func-tioning. Of course, the specter of suicide should be of concern. Al-though hopelessness is common in those with major depression, it is also a risk factor for suicide as are increased alcohol use, prior history of suicidal behavior, and subtle or overt attempts to "say good-bye" to loved ones. In the case of major depression, the pastor may need to make an emergency mental health referral (including hospitalization), particularly when the parishioner has articulated some suicidal thinking or their level of functioning is so impaired that they require intensive and monitored treatment.

Bipolar ("Manic-Depressive") Disorder

Bipolar disorder is distinguished from major depression by the presence of one striking and unique syndrome—the manic episode. Mania is a very extreme condition and it nearly always interferes with social and occupational functioning. A person who experiences a manic episode has a markedly elevated, euphoric, and expansive mood, often interrupted by occasional outbursts of irritability or even rage—especially when others refuse to go along with the sufferer's odd plans or behavior. Manic individuals may also have seemingly boundless energy and restless thoughts that seem to "race." Their speech is often extremely rapid and they have great difficulty focusing on one topic. Persons with this disorder will alternate between depressive episodes (see the Major Depression Key Indicators) and manic episodes, which will be less frequent and shorter in duration.

Bipolar Disorder: Key Indicators

- For a period of at least one week, the person has persistently elevated, expansive, or irritable mood.
- During this time, at least three of the following symptoms are present: (1) inflated self-esteem or a grandiose assessment of oneself; (2) decreased need for sleep; (3) more speech, and speech seems "pressured"; (4) racing thoughts; (5) distractibility; (6) increased goal-directed activity (socially, at work or school, or sexually) or increased physical-motor agitation; (7) excessive involvement in pleasurable activities that have high potential for painful consequences (e.g., unrestrained buying sprees, sexual indiscretions, or foolish business investments).
- The person's relationships or work performance are impaired.
- There is typically some history of previous episodes of major depression (although it is possible to have an initial manic episode in the absence of prior depression).

The manic parishioner will likely be quite disruptive at work, in relationships, and in the church. He or she will engage in very uncharacteristic and potentially injurious behaviors. Often, these high-risk and inappropriate behaviors will be a source of great shame and embarrassment after the person has received treatment and the manic episode has resolved. It is important to keep in mind that this person needs professional treatment immediately. A referral to a psychiatrist is indicated so that the person can begin a trial of medication, usually lithium. Once the current manic episode has been treated, the real challenge may be encouraging the person to remain on medication (as long as the physician recommends) to prevent further occurrences.

Summary and Guidelines

Mood disorders are among the most common problems the pastor will see in day-to-day interaction with parishioners. Such disorders may range from "normal" depression to major depression with suicidal planning. Although bereavement, adjustment disorders, and, in some cases, major depression may have specific precipitating causes, most severe mood disorders are caused by a combination of biological, genetic, social, and even cultural factors. In the case of mild forms of depression, the pastor must consider how well prepared he or she feels to counsel a parishioner with mood problems. Good social support, good insight about the problem, and a willingness to seek and engage in assistance through the church are all positive indicators.

In the case of more serious mood problems such as major depression and bipolar disorder, the pastor should nearly always encourage the parishioner (and the parishioner's family) to pursue professional mental health treatment. Again, a joint referral to a physician (preferably a psychiatrist) and a mental health provider with expertise in psychotherapy for mood disorders is highly recommended. It is quite likely that antidepressant medications will be prescribed for the person with a major depressive episode. Increasingly, physicians and psychiatrists are prescribing a new category of drugs—*SSRIs* (selective serotonin reuptake inhibitors), which change levels of the neurotransmitter in the brain and often create remarkably positive changes in mood. Prozac, Zoloft, and Paxil are among the most commonly prescribed antidepressant medications. Antidepressant medications may play a critical role in an individual's recovery from depression. Unfortunately, antidepressant medications usually require several weeks to take effect. In the meantime, the severely depressed person may require hospitalization (especially if suicidal) or other intensive care to ensure their well-being and safety.

In the most severe cases of major depression that do not respond well to therapy and medication, a psychiatrist may employ electric shock treatment (*electroconvulsive therapy*—ECT). Electroconvulsive therapy is typically indicated only in the case of an older adult for whom all other treatment approaches have failed. Lithium therapy is the medical treatment most likely to be effective in treating bipolar illness, although it is also used in some cases of major depression. Lithium is often effective in preventing the cycling between manic and depressive episodes common among persons with this disorder.

A range of psychotherapies, most preferably cognitive-behavioral or interpersonal, are also helpful in treating major depression. These therapies often focus on helping depressed persons to change their depressing self-statements and irrational beliefs. They may also address the sufferer's lack of rewarding experiences during the day and his or her need for more social reinforcement. Most often, a combination of therapy and medication will produce the most rapid recovery.

Finally, the pastor must recognize that he or she can often be a critical component in the parishioner's recovery from depression.[7,8] This may involve making an immediate referral in the case of the severely depressed, serving as a supportive person in the parishioner's environment, and helping the parishioner and his or her family negotiate conflicts and understand the common symptoms of the disorder. The pastor will often be very influential in encouraging the afflicted person to seek treatment and in helping him or her deal with the guilt and shame that can often accompany depressive syndromes. Finally, the use of spiritual resources, prayer, and religious imagery have been shown to be very helpful for parishioners suffering from depression.

PSYCHOTIC DISORDERS

Presenting Complaints

Frank, a twenty-three-year-old parishioner, has been a member of the church since childhood. During the past two years, he has

evidenced some odd changes in behavior. Frank began withdrawing from social activities, stopped attending church, and began
spending most of his time in his college dorm room. He appeared
emotionally "blank" and stopped basic personal hygiene. Eventually, Frank dropped out of college and has been living with his
parents. His parents report that Frank now hears voices calling
him bad names. He believes that authorities from his college are
attempting to kill him using microwaves.

*   *   *

Linda, age thirty-two, comes for counseling with her husband.
Her husband is exasperated by Linda's constant preoccupation
with Tom Cruise. It seems Linda believes this actor is deeply in
love with her and that he communicates to her via subtle comments and gestures (which only she can translate) in his various
movie roles. When she reads interviews with the actor, Linda
detects "special notes" to her. Linda appears normal with the
exception of her firm belief that Mr. Cruise is communicating
intense love for her.

*   *   *

You are asked to visit fifty-year-old Reggie in the hospital. He
has apparently "gone crazy" after accidentally hitting and killing
a child who ran out in front of his car. In the hospital, Reggie is
staring and mumbling to himself. He does not respond to you or
anyone else. One week later, Reggie is back in church. He has no
memory of the accident or your visit and he appears to have
completely returned to normal.

Common Features and Symptoms

The psychotic disorders represent the ultimate in personal psychological breakdown. Parishioners who are psychotic will present with
some of the most extreme and disturbed behaviors the pastor will ever
see. The term *psychosis* implies a profound loss of contact with reality.
In essence, the psychotic person has become detached from basic
connection points with society and the larger world around him or her.

To people who interact with them, psychotic persons appear bizarre, incomprehensible, and even frightening. Psychotic individuals are so detached from reality that they are sometimes not held responsible for acts committed while psychotic. Hospitalization and medication are nearly always indicated. In this section, we describe *schizophrenia* (undoubtedly the most common and well-known of the psychotic disorders), *delusional disorder,* and *brief psychotic disorder.*

Subtypes

Schizophrenia

Schizophrenia is a debilitating psychotic disorder that occurs in all cultures. This disorder is among the most costly of world health problems with respect to financial loss, personal suffering, and treatment intensity.[2] About 1.1 percent of the U.S. population, roughly 2 million Americans, suffer from schizophrenia.[9] The word schizophrenia literally means "split mind," and the disorder is characterized by disorganized thought processes, lack of coherence between thought and emotion, and an inward movement away from reality. The disorder is particularly tragic because its onset is typically in late adolescence or early adulthood, and the prognosis for full remission is poor.

Schizophrenia typically develops gradually. The afflicted person becomes progressively more seclusive, loses interest in the outside world, and the capacity for emotional responsiveness declines. Although most cases show this gradual onset in late adolescence or early adulthood, a smaller percentage are more sudden in onset and may be triggered by a stressful life event. Although the causes of schizophrenia are not well understood, research has confirmed a strong genetic component. For example, when one identical twin has the disorder, a 60 percent chance exists that the other will also have it—even when the two are reared apart. Undeniable evidence indicates that brain chemistry plays a central role in causing this disorder. An excess of the neurotransmitter dopamine has been a consistent finding among schizophrenic patients. The medications that effectively treat this disorder actually alter neurotransmitter levels.

Schizophrenic symptoms are usually divided into *positive symptoms* and *negative symptoms*. Positive symptoms are behavioral excesses such as emotional turmoil, motor agitation, inappropriate emotional expression, disorganized speech and behavior, and the two hallmark symptoms of schizophrenia, *hallucinations* and *delusional beliefs*. Hallucinations are false perceptions such as voices, sights, or smells that no one else perceives. Delusions are clearly false beliefs such as "my thoughts are being broadcast to the CIA" or "someone is using microwaves to control me." Inappropriate emotional expression refers to such things as giggling when describing something morbid (e.g., the death of a family member). Disorganized speech refers to the fact that the schizophrenic's speech does not make sense (sometimes called "word salad"). Negative symptoms are behavioral deficits in such areas as emotional expression (flatness of expression), communicative speech (low verbal output), reactivity to the environment (withdrawal, fantasy, daydreaming), and goal-directed activities (self-care, work).

Schizophrenia: Key Indicators

- At least two of the following must have been present most of the time for at least one month: (1) delusions; (2) hallucinations; (3) disorganized speech; (4) disorganized behavior; (5) negative symptoms (see text) such as loss of emotional expression.
- The symptoms cause interference in the person's social and/or occupational functioning.
- There must be continuous signs of the disturbance for at least six months (including at least one month of the symptoms described above), perhaps followed by periods of less intense disturbance.

It is worth noting that parishioners who suffer from schizophrenia do not always exhibit the same symptoms. In addition to the varied causes of this disorder (genetics, biology, social stressors, trauma, etc.), it has several subtypes. *Paranoid schizophrenia* is characterized by bizarre and illogical delusions, which often have a grandiose or suspicious quality (e.g., "I am God's chosen one and many are jealous of that and trying to kill me."). A great deal of impaired judgment, erratic behavior, and even dangerous acting out occurs. Although the paranoid schizophrenic is less withdrawn socially, he or she may be more hostile and dangerous by interpreting the behavior of others as a direct personal threat. The *disorganized schizophrenic* is likely to develop the disorder at an earlier age and is considered more seriously fragmented than other types. Symptoms of emotional distortion and inappropriateness, bizarre behavior, and odd mannerisms are most common with this subtype. Finally, a person with *catatonic schizophrenia* may remain motionless for hours or even days—seemingly entirely cut off from external reality. These periods of "frozen" behavior may alternate with periods of excitement as well as emotional and physical acting out.

Treatment for schizophrenia nearly always begins with hospitalization. This is especially true during initial episodes when the person begins acting quite erratically. For example, the person may be hearing voices or staring vacantly while ignoring basic self-care. Stabilizing schizophrenics often involves having them carefully monitored lest they harm themselves or others. In most states, there are provisions for hospitalizing psychotic persons, involuntarily if necessary, in order to protect and treat them. Antipsychotic medications are nearly always indicated and long-term management by a psychiatrist is to be expected. Although the medications will often help alleviate the most severe symptoms of schizophrenia, family members and friends should anticipate a long road to recovery. About two-thirds of those with this disorder will evidence at least mild symptoms for the rest of their lives.

Delusional Disorder

Delusional disorder (sometimes called *paranoid disorder*) is much less serious than schizophrenia. The psychotic person with this disorder is often able to function reasonably well both socially and at work. The hallmark symptom of delusional disorder is the presence of *nonbizzare delusions* that persist for at least a month. A person who has other psychotic symptoms or has ever been diagnosed with schizophrenia cannot be diagnosed with this disorder.

The person often feels singled out and taken advantage of, plotted against, stolen from, spied on, ignored, or otherwise mistreated. The delusions to which this person firmly clings are nonbizarre, meaning that they involve situations that can conceivably occur in real life (e.g., being followed, poisoned, infected, loved at a distance, or deceived by one's spouse or lover).[1] The delusional system usually centers on only one of these themes. For example, a parishioner may believe that his co-workers are attempting to steal his plans and that they have begun following him, tapping his phone, and collaborating with government agencies to collect information about him. Another parishioner may believe her husband is being unfaithful, although no real evidence for this exists. Because he returns ten minutes late from the store one evening, she concludes he has rendezvoused with a lover. She becomes convinced that each of his behaviors (taking slightly more time in the shower, smiling when a certain song plays on the radio, or wearing a specific tie to work) hint at his unfaithfulness. She will be unresponsive to reason from others and will hold firmly to the belief that he is unfaithful.

Several subtypes of delusional disorder include:

- *Persecutory type:* The person believes that he or she, or a loved one, is being subjected to maltreatment such as spying, stalking, or spreading of false rumors. The person may take legal (or more hostile) actions against those believed to be responsible.
- *Jealous type:* The person believes firmly that his or her sexual partner is being unfaithful.
- *Erotomanic type:* Someone of higher status (e.g., a movie star) is believed to be deeply in love with the person and interested in a sexual relationship (some people who "stalk" others may fit this category).
- *Somatic type:* This person has an unshakable belief that he or she suffers from some physical illness—often of a very exotic nature.
- *Grandiose type:* The person has a fixed belief that he or she has extraordinary status, power, ability, talent, beauty, etc.

Delusional Disorder: Key Indicators

- Nonbizarre delusions (events that could conceivably occur) for at least one month.
- The person has never been schizophrenic.
- Aside from the impact of the delusions (e.g., rejection by others), there is no obvious impairment in functioning and behavior is not otherwise odd or bizarre.

The exact causes of delusional disorder are unclear. We do know that these persons have often gone through life feeling unappreciated, frustrated, and unjustly treated. As children, they were probably aloof, suspicious, stubborn, secretive, and resentful of punishment. They rarely have warm relationships with others.[10]

Once a delusional disorder is firmly in place, it is very difficult to help these people. They may be quite frustrating for the pastor and their own family members because they seldom seek treatment; they are much more interested in seeking justice for all the wrong that has been done them. Because their lives may remain marginally intact, in spite of their fixed false beliefs, they may effectively thwart all attempts at intervention; they are seldom at such great risk that they merit involuntary hospitalization. They cannot be "talked out of" their delusions and attempts to do so may merely convince them that the pastor is an accomplice to those who persecute them. Although some medications may be helpful, it is seldom that a person with this disorder will consent to take them. Unconditionally accepting the delusional parishioner and providing support for the family may be key pastoral roles.

Brief Psychotic Disorder

On very rare occasions, a person may become psychotic only for a brief time. In these unusual cases, the individual appears to be fine one day and delusional, disorganized, or hearing voices the next. The symptoms last only a short while and the person can be expected to return to normal functioning again. The person does not have schizophrenia or a delusional disorder, but does evidence one or more of the psychotic symptoms for a brief period of time. Most often, an identifiable stressor precipitates the psychosis (e.g., loss of a loved one, combat experience), but an identifiable stressor is not required for this brief disturbance to occur. Finally, there are some cases of these brief reactive states in women shortly after giving birth (postpartum onset).

Brief Psychotic Disorder: Key Indicators

- The person experiences at least one of the following symptoms: (1) delusions; (2) hallucinations; (3) disorganized speech; (4) grossly disorganized behavior.
- Symptoms last for at least one day but less than one month.
- The person returns to a completely normal level of functioning.

It is important to be sure that the parishioner who demonstrates sudden psychotic behavior has not been using illicit drugs or prescription medications that might explain his or her symptoms. Sudden symptom onset also raises concerns about medical problems such as brain accidents (e.g., strokes). Also, there are cultural explanations for certain behaviors which might otherwise seem bizarre. Certain religious ceremonies and religious groups may endorse speaking in tongues, "receiving a word" from outside of oneself, or having spiritually based experiences such as visions. The pastor should be sensitive to the specific symptom and its meaning to the parishioner in the context of his or her religious community.

Summary and Guidelines

Psychotic disorders are extremely serious. They are chronic mental health afflictions. As a pastor, you may be the first to recognize signs of psychosis in a parishioner. You may be the one to organize and leverage hospitalization for a seriously disorganized and potentially dangerous person. More often, you will be called upon to support this person's family as they struggle to understand the gravity of their loved one's illness. Alleviating guilt or shame for the family is important as parents may often assume that they have "caused" schizophrenia in their child. Helping the family to understand the biological contributions to psychosis, the need for psychiatric treatment, and the long-term nature of the disorder are critical tasks. Research has shown that helpful communities for schizophrenic persons are gentle, accepting, consistent, and knowledgeable about the signs and treatments of the disorder. Larger churches or groups of churches might consider establishing day treatment or support programs for schizophrenic members and their families. The pastor should keep in mind that psychiatric medications are typically a must in the effective treatment of these disorders and that hospitalization can be critical as well. Understanding the chronic nature of schizophrenia while also maintaining and expressing hope for recovery is essential.

BRAIN-INJURY/DISEASE DISORDERS

Presenting Complaints

Sally is a sixty-one-year-old mother of four. She has always been exceptionally active in the church and a leader in many areas. During the last year, Sally's family has grown concerned about her slow withdrawal from social activities. Sally has some trouble remembering new things. She seems more fatigued and less alert than before. Her husband is especially concerned that Sally has slowly grown less concerned with hygiene and the appearance of their home. Her daughter wonders why her mother has become more childlike in her emotional expression. The family asks if you will "counsel" Sally.

*   *   *

Earl is a twenty-five-year-old who lives with his mother. She approaches you and expresses guilt about feelings of anger toward her son. For several years, she has been encouraging Earl to get a job and move out. Earl has only succeeded in securing very menial jobs that do not pay well. Although Earl is kind and even tempered, he struggled in special education classes and dropped out in the ninth grade. His mother admits that the school psychologist said Earl had a "very low IQ." However, she dismisses this and wonders why her son "has to be so lazy."

*   *   *

Stephen is a forty-seven-year-old accountant. He has been a steady and reliable parishioner for many years. He is a model family man and a responsible member of the elder board. Stephen's wife demands that he accompany her to see you for counseling. During the past week, Stephen has behaved in a very uncharacteristic fashion. His mood fluctuates rapidly and can swing from irritability to tearfulness with little warning. He has also made inappropriate sexual comments at home and at work. Stephen admits being involved in a "fender bender" the week before, but he minimizes the "tiny bump on the head" he received.

Common Features and Symptoms

In contrast to other varieties of psychiatric impairment, brain-injury/disease disorders are usually a consequence of structural defects or damage to brain tissue—often the result of injury or disease. This loss of integrity of brain tissue (destruction of nerve cells in the brain) results in emotional and behavioral disorders that, at times, mimic other psychiatric problems. Brain-injury disturbances are referred to as *organic* disorders. One of these disorders, *mental retardation,* occurs early in life (sometimes prior to birth) and is characterized by poor intellectual skills and impaired adaptive functioning. In contrast, *brain injuries* and *dementia* are indicative of actual damage to or deterioration of the brain sometime after the brain has developed. Brain impairment may result from focal damage (e.g., a bullet wound) or from diffuse damage resulting from disease, exposure to toxic substances, oxygen deprivation, or a head injury that affects more than a single region.

Persons with "organic" brain disorders often share certain presenting symptoms, although these will vary in each case. Symptoms may include memory impairment (especially for more recent events), forgetting one's own identity or the identities of loved ones, inability to learn new material, poor judgment (behavior becomes improper or unethical), apathy, lack of initiation of behavior (e.g., working, conversing), poor visual-spatial perception, and problems understanding and using language.

Parishioners with organic brain disorders will often be elderly. One of the premier challenges to clergy is to provide good support and direction to family members who may be understandably horrified by or depressed about the sudden (and often irreversible) changes to the personality of their loved one. In some cases, organic brain disorders are progressive and terminal. In others, they result in permanent disability with little potential for return to previous levels of functioning.

Subtypes

Head Injuries

There are three types of head injuries. In *closed-head* injuries, the cranium remains intact, but damage occurs to brain tissue nonetheless. Closed-head injuries are by far the most common organic brain disorders. Auto accidents, accidental falls, sports-related accidents, and many other events frequently result in closed-head injuries, which may be quite mild or life threatening depending on severity of damage to brain tissue. Less common head injuries include *penetrating* injuries (such as those from bullets or shrapnel in combat situations) or *skull fractures* in which the impact is substantial enough to break the skull bone.

Regardless of the cause of the injury to a person's brain, brain damage due to head injury can produce some predictable symptoms. The most common are *retrograde amnesia* (loss of memory for events immediately preceding the injury), *anterograde amnesia* (inability to effectively store new memories following the injury), poor concentration, problems with speech, impaired judgment, poorly controlled moods, increased or decreased sleep, fatigue, irritability, dizziness, and headaches. Any of these symptoms, if sudden in onset, may be an indicator of a head injury. It is a good idea for the pastor to inquire about recent accidents. In some instances of closed-head injury, a parishioner may have received what he or she believes was merely a "bump on the head," when in fact there is sustained bleeding inside the brain which produces pressure on the brain tissue, impairment, and the necessity of surgery to relieve the pressure. It is also important to note that these symptoms could be indicative of a brain tumor—particularly when accompanied by headaches, nausea, and dizziness.

Head Injury: Key Indicators

- The person has sustained some injury to the brain, even when the event was apparently not traumatic.
- Following the injury, the person experiences symptoms such as impaired memory, irritability, poor control of emotions, impaired judgment, changes in sleep pattern, fatigue, poor concentration, headaches, dizziness, and anxiety.

Head injuries are a distinctly medical matter. When the pastor becomes concerned that a parishioner is experiencing symptoms related to a recent injury to the head, an immediate referral to a physician is indicated. If the symptoms appear severe, transportation to a hospital or consultation with a neurologist are recommended. Prognosis for recovery hinges on the extent of damage to the brain and the speed at which medical intervention occurs. Prognosis is nearly always more positive in children as younger brains have greater potential for recovery and adaptation.

Dementia

Dementia is the most common and feared organic brain disorder among older adults. Dementia involves the progressive deterioration of the brain sometime after early adulthood. The parishioner with dementia will typically be elderly, although the disorder can strike people as young as forty. The earlier the onset, the more rapid the progression of the disorder. One in every six Americans over the age of sixty-five has some form of dementia. In those eighty-five or older, the rate jumps to 50 percent.[11] Although the brain begins to deteriorate in all older adults (often called senility), earlier degeneration of the brain is known as *presenile dementia*. Presenile dementia is characterized by permanent degeneration of the brain tissue, which is sometimes caused by strokes, infections or disease, tumors, lack of oxygen, or repeated head injuries. However, the cause of dementia is not always clear and genetics contribute strongly to this disorder.

Among the dementias, dementia of the *Alzheimer's type* (DAT) is most common.[1] Dementia of the Alzheimer's type is a very subtle disorder, which develops slowly in most cases. In early stages, the person remains reasonably alert and aware—though he or she may have trouble remembering some recent events. This subtle beginning often makes the onset of dementia nearly impossible to date. As the disorder progresses, the person experiences difficulty with abstract thinking, learning new things, judgment, problem solving, and control of muscle activity. His or her personality may begin to deteriorate, emotional control declines, and the person appears to lose motivation in most areas. Persons with dementia may become upset by changes to their routine. They become progressively more childlike, unaware of hygiene, and ultimately entirely dependent on others for care.

Dementia of the Alzheimer's Type: Key Indicators

- The person develops several cognitive problems such as loss of memory, an inability to use language, failure to recognize or identify objects or people that one should be familiar with, loss of ability to effectively plan or organize, and disturbances in motor functioning.
- In later stages, the person disengages from activities and interests previously enjoyed, becomes less alert, less emotionally balanced and inflexible with regard to daily routine.
- These changes cause disruption in the person's social or occupational functioning and represent a loss or decline.
- The development of the symptoms is gradual and progressive.

Unfortunately, this disorder is terminal and slowly decreases the parishioner's quality of life until death. Regardless of the cause, the disorder will gradually diminish the person's ability to enjoy life, remain independent, and even understand who he or she is. Not only may the pastor be called upon to assist the parishioner with accepting and coping with this frightening disorder, the family typically has a substantial need for support and encouragement from the pastor as they deal with grief issues, adjustment to caretaking, and preparation for gradual loss of a parent or spouse. The person's faith, and that of his or her family members, may be understandably shaken at times during this process. Although there is no cure for dementia, referral of the parishioner and family for medical support and social services (such as adult day care) is highly recommended.

Mental Retardation

Mental retardation indicates significantly below average intellectual functioning, accompanied by substantial limitations in adaptive skills such as self-care, ability to work, health maintenance, and safety. Mental retardation occurs worldwide and is present in approximately one percent of the U.S. population.[12] This disorder usually begins prior to age eighteen and it is almost always evident by the time a child begins formal education. A diagnosis of mental retardation can officially be made when a person's level of intelligence, or IQ,[1] as measured by a standardized intelligence test, is below 70 and there is evidence of specific deficits in adaptive skills, or the person's behavior is unmanageable. Mental retardation has many potential causes including genetic-chromosomal factors (e.g., *Down's syndrome*), exposure to infections or toxic agents (e.g., if the mother is HIV positive or syphilis-infected during pregnancy), malnutrition, and brain injury (including injury prior to birth).

There are different levels of severity among persons diagnosed as mentally retarded. *Mild mental retardation* (IQ range from 70 to 50-55) comprises by far the largest group of retarded persons. Mildly retarded individuals will have an intellectual level comparable to children between eight and eleven years old. Social adjustment may be similar to the typical adolescent and, with early intervention and good social support, such individuals can become reasonably well adjusted and self-supporting. *Moderate mental retardation* (IQ range from 50-55 to 35-40) indicates an intellectual level common to children between ages four and seven. These people can master certain routine skills and may achieve partial independence, but usually work and reside in sheltered environments. They are often physically clumsy and poorly coordinated. Finally, persons with *severe* or *profound mental retardation* (IQ from 35-40 or below) are extremely limited and absolutely dependent on others. They have very low intellectual functioning and minimal ability to care for themselves. Extreme speech and motor deficits are usually evident.

Mental Retardation: Key Indicators

- Significantly below-average intellectual functioning as determined by a psychologist administering a standardized intelligence test or, in the case of infants, clinical judgment of significantly below-average intelligence.
- Also, the person has clear deficits in adaptive functioning in some of the following areas: (1) communication; (2) self-care; (3) home living; (4) social/interpersonal skills; (5) academic skills; (6) self-direction; (7) work; (8) health; (9) leisure; (10) safety.

Although mental retardation can be extremely stressful for family members, many resources are available on both the local and federal levels for developmentally disabled persons and, at times, family members.[12] Although mental retardation is not treatable, nor can the intellectual functioning of the retarded person be substantially improved, early diagnosis and family support are critical for reducing the stress of this condition for all concerned. The pastor may find himself or herself in the role of helping new parents with accepting and coping with their child's intellectual limitation. Arranging support groups or services for parents and families of retarded parishioners is an excellent opportunity for local ministry. In addition, the pastor may serve as an important model of unconditional love and acceptance for retarded persons in the church. For example, encouraging public involvement of retarded children in worship services and other church gatherings is important in setting a tone for other parishioners.

Summary and Guidelines

Brain-injury/disease disorders or "organic" mental health problems may be among the most tragic and difficult for the pastor and family members to address. Because these disorders involve the structure and functioning of the brain itself, they are often not treatable. Perhaps the most important task for the pastor is helping brain-impaired parishioners and their families with acceptance. Helping young parents accept the cognitive limitations of a mentally retarded child, helping adult children accept the steady and permanent decline of a parent with Alzheimer's, and helping a spouse accept the severe loss of functioning in a brain-injured spouse are examples of this task. Modeling patient acceptance and sturdy faith in the face of such adversity can be powerful interventions.

Serving as an effective referral source is another critical pastoral role. As a pastor, you may be the first to recognize the signs of a stroke or subtle head injury and should initiate an immediate referral to a physician. You may be the first to spot signs of "caretaker stress" in the spouse of a parishioner with dementia. In this case, you might recommend a day care facility for such impaired church members or even work with other local churches to create a day care consortium for Alzheimer's patients. You may also be the first to inform parents of retarded children of the services available through state agencies to persons with developmental disabilities.

Chapter 3

The Parishioner in Distress:
Major Psychological Disorders, Part II

In this chapter, we continue to describe several major psychiatric disorders that the pastor may encounter in the congregation. Although these disorders are certainly less prevalent than depression and anxiety problems, they will occur nonetheless. In this chapter we summarize trauma-related disorders, substance abuse disorders, sleep disorders, and sexual disorders. As in Chapter 2, we provide subsections that address presenting complaints, common features and symptoms, *subtypes,* and key indicators for each disorder. A summary and guidelines section encapsulates the primary factors for the pastor to consider when responding to a parishioner who may suffer from a particular disorder.

TRAUMA-RELATED DISORDERS

Presenting Complaints

Jennifer is a seventeen-year-old high school student who was involved in an auto accident three weeks ago. Although Jennifer sustained only minor injuries, a close friend was killed in the accident. Jennifer was trapped in the car with her deceased friend for nearly thirty minutes before help arrived. Since then, Jennifer can barely recall events surrounding the accident and she reports feeling "numb." She describes feeling as though things are no longer "real" and she avoids all reminders of the accident.

* * *

Bob has been a church member all his life. He is employed at a local service station and has held numerous jobs over the years. He has never been married and he seems to avoid relationships. He sometimes gives little attention to hygiene and others see him as "jumpy" and aloof. When Bob was in his early twenties, he was stationed aboard the *USS Iowa* when one of the main gun turrets exploded and many sailors were killed. Bob was involved in recovering bodies from the turret. Years later, Bob continues to have nightmares about the event, avoids anything having to do with ships or the ocean, and appears easily startled.

*   *   *

Angela is a single twenty-eight-year-old who has been actively involved in church support groups for several years. She struggles with a weight problem and poor self-esteem. Angela has disclosed a history of having been severely sexually abused as a young girl. While describing her abuse in a counseling session, she begins speaking with a young girl's voice. She also curls up in her chair and takes on the mannerisms of a child. She seems to be a different person and she refers to herself as Bonnie. The counselor learns that although Bonnie is aware of Angela, Angela does not seem to know about Bonnie.

Common Features and Symptoms

In each of these cases, a common theme is the experience of a very painful life event (or series of events) that can be considered traumatic. Traumatic events are unusual and often catastrophic events that most people never experience. In traumatic situations, people believe that death or serious injury to themselves or others is imminent. During the trauma, the person responds with understandable fear, helplessness, or horror. Trauma can occur upon hearing that a family member or close associate has been unexpectedly killed or harmed. Traumatic events may include auto or plane accidents, military combat, rape, and natural disasters such as hurricanes and earthquakes. In this section, we will describe three of the most common examples of traumatic event-induced disorder. *Post-traumatic stress disorder* and *acute stress disor-*

der frequently occur following a traumatic and life-threatening experience. *Dissociative identity disorder* is more often the result of trauma experienced in childhood (most often, the trauma relates to child abuse of some sort).

Subtypes

Post-Traumatic Stress Disorder

Post-traumatic stress disorder or PTSD may follow exposure to a specific traumatic life event (e.g., terrorist attack, sexual assault, combat, tornado, or other calamity). The trauma typically involves the threat of death or serious injury to oneself or to others. It appears that the more severe the trauma and the longer the span of time between the event and the symptoms, the more severe and chronic the PTSD will be. In the hours and days following the traumatic event, the person may fluctuate between reexperiencing the trauma and avoidance of it altogether. During the avoidance phase, the person may feel numb, minimize the importance of the event, and report amnesia for the time surrounding the event. During the reexperiencing phase, the person is unable to stop thinking about the trauma; these thoughts may be experienced as "intrusive" and beyond the person's control. He or she is likely to have sleep problems, be easily startled, and somewhat "paranoid" or guarded. The person will often feel anxious and may feel as though he or she is going "crazy."

Mental health professionals first became aware of PTSD during World War II. At that time the disorder was known as "shell shock," "battle fatigue," or "war neurosis." A substantial number of Vietnam veterans suffer from very severe cases of PTSD. Many Veterans Administration (VA) medical centers specialize in treating PTSD among combat veterans. Persons suffering from PTSD may avoid getting assistance and may withdraw from important relationships altogether. They may use alcohol and drugs to manage their symptoms. Children and elderly persons are more vulnerable to PTSD. Individuals with a previous history of psychiatric problems are also more likely to develop PTSD following a traumatic event.

Post-Traumatic Stress Disorder: Key Indicators

- The person has experienced or witnessed a traumatic event that involved actual, or threatened, death or injury.
- The traumatic event is persistently reexperienced for more than a month via intrusive, uncontrollable recollections and dreams.
- The person avoids reminders of the trauma by avoiding persons, situations, conversations, and activities that are linked to the event.
- There is evidence of physical arousal related to the trauma such as sleep disturbance, irritability, poor concentration, being easily startled, and being excessively vigilant about one's surroundings.
- The person is distressed about these symptoms; the person's work and relationships are impaired as a result.

Ideally, persons who have experienced a traumatic event will undergo a "debriefing" immediately following the event. A debriefing involves talking about the trauma—preferably with others who were also present—as a way of normalizing their responses. Research suggests that those who undergo such debriefing procedures are less likely to develop PTSD. For those who do, treatment often involves individual and group therapy and medication. The pastor should make every effort to get the traumatized parishioner into treatment as soon after the event as possible. Ongoing support groups for PTSD are probably the most effective, especially for combat veterans, persons who have been raped, emergency personnel, and others who experience traumas. In individual counseling, cognitive-behavioral interventions are often used that typically focus on gradual exposure to the traumatic memories and environmental cues (e.g., specific locations and situations) in order to reduce fear responses. Therapy may also help to change the person's distorted (often self-blaming) thoughts and beliefs about the traumatic event. Medications for more severe PTSD may include both antidepressant and antianxiety drugs. These medications should be managed by a psychiatrist with experience in treating trauma-related disorders. Although PTSD can, at times, improve and even dissipate altogether without treatment, this is very unusual. In most cases, untreated PTSD results in chronic disturbance, substance abuse, and both work and relationship failures.

Acute Stress Disorder

In acute stress disorder, the parishioner will have been exposed to some traumatic event—similar to those previously described for PTSD. That is, the person experiences or is confronted with events involving real or threatened death or serious injury. After the event, the person experiences a number of symptoms of anxiety or *dissociation* (feeling as though things are not real, feeling detached from one's own body, or having difficulty recalling specific details about the traumatic event). The difference between this disorder and the more serious PTSD is simply time. While PTSD requires the presence of these symptoms for at least one month, acute stress disorder is diagnosed immediately after the trauma (within two days). If it persists for more than four weeks, it is considered a more serious and chronic posttrauma problem (PTSD). It is not uncommon for a person to show signs of anxiety and dissociation following an extreme stressor. These symptoms often decline within several weeks and there is no need for ongoing mental health care. If these symptoms do not dissipate or if they become more acute, it is reasonable to suspect that the person's reaction to the trauma has progressed from acute stress disorder to PTSD.

Acute Stress Disorder: Key Indicators

- The person is exposed to the same kind of trauma described in the PTSD key indicators.
- Either during or following the traumatic event, the person experiences some of the following symptoms of dissociation: (1) emotional numbing or detachment; (2) a sense of being "dazed"; (3) feeling as though things are not real; (4) feeling detached from oneself; (5) having amnesia for some events surrounding the trauma.
- The person has flashbacks or nightmares about the event.
- He or she avoids situations or stimuli that remind him or her of the trauma.
- There are significant symptoms of anxiety or arousal following the event.
- These symptoms have lasted for at least two days, but not for more than four weeks.

Because many cases of acute stress disorder resolve during the month following the trauma and because this reaction is such a normal response to uncommon trauma, the pastor may be most helpful to the parishioner by simply remaining patient and understanding. Inviting the parishioner to tell his or her story about the event and describe feelings connected to it is also usually helpful. Normalizing (without minimizing) the parishioner's feelings of anxiety and distress is also indicated. Of course, if the symptoms do not dissipate or if they significantly worsen, a referral for mental health intervention is wise.

Dissociative Identity Disorder

Dissociative disorders occur when the normal integration or blending together of a person's consciousness, personal identity, and memory are disrupted. Dissociation is a psychological process in which the mind splits off, or compartmentalizes, certain memories or events from conscious awareness. Dissociation is often a response to trauma—especially trauma experienced at an early age when dissociation or psychologically "going away" from the situation was the best defense. Most dissociative states are triggered by a significant or stressful event. Major types of dissociation include *dissociative amnesia* (the person is unable to remember important personal information), *depersonalization disorder* (the person feels detached from his or her body and as though he or she is an outside observer), and *dissociative fugue* (the person suddenly leaves his or her locale, forgets his or her identity, and assumes a new one). Dissociative disorders are thought to affect 4 to 5 percent of the population at some time.[1] Amnesia and fugue are most common during natural disasters and combat. Age at onset is usually quite young and these disorders rarely develop after age forty.

Dissociative identity disorder (DID) is the new name for a severe psychiatric disorder previously known as *multiple personality disorder*. It is the most commonly known and most severe of the dissociative disorders. Nearly all persons with DID report severe physical or sexual abuse as children. The hallmark of DID is the existence of two or more distinct identities or personalities within the same individual. Each of these distinct identities, or *alters*, is a complex and integrated personality with a name, gender, history, personality features, medical problems, social relations, and even distinct intelligence levels. The number of alters may vary from two to fifty in the same person. The original person is sometimes called the "host alter" and is usually not consciously aware of the other alters, although they are aware of the host and may be aware of one another. The alters often show extreme departures from the host's normal personality. For example, a shy host may have alters including a prostitute, transvestite, or devil. Alters may differ in age, gender, and race from the host.

Persons with DID are often in therapy for years before being officially diagnosed with the disorder since they often come to treatment for other reasons (such as depression), and the alters are difficult to detect. Signs of DID include use of the pronoun "we" instead of "I" in conversation, being charged for things the person (host) does not recall buying, or hearing voices coming from inside one's head (versus outside as in the case of psychotic disorders). It is very important that a professional, with *substantial* experience, assess and diagnose DID. This disorder is occasionally faked by persons who have a significant need for the attention that DID nearly always generates.

Dissociative Identity Disorder: Key Indicators

- Two or more distinct identities or personality states are present in one person.
- At least two of these personality states occasionally take control of the person's behavior.
- The person shows inability to recall important personal information that is too extensive to be explained by ordinary forgetfulness.

Dissociative identity disorder has often been falsely diagnosed in persons with other trauma-related disorders, depression, psychosis, or personality disorders. When this disorder is suspected, the person should be referred to a psychiatrist, psychologist, or clinical social worker with specialized training and experience. Therapy for DID can be long, tedious, and only marginally successful. The goal is to integrate the alters into a single unified personality, which requires bringing to awareness those traumatic memories that the person's alters have successfully allowed him or her to avoid. Medications are generally not helpful and hypnosis can be dangerous because these people are so suggestible (new alters may be easily and inadvertently created).

Although the prognosis for full recovery is guarded, full recovery does occur and maintenance of hope is critical for both parishioners with DID and their loved ones.

Summary and Guidelines

When a pastor learns that a parishioner has experienced a traumatic life event, he or she is encouraged to review the symptoms of acute stress disorder with the expectation of encountering symptoms of dissociation, avoidance, and heightened anxiety and arousal. Parishioners may feel as though they are going "crazy" or they may be ashamed about their level of fear following the experience. Normalizing posttrauma symptoms is a first step, followed closely by an invitation to meet with the parishioner to hear his or her story. When groups of parishioners are involved, arranging a formal debriefing by a counselor experienced with this procedure is recommended. Keep in mind that speedy intervention following a traumatic event is the most effective method of reducing the risk of eventual PTSD. Finally, when a parishioner appears to have an alter personality, or there are reports from others that this is so, we recommend rapid referral to a practitioner who is well trained and experienced in the treatment of dissociative identity disorder. This disorder is both rare and particularly difficult to resolve. It is often associated with severe childhood abuse and serious adult personality disturbance, which make therapy challenging for even the most skilled clinician.

SUBSTANCE ABUSE DISORDERS

Presenting Complaints

Alex is a twenty-year-old college junior who is facing expulsion from a local university following his third alcohol-related incident on campus. During the past two years, Alex has been involved in two altercations with other students and campus police while drinking. Most recently, he was arrested at a basketball game for public drunkenness. He is also on probation for driving while intoxicated. Although Alex does not use alcohol on a daily basis, he tends to drink to intoxication on weekends in spite of his arrests and the threat of expulsion.

*   *   *

Megan is a forty-seven-year-old married mother of two adult children. She comes to counseling with her husband who is "fed up" with her refusal to cut down on her alcohol consumption. Although Megan denies she drinks excessively, her husband notes that her drinking has increased dramatically since the children left home. He also mentions that Megan drinks in the morning and continues throughout the day. Megan appears unable to skip a day of drinking, and her husband has discovered alcohol hidden in unusual places around the home. Megan admits having attempted to reduce her alcohol consumption without success.

*   *   *

Jeffery is an attorney for a large and competitive law firm. He began using amphetamines a year ago in an attempt to increase his alertness late at night so that he could work longer and accrue more billable hours. He is up for promotion to partner in the firm and feels tremendous pressure to succeed. Jeffery became alarmed recently when he realized he is now using eight times the dosage of amphetamines to achieve the same sense of alertness. When he has attempted to reduce the amount he uses, he becomes fatigued, has unpleasant dreams, feels agitated, and has trouble sleeping.

Common Features and Symptoms

Addictive behavior may include any behavior based on the excessive or uncontrollable "need" for a substance or activity. By *substance,* we mean alcohol or legal and illegal drugs. Legal drugs may include both prescribed and over-the-counter medications. Addictive behavior may include excessive or harmful use of substances such as alcohol, cocaine, or marijuana. A food addiction may involve excessive intake of high-calorie food—resulting in obesity. Addictions may also be present when sexual behavior becomes so disruptive that it interferes with relationships or employment.

In this section, we focus on the most commonly abused substances or *psychoactive drugs:* alcohol, narcotics, amphetamines, barbiturates, hallucinogens, and marijuana. For all substances, there are two levels of substance-related disorder: *abuse* and *dependence.* We describe the major characteristics of substance abuse and substance dependence. We then very briefly describe the distinctive elements of each type of addictive substance.

Subtypes

Substance Abuse

Substance abuse always suggests a maladaptive pattern of using a substance in spite of serious and repeated negative consequences that are caused by the substance. The substance abuser will use the drug despite failing to fulfill important role expectations or in situations that could be physically dangerous (e.g., driving while intoxicated). He or she may also continue to use the substance despite serious legal problems or social and occupational problems resulting from the substance use. The substance abuser may neglect children, end up in altercations, and face serious marital problems, which are directly caused by the substance abuse.

Substance Abuse: Key Indicators

- The person uses the substance repeatedly despite serious impairment or distress, as indicated by one or more of the following during a twelve-month period: (1) failure to fulfill major role obligations at home, work, or school; (2) using the substance in a potentially hazardous situation; (3) recurrent substance-related legal problems; (4) serious social or interpersonal problems.

Substance abuse may be applied to nearly any psychoactive drug that a person might use in a maladaptive way. It is different from substance dependence because it is less severe and does not involve increasing tolerance for the substance, or withdrawal symptoms if the substance is discontinued. For example, a parishioner may have several DUI arrests, yet use alcohol only infrequently. Although the parishioner is not dependent on the substance, he or she repeatedly uses it in harmful and self-defeating ways.

Substance Dependence

Substance dependence is more severe than substance abuse. As in the case of abuse, those who have become dependent on substances continue to use them despite significant problems. A person may become dependent on nearly any drug or psychoactive substance. In addition, substance dependence involves repeated use resulting in tolerance, withdrawal, and compulsive-use behavior.[2] *Tolerance* for a psychoactive substance occurs when the user begins to need greatly increased amounts of the substance for intoxication (or the desired effect). Using the same amount becomes unsatisfying. The degree to which increasing tolerance occurs varies across substances. For example, amphetamine dependence can result in a tenfold increase in the dosage used, while hallucinogenic drugs produce comparatively little tolerance.

Withdrawal is a physical response that occurs when blood or tissue levels of a substance decline—usually after prolonged and heavy use. This decline results in maladaptive (and possibly deadly) symptoms. Although the typical withdrawal symptoms vary with each substance type, frequently occurring withdrawal symptoms include: tremors, sweating, insomnia, nausea/vomiting, anxiety, seizures, agitation, hallucinations, fatigue, restlessness, poor concentration, depressed mood, and increased or decreased appetite. The substance-dependent person will typically find withdrawal symptoms so aversive that they will continue to use the substance to avoid them. This may result in a pattern of repeated use that begins in the morning and continues throughout the day.

Compulsive use of the substance is yet another indication of substance dependence. Several behavior patterns may suggest that someone is using a substance in a compulsive manner. For example, a person may use more of a substance than he or she intends to use or may make unsuccessful attempts to reduce the amount used. The person may also spend a great deal of time obtaining, using, and recovering from the substance. At the same time, he or she may begin to withdraw from important family, occupational, and social activities. A final indicator of compulsive use is the continued use of the substance despite clear links between the substance and the person's psychological and physical problems.

Substance Dependence: Key Indicators

- The person continues to use a substance in spite of consistent evidence of impairment or disturbance (socially, relationally, occupationally, or physically) in his or her life.
- There may be increasing tolerance of the substance, meaning that higher doses are required to become intoxicated.
- When the person attempts to discontinue the substance, he or she may experience serious physical withdrawal symptoms.
- The person usually cannot cut down on the amount of the substance used and he or she often uses more than intended.
- The person spends a great deal of time obtaining, using, or recovering from the substance.
- There is a pattern of withdrawal from family, friends, social activities, and job-related activities.

Substance dependence is an extremely serious condition. Not only is it among the most common and costly of all health problems in the United States each year, substance dependence is devastating for children and families. It is very important for pastors to know the indicators of substance abuse and dependence. They must be ready to assist family members in identifying the problem, confronting the abuser, and assisting with arrangements for treatment and follow-up support. It is worth noting that withdrawal symptoms from many substances can be lethal and often require medical support. When a parishioner expresses an intention to "go cold turkey," it is recommended that a referral to his or her physician be made.

Major Substances

The following section briefly identifies and describes the major psychoactive substances that parishioners may abuse or become dependent upon. Keep in mind that the previously listed key indicators for abuse and dependence apply to each of these substances. Although the specifics for tolerance and withdrawal symptoms may change, the overall characteristics of the substance-abusing dependent person will remain consistent across substances.

Alcohol

Alcohol is the most frequently abused of the psychoactive substances. Although many use alcohol moderately, millions abuse it daily and millions more will become alcohol dependent (alcoholic) during their lifetimes.[3] Each year, 100,000 Americans die from alcohol-related causes. Genetic, biological, psychological, and social factors all play a role in determining who may become alcoholic. Alcohol is a central nervous system depressant that may eventually produce chronic health problems such as impotence, stomach problems, memory impairment, liver cirrhosis, cancer, and even brain shrinkage. As a drug, it affects the higher brain centers, impairing judgment, impulse control, and rational processes. Alcoholics are considerably more prone to suicide, mental health problems, and family and work problems than people who consume alcohol moderately.

Narcotics

Morphine and heroin are the most frequently abused of the narcotic drugs. Narcotics are derivatives of opium, and their use dates back 5,000 years. Morphine and heroin have often been used to treat pain and they are effective pain relievers. Unfortunately, they are extremely addictive drugs that quickly lead to increasing tolerance and serious (even life-threatening) withdrawal symptoms. Those who begin using heroin are most likely to state that pleasure, curiosity, and peer pressure were the primary reasons for using the drug initially. The causes of narcotic addiction include brain receptivity to the substances, personal pathology, and social/cultural influences. Those who become dependent on narcotics become increasingly withdrawn, indifferent to relationships and events around them, and progressively more reliant on the effects of the drug to reduce tension and keep withdrawal symptoms at bay.

Amphetamines

In contrast to narcotics and alcohol, which slow down or depress the nervous system, amphetamines stimulate and speed up the nervous system by stimulating the cortex. This is why they are known as *stimulants.* Cocaine is the most common of the stimulant drugs. It may be ingested by sniffing, smoking, swallowing, or injecting, and it typically produces a euphoric state for four to six hours after use. During this time, the user may experience confidence and contentment. As the user becomes increasingly addicted to cocaine, symptoms such as dizziness, headache, depressed mood, and restlessness may occur between doses. In more advanced cases, those who are dependent on cocaine may experience psychotic hallucinations (much like schizophrenics) and severe depression as well as serious legal, family, job, and marital problems. Because the drug is quite expensive, criminal activity may begin as a way of supporting the dependency. Other amphetamine drugs include Dexedrine and Methedrine. Persons may begin using these medications or cocaine to curb appetite, decrease fatigue, or achieve a sense of arousal with respect to attention and sexual interest. Unfortunately, amphetamines have been widely accepted by middle-class culture.

Barbiturates

Barbiturates are powerful *sedatives* that have some important medical uses, but are extremely addictive and possibly lethal when used excessively. Similar to alcohol in their effect on the central nervous system, barbiturates act as depressants, causing the person using them to experience relaxation, reduction in tension, and eventually drowsiness and sleep. Although mild doses may produce only relaxation, higher doses can produce sleep almost immediately. Overdoses can paralyze the brain's respiration center, resulting in death. Repeated use of barbiturates can lead to increased tolerance, compulsive use patterns, and withdrawal symptoms if discontinued. Side effects from chronic use may include sluggishness, slow speech, reduced comprehension and memory, sudden mood shifts, loss of motor coordination, and depression. Even though tolerance may increase, the amount of barbiturate needed to cause death does not increase, which makes overdose increasingly more likely as use continues. Barbiturates are not typically considered "fashionable" and are seldom used experimentally. The typical barbiturate-dependent person will be middle-aged and will use the drug to reduce anxiety or help with sleep. Barbiturates are especially lethal when mixed with alcohol.

LSD

Hallucinogens or *psychedelic* drugs have the effect of distorting perceptions such that people see and hear things in unusual ways. These drugs include LSD, mescaline, psilocybin, and PCP ("angel dust"). The most potent of the hallucinogens, LSD, can cause intoxication with an amount smaller than a grain of salt. Following ingestion of LSD, the person will typically experience approximately eight hours of sensory perception distortions, mood swings, and feelings of detachment. The experience of perceiving distorted objects, intense colors, and new thoughts and images can be extremely pleasant or terrifying. Traumatic responses to hallucinogens have been described as "bad trips," which can cause people to jump from high places or set themselves on fire in response to their distorted perceptions. One interesting side effect of hallucinogen use is the flashback (i.e., the involuntary reoccurrence of a perceptual distortion or hallucination weeks or months after taking the drug). Although LSD and other hallucinogens were touted as therapeutic and possibly consciousness-expanding drugs in the 1960s, no research has supported their usefulness in that regard. Hallucinogens are not among the most addictive drugs, yet they may produce extremely dangerous behavior and even psychosis when used repeatedly.

Marijuana

Marijuana and its derivative, hashish *(hash),* are technically hallucinogens. However, the intensity and duration of their effects make them distinct from the drugs discussed previously. Marijuana comes from the leaves and tops of the hemp plant. Both marijuana and hash are typically smoked in the form of cigarettes or in pipes. Marijuana has been used for centuries, but became particularly popular in America during the 1960s. Today, the majority of young adults have experimented with this drug. Although the precise effects of marijuana vary depending on the dose, purity of the drug, social setting, and the user's experience and expectations, common effects include mild euphoria, pleasant relaxation, sensations of drifting or floating, a distorted perception of time, and interruption of short-term memory. The effects of marijuana rarely last longer than two or three hours. When marijuana is used chronically, as is often the case, symptoms may include decreased self-control, memory impairment, and problems with sexual functioning in men. There is also evidence that depression is linked to chronic marijuana use.

Summary and Guidelines

Substance-related disorders are among the most common and costly disorders the pastor is likely to face. In fact, abuse of and dependence on alcohol or drugs may be one of the most underidentified yet widespread problems in the church today. The causes of substance abuse and dependence range from genetic predisposition (as in the case of alcohol) to social pressure and intentional experimentation (especially with marijuana and LSD). The pastor may first become aware of a substance disorder through family members of the addicted person. Physical abuse, neglect of family or spouse, financial distress, and occupational troubles (or actual job loss) may all be initial markers of substance dependence.

Because denial of the problem is a hallmark symptom of dependency, the pastor may play a critical role in empowering those who love the addict or alcoholic to organize a clear confrontation with the person about his or her substance problem. Family members must focus on what the person will have to do to remain in the home and salvage his or her job and relationships. It is best if this intervention is arranged by a professional who is trained in the treatment of substance-related disorders. Treatment in severe cases may begin with hospitalization to manage the most severe symptoms of physical and psychological withdrawal from the substance. This will typically be followed by outpatient treatment designed to keep the individual completely abstinent from substances while focusing on a program of counseling and social support from others recovering from dependency. Many churches host meetings of Alcoholics Anonymous and other substance-related disorder recovery groups. This is often an excellent way for the church to blend stewardship, ministry, counseling, and discipleship. Since alcoholism and other forms of substance dependence are chronic problems, and the dependent person is always at risk for a relapse, the pastor and family members will need to remain vigilant for signs of continued use. The pastor will also need to support and empower loved ones in their attempts at setting limits with the substance-dependent person.

SLEEP DISORDERS

Presenting Complaints

Martin is a twenty-seven-year-old parishioner who comes to you for pastoral counseling. He looks fatigued and you note bags under his eyes. He complains of not sleeping well in spite of exercising, getting to bed on time, and avoiding all caffeine after lunchtime. He has tried praying and talking with his wife before bed, but he still stays awake until well after one o'clock in the morning. He has a new job as chief of security at a major bank. Although he was initially anxious about performing well at work, he now feels most upset about his inability to sleep and believes work is only a minor problem in comparison.

*   *   *

Tonya is a thirty-four-year-old mother of one. She comes to counseling due to an increasing problem with sleeping too much. During the last year, Tonya has slept longer and longer at night. She currently sleeps twelve hours at night and still wakes up feeling exhausted in the morning. She also reports "uncontrollable catnaps" during the day. She may fall asleep for an hour while at home or on a break at work. Her boss is growing increasingly irritated with her sleepiness. Tonya denies using drugs or medications.

*   *   *

Stanton is a six-year-old whose parents bring him to you out of concern for his spiritual well-being. During the last two months, he has been waking at night with seemingly uncontrollable "fits" of terror and he cannot be comforted. Though his parents have tried many methods of waking him during these "terrifying bouts," nothing seems to rouse him from his very deep but troubled sleep. Stanton often screams, trembles, and writhes during these episodes. His parents fear he is being troubled by evil forces at night.

Common Features and Symptoms

Good sleep is often taken for granted by most of us. Unfortunately, millions of Americans experience the negative effects of sleep problems, which can become extremely severe at times. Research suggests that sleep serves to restore us physically and psychologically and that it is a critical form of self-protection or energy conservation. The significance of sleep is evident in the effects on those who are deprived of it. In both experimental and natural cases of sleep loss, people lose the ability to perform physical and mental tasks, and eventually show numerous health problems including decreased immune system effectiveness. Our need for sleep declines slowly over the life span. Americans are notorious for being chronically sleep deprived. Sleep researchers have commented that our fast-paced lifestyle has meant that few Americans know what it feels like to be fully alert![4]

Human beings experience a rather predictable sleep cycle consisting of movement through five distinct stages about every ninety minutes. Starting with stage 1 and moving through stage 4, we become more relaxed and more deeply asleep. Electroencephalograph (EEG) readings of brain activity show that our brain waves move from high frequency *beta* waves to lower frequency *theta* and *delta* waves. Our breathing deepens, our heart rate becomes regular, and our blood pressure decreases. Eventually, we will enter the fifth stage, which is called rapid eye movement (REM) sleep. Immediately, our eyes begin rapid movement as active dreaming starts. Our heart rate and blood pressure increase and brain wave activity returns to higher frequencies. In fact, the person in REM sleep appears to be physiologically awake. Actually, they are physically paralyzed, but actively dreaming. REM sleep is critical for physical and emotional restoration. Following deprivation of REM sleep, a person will experience a "REM rebound" or an extended period of REM sleep.

In this section, we briefly cover several of the *primary sleep disorders,* which are caused by abnormalities in a person's sleep-wake cycle. This may mean problems in the mechanisms that cause the onset or timing of sleep. The DSM-IV[3] divides primary sleep disorders into *dyssomnias* and *parasomnias*. Dyssomnias are disturbances in the amount, quality, or timing of sleep while parasomnias describe abnormal behavior or bodily events that occur during sleep—usually during specific stages of sleep or in the transition between sleep and waking.

When sleep difficulties are caused by psychiatric problems, medical problems, or substance abuse, they are referred to as *secondary sleep disorders*, but we will not address these here. When a pastor learns that a parishioner is suffering from a sleep problem (most typically insomnia), several common contributors can be explored. First, stress or a significant life change often produces sleep difficulties. This may include a loss, anxiety about an upcoming event, or a recently disturbing experience. Second, the pastor may inquire about substance use. Caffeine or alcohol use is often a primary cause of insomnia. Is the person using caffeinated drinks late in the day or using alcohol to become drowsy? Both can disrupt normal sleep patterns. Finally, depression and anxiety are commonly linked to sleep disturbance. A parishioner's report of insomnia may actually be the first sign that he or she is struggling with depression.

Two dyssomnias *(primary insomnia* and *primary hypersomnia)* are covered first. These problems involve difficulty falling and staying asleep or excessive sleepiness. Next, we address three parasomnia disorders *(nightmare disorder*, *sleep terror disorder,* and *sleepwalking disorder)*.

Subtypes

Primary Insomnia

Between 20 and 30 million Americans suffer from insomnia each year.[5] Insomniacs cannot fall asleep or remain asleep, or feel fatigued even after sleeping a normal amount of time. Most commonly, the parishioner with insomnia will describe difficulty falling asleep or a pattern of waking up during the night and having trouble returning to sleep. The insomniac often develops a vicious conditioned cycle of disturbance *about* not sleeping. As the parishioner becomes increasingly preoccupied with his or her lack of normal sleep, he or she may become more upset and anxious, which further disrupts normal sleep. Paradoxically, insomniacs will begin to sleep normally when they stop trying to make themselves sleep. That is why encouraging people with insomnia to try to stay awake while lying in bed often causes them to fall asleep.

Parishioners who may be most prone to insomnia are those with personality styles characterized by worry. Those preoccupied with physical health and various medical symptoms are also likely to over-react to the first signs of difficulty sleeping. Very often, insomniacs use sedatives such as alcohol or barbiturates to get to sleep. Although these drugs may produce some initial drowsiness and even sleep, they eventually disrupt the sleep cycle even further. They also lose their effectiveness over time and can be quite addictive. Although typically a response to a life stress, caffeine use, mood problems, or other factors, insomnia may also signal a physical condition that can only be detected by a physician.

Primary Insomnia: Key Indicators

- The person complains of difficulty in falling or staying sleep, or feeling fatigued after sleeping.
- Because the person feels fatigued during the day, he or she becomes upset, or experiences problems socially or at work.
- The insomnia lasts for at least a month and is not due primarily to a physical or psychiatric disorder.

Primary Hypersomnia

The parishioner with hypersomnia also has a dyssomnia problem; however, in this case the person describes excessive sleepiness that has lasted for at least a month. The individual will describe sleeping longer than he or she intended at night or episodes of sleeping (planned or not) during the day. Very often, the hypersomniac will sleep considerably longer than eight hours at night, yet have tremendous difficulty waking. Long naps often leave the person feeling unrefreshed or experiencing "sleep drunkenness." The person may also be prone to "dropping off" when in a low-stimulation environment, which could be embarrassing or dangerous. In cases of primary hypersomnia, the pastor should be concerned about major depression, substance abuse, or a potentially serious medical problem such as a recent head trauma or an endocrine abnormality. Only about 5 to 10 percent of those with sleep disorders have hypersomnia.[3]

Primary Hypersomnia: Key Indicators

- For at least a month, the person complains of excessive sleepiness and sleeps for prolonged periods at night, or has daytime sleep episodes almost daily.
- This excessive sleepiness causes the person to become upset or results in social or work-related problems.
- The sleepiness is not due primarily to a physical or psychiatric disorder.

Nightmare Disorder

On occasion, a parishioner or a family member may describe a pattern of disturbing or terrifying nightmares. Persons with nightmare disorder often have very elaborate and extremely anxiety-provoking dream experiences. The individual will often awaken from nightmares abruptly, have a clear memory of the nightmare content, and be fearful of returning to sleep. The nightmares usually involve some real physical threat (being pursued or attacked) or, less frequently, extreme failure or embarrassment. If the person has experienced a traumatic event, the content of the nightmares may reflect that experience. Because nightmares are dreams, these episodes occur almost exclusively during REM sleep. As people go through several sleep cycles each night (including several episodes of REM), the nightmares can occur almost anytime. Most often, the person wakes during the second half of the night. Typically, he or she will awake abruptly from the nightmare and experience extreme arousal in the form of palpitations, increased heart rate, and sweating. Obviously, frequent nightmares are quite distressing for the person experiencing them, but they can also be upsetting to those around them. As a result, these nightmares may lead to insomnia and job-related problems.

Nightmare Disorder: Key Indicators

- The person describes a pattern of waking suddenly from sleep with vivid recall of lengthy and extremely frightening dreams.
- After waking, the person rapidly becomes alert and aware that he or she has been dreaming.
- The person is upset by the dreams, which may cause disturbance in relationships or work performance.

Sleep Terror Disorder

Sleep terror disorder also involves an experience of extreme terror during sleep. However, in contrast to nightmare disorder, this person does not wake up following the event and does not remember specific details of a nightmare. During a typical sleep terror episode, the person will sit up abruptly, often screaming or crying, with a frightened expression and physical signs of panic such as rapid breathing, racing heart, and sweating. Attempts to wake this person are typically futile—which can be frustrating for parents attempting to wake their terrified child. If the person does wake up, he or she will usually be disoriented and confused. The following day, the person will usually be unable to recall anything about the event. Sleep terrors occur during the deepest stages of sleep. They often cause distress for the people sleeping with or near the person affected and can lead to relationship problems or embarrassment.

Sleep terror disorder is most common in children but can persist into adulthood. In children, the disorder is not related to any emotional disturbance and usually begins between the ages of four and twelve and resolves on its own by adolescence. In adults, however, sleep terror disorder is correlated with other psychiatric problems such as post-traumatic stress disorder (PTSD). In general, it is best to simply calm the person experiencing a sleep terror, without trying to wake him or her, because he or she will sometimes resist with physical force such as punching or kicking.

Sleep Terror Disorder: Key Indicators

- The person has repeated episodes of waking abruptly, usually with a scream, from deep sleep.
- The person shows symptoms such as intense fear, rapid breathing, and sweating, and resists, or does not respond to, attempts by others to calm or wake him or her.
- There is little recall of the event and the episodes may lead to some impairment in functioning—especially social functioning.

Sleepwalking Disorder

The final parasomnia we discuss is sleepwalking disorder. Between 10 and 30 percent of all children have had at least one episode of sleepwalking, while only 1 to 7 percent of adults have an episode.[3] Sleepwalking disorder involves repeated episodes in which an individual sits up or rises from bed and engages in some motor behavior, such as walking about, before waking spontaneously or returning to bed. During sleepwalking episodes, it is not uncommon for people to walk around the bedroom, up and down stairs, and even outside. They may even engage in complex tasks (some sleepwalkers have driven cars!) and respond to questions in a vague way. They may wake on their own, be wakened by others, or simply return to sleep. (They may wake up in strange places in the morning.)

Although there is some danger that sleepwalkers may inadvertently harm themselves or others, this happens only rarely, as pain or other sudden stimuli often cause them to wake up. Sleepwalking may be disturbing for other family members or roommates and, therefore, embarrassment or other social problems may occur. Also, sleepwalking will cause a person to be discharged from military service for obvious reasons. During the sleepwalking episode, a person typically has a blank stare and is only minimally responsive (or not at all) to questions or verbal directions from others. He or she may or may not report memory of the event and does not necessarily dream during these episodes.

Sleepwalking Disorder: Key Indicators

- The person routinely rises from bed and walks about during the night.
- The person has a blank expression, is relatively unresponsive, and may be difficult to wake.
- There is very little memory of the event, but these repeated episodes may cause embarrassment, distress, and social or work-related impairment.

Summary and Guidelines

Sleep disorders, especially primary insomnia, are exceptionally common. In any congregation, the pastor can reasonably assume that a significant proportion (perhaps 10 percent or more) of parishioners suffer with sleep disruptions or abnormalities. Although the causes of sleep problems are wide-ranging, the most common include lifestyle factors (substance abuse, excess caffeine use, eating before bed, lack of exercise, or intentional sleep deprivation), anxiety (regarding upcoming events or preoccupation with lack of sleep), recent trauma or loss, and mood-related factors—primarily depression—which nearly always produces insomnia or hypersomnia. Very often, the pastor may provide powerful reassurance to the parishioner by simply informing him or her that sleep problems are quite normal. For example, telling parents of a child with sleep terrors that this is a rather common occurrence in children, that they need not wake the child, and that sleep terrors decline with age, may be very helpful. Similarly, suggesting to a parishioner plagued with anxiety about not being able to fall asleep that he or she should stop trying to sleep and instead try to remain awake while lying in bed may be very effective. Prayer and scripture reading are excellent substitutes for lying in bed and worrying about lack of sleep.

It is also worth repeating, however, that sleep disturbance may be an initial signal of a physical difficulty. Suggesting that the parishioner seek out his or her physician for a physical exam is always wise. Subtle head injuries, neurological problems (e.g., brain tumor), endocrine changes, and other disorders may cause sleep difficulties. Also, sleep apnea and other potentially serious breathing problems may first become evident when a person reports feeling fatigued, hypersomniac, or insomniac.

SEXUAL DISORDERS

Presenting Complaints

Hugh is a twenty-eight-year-old parishioner who comes to see you, with his wife Barbara, for pastoral counseling. Both Hugh and Barbara appear uneasy about discussing exactly why they have come to see you at this time. After some vague statements about their sexual relationship, Hugh states that his wife is making a "big deal" about the fact that he enjoys it when she wears shoes during sex. Barbara insists that Hugh appears most aroused by her shoes. She has discovered him masturbating with her shoes on occasion and he is unable to perform sexually unless shoes play a prominent role in the sexual scenario.

*   *   *

Sally and Tom also come for marital counseling. Sally appears extremely embarrassed while Tom appears both weary and angry.

The two have been married only two months, but Tom notes they have had "relations" only twice. He states that Sally is the problem and insists she has no interest in sex, although Tom has gone to great lengths to create a comfortable and enjoyable experience for her. Sally hesitantly acknowledges being "repulsed" by the idea of sexual intercourse and admits she finds it "filthy" and "disgusting." She denies any interest in sexual contact with her husband.

*   *   *

Stuart is a fifty-eight-year-old widower who has been active in the church for years. He has been a friend of yours for some time. Over coffee one day, he sheepishly states recent trouble "raising the flagpole." When you correctly clarify that he is referring to trouble with erections, he becomes forlorn and insists it just means he is getting old. He notes that his erection problems have happened a few times in the last year and that they have caused him extreme embarrassment with his new wife. He confides that he is considering leaving his marriage and says, "It doesn't seem fair to my new bride, you know."

Common Features and Symptoms

Sexual dysfunction refers to impairment in either the desire for sexual gratification or in the ability to achieve it. In this section, we highlight the four major types of sexual dysfunction and also discuss *paraphilias.* Parishioners suffering from sexual dysfunction experience disruption in the normal sexual response cycle, which leads to distress and, often, relational problems. The four major categories of sexual dysfunction include *dysfunctions of sexual desire, dysfunctions of sexual arousal, dysfunctions of orgasm,* and *sexual pain disorders.* Each of these categories involves disruption in the normal sexual response cycle or pain with intercourse. The four phases in the human sexual response cycle are as follows:

1. *Desire:* Fantasies about and desire to have sex.
2. *Excitement:* Experience of sexual pleasure and physical changes (penile erection in men, and lubrication and vaginal swelling in women).

3. *Orgasm:* Peaking sexual pleasure and release of sexual tension (ejaculation in men and vaginal contractions in women).
4. *Resolution:* Sense of relaxation and well-being.

In contrast to sexual dysfunctions, which typically involve disturbance in this sexual response cycle, *paraphilias* are recurrent, intense sexual urges, fantasies, or behaviors that involve unusual objects, activities, or situations. Repetitive acting out of these unusual sexual behaviors leads the parishioner to significant personal distress or impairment of relationships or work performance.

The paradox of sexual disorders is that, although they are among the easiest mental health problems to treat, they are often the most difficult for parishioners to discuss with one another, let alone their pastor. Unfortunately, some medical doctors and counselors are equally uncomfortable talking frankly about sexuality, which can certainly make the experience more harrowing for the individual or couple. Because of this discomfort with the topic of sexuality and sexual dysfunction, we recommend that pastors be very willing to introduce the topic of sexuality early on in counseling with couples.

A matter-of-fact statement about the normalcy of sexual concerns among Christian couples may be enough of an icebreaker so that the couple will feel comfortable enough to broach problems in this area. We have also found that some parishioners are considerably more likely than the general population to view sex as dirty or pathological. Thankfully, classic research by Masters and Johnson has largely served to dispel this thinking among most medical and mental health practitioners.[6] Nonetheless, the pastor may need to educate parishioners regarding the basics of the human sexual response and dispel myths linking sexuality, or sexual difficulty, with evil in the minds of some couples.

Subtypes

Disorders of Sexual Desire

A parishioner may present with one of two major forms of sexual desire dysfunction that involve the absence of sexual fantasies as well as desire for sexual activity. *Hypoactive sexual desire disorder* may be present when a man or woman has little or no sexual drive or interest.

Although there is nothing medically wrong with this person, sexual motivation is somehow blocked. Such a parishioner will rarely come to the pastor's attention on his or her own. Instead, the person's partner will complain of inadequate sexual activity. The second dysfunction of sexual desire is *sexual aversion disorder*. In this case, the parishioner shows extreme aversion to, and avoidance of, all genital sexual contact with a partner. This disorder appears equally prevalent in men and women, and may be linked to parental or community messages equating all sexual behavior with sin or filth.

Disorders of Sexual Desire: Key Indicators

- Persistent deficit or absence of sexual fantasies and/or desire for sexual activity or persistent aversion to, and avoidance of, all genital sexual contact with a sexual partner.
- The disturbance causes the person considerable distress or problems with relationships.

Sexual Arousal Disorders

There are two major types of sexual arousal disorder. *Male erectile disorder* involves an inability to achieve or maintain an erection (formerly known as impotence). *Female sexual arousal disorder* refers to nonresponsiveness to erotic stimulation both physically and emotionally (formerly known as frigidity). A very small number of men are never able to achieve an erection. The cause of this lifelong erection problem is thought to be biological or medically based. The vast majority of men who experience problems with erectile functioning have what is known as acquired or situational erectile disorder. In these cases, the male has had satisfactory erections in the past, but now suffers complete or occasional difficulty achieving erections. Most often, relational problems or anxiety are to blame for erectile problems. For example, it is extremely common for men to engage in "spectatoring" following a single experience of incomplete erection. The male becomes anxious and preoccupied with the experience of not "performing" sexually. He is then so nervous about his erection that he ensures subsequent episodes of erection difficulty. Of course, erection problems become more common as a man ages. By the age of seventy, for example, about half of married men report having had some experiences of erectile difficulties.[7] Although many men remain capable of sustaining normal erections to the age of 100 and beyond, it is important to expect that older male parishioners may experience increasing rates of erectile difficulty and frustration.

In many ways, female sexual arousal disorder is the female counterpart to erectile disorder. Women with this difficulty do not produce the characteristic swelling and lubrication of the vulva and vaginal tissues during sexual stimulation. This, of course, may make intercourse painful and lead to avoidance of sexual activity. In many, cases, the cause of the deficit in sexual arousal is situational and may be correlated with factors such as dislike of, or disgust with, one's current sexual partner, distorted views regarding the evil nature of sex, or some experience of sexual trauma.

Sexual Arousal Disorders: Key Indicators

- Persistent inability to achieve or maintain an adequate erection or adequate lubrication-swelling response of sexual excitement.
- The disturbance causes the person considerable distress or problems with relationships.

Orgasmic Disorders

Three sexual disorders are characterized by an inability to achieve an orgasm or problematic timing of the orgasm. *Premature ejaculation* is defined as an unsatisfactorily brief period between the beginning of sexual stimulation and the occurrence of ejaculation. Whether ejaculation occurs during initial stimulation or shortly after intercourse begins, the timing of the male's orgasm causes him embarrassment or inhibits the couple's mutual satisfaction in the sexual encounter. Not surprisingly, premature ejaculation is most common when there has been a lengthy period of abstinence from sexual activity. Younger men are also more prone to have at least occasional experiences of ejaculating earlier during intercourse than they wish.

Male orgasmic disorder is quite the opposite problem. In this case, a man is unable to ejaculate during intercourse. Because men often feel ashamed of an inability to achieve an erection or to have an orgasm during sex, it is not uncommon for this problem to be mentioned initially by a spouse or partner during pastoral counseling. Often refusing to disclose the problem to others, men may suffer significant anxiety about their perceived "defect" and may simply avoid sexual activity with their spouses, creating additional relational problems. Men who cannot achieve orgasm through any means (e.g., masturbation) are extremely rare. More often, the problem is situational—indicating anxiety problems or dislike of one's partner.

Finally, *female orgasmic disorder* is largely equivalent to the male version just discussed. Women struggling with this problem report an inability to achieve an orgasm either through sexual intercourse or direct manual stimulation. Although they may enjoy sexual stimulation and be responsive sexually, they remain unable to achieve orgasm. Of course, the range of orgasmic experiences varies widely among women and it is important to rely on the woman's own report of satisfaction with her sexual responsiveness before assuming any dysfunction.

Orgasmic Disorders: Key Indicators

- In either a male or female, persistent delay in or absence of an orgasm following normal sexual stimulation.
- In a male, excitement or persistent ejaculation with minimal sexual stimulation, or before the person wishes to ejaculate.
- The disturbance causes the person considerable distress or problems with relationships.

Sexual Pain Disorders

Two sexual problems, *vaginismus* and *dyspareunia,* involve painful experiences during intercourse. These disorders nearly always necessitate a medical referral in order to rule out a physical problem before a parishioner can be referred for sex therapy. Vaginismus describes an involuntary muscle spasm at the entrance to the vagina that prevents penetration and sexual intercourse. Because the woman with vaginismus experiences considerable discomfort during intercourse, the problem is likely to be extremely distressing to both her and her partner. In this case, the vaginal muscles appear conditioned to respond with contraction to impending penetration. Although women with this disorder may also have a sexual arousal deficit, it is possible to experience vaginismus following normal arousal. Previous experiences of sexual trauma are correlated with this disorder.

Dyspareunia, or painful intercourse, is possible in men, but is much more frequent in women. There is often a physical cause for this problem (e.g., infection or an actual structural problem with the genitals). However, it may also be caused by psychological factors. For example, a woman with a strong aversion to sex may express and experience her displeasure in the form of painful intercourse. Thankfully, dysfunctions involving pain are among the rarest of the sexual problems. Physical explanations must always be ruled out for these problems before treatment is attempted.

Sexual Pain Disorders: Key Indicators

- Persistent genital pain during intercourse in either a male or female, or persistent involuntary spasm of the vaginal muscles that interferes with sexual intercourse.
- The disturbance causes the person considerable distress or problems with relationships.

Paraphilias

In contrast to the sexual disorders discussed previously, paraphilias typically involve what most people would consider "aberrant" or disturbed sexual behavior. The essential component of a paraphiliac disorder is that the person experiences recurring and intense sexual fantasies, sexual urges, or engages in sexual behavior involving non-human objects, the suffering or humiliation of oneself or one's partner, children, or other nonconsenting adults.[3] Although many well-adjusted men and women report mild or episodic enjoyment of fantasies or behavior of a paraphiliac nature, a disorder is indicated when the focus of sexual arousal and gratification is almost exclusively on suffering or humiliation, a nonhuman object, or a nonconsenting partner. Paraphiliac behavior is often very compulsive, and it is not uncommon for such individuals to require orgasmic release as often as four to ten times per day.

The DSM-IV recognizes eight categories of paraphilia,[3] including the following:

1. *Fetishism:* Sexual interest in an inanimate object such as a piece of clothing or body part.
2. *Transvestic fetishism:* Achievement of sexual arousal and satisfaction by "cross-dressing."
3. *Voyeurism:* Achievement of sexual pleasure through secretly peeping at others.
4. *Exhibitionism:* Sexual gratification through intentional exposure of the genitals to others (usually strangers) in inappropriate circumstances and without their consent.
5. *Sadism:* Achievement of sexual gratification through inflicting suffering or humiliation (physically and psychologically) on a sexual partner.
6. *Masochism:* Sexual satisfaction achieved through experiencing pain—whether self-administered or caused by a sexual partner.
7. *Pedophilia:* Sexual arousal and satisfaction achieved through fantasy about or actual sexual activity with prepubescent children.
8. *Frotteurism:* Achievement of sexual gratification by rubbing against a nonconsenting person.

Although the causes are unclear, it is true that nearly all paraphiliacs are male and that paraphiliacs nearly always have more than one paraphilia. The fact that men are more sexually responsive to visual stimuli may make them more vulnerable than women to developing paraphilias. Men are also more prone to developing sexual associations with nonsexual stimuli. Parishioners with paraphilias are unlikely to come to the attention of a pastor until one of two situations occurs. Either the parishioner will be apprehended in a paraphiliac act (peeping, cross-dressing, or masturbating with a child) or his partner will complain about his sexual focus (she may report feeling like an accessory or "prop" in his sexual scenario).

Paraphilias: Key Indicators

- During a period of at least six months, the person has recurring and intense sexually arousing fantasies, sexual urges, or behaviors involving nonhuman objects, inflicting or experiencing pain or humiliation, or children and other nonconsenting partners.
- The disturbance causes the person considerable distress or problems with relationships, the legal system, or employment.

Summary and Guidelines

The pastor should be alert to the fact that complaints of a sexual nature may indicate a host of concerns and should lead to the possibility of a referral. Some sexual problems (e.g., erectile problems or pain with intercourse) may indicate a medical problem, which should be investigated by a physician. Substance abuse (especially alcohol abuse) is also frequently implicated in sexual problems; careful assessment of medication and substance use is crucial. For example, many common antidepressant medications lead to erection or lubrication difficulties. Sexual dysfunction may also be one of many symptoms of a pervasive personality problem (see Chapter 4). This may be most evident in the case of male parishioners with paraphilias. Finally, complaints about the sexual side of a couple's relationship rarely indicate sexual difficulty alone, but may be symptomatic of a more pervasive conflict or incompatibility.

The pastor will be most helpful to parishioners with sexual problems when he or she is open and receptive to discussing sexual concerns. But, unless the pastor has specialized training in treating sexual dysfunctions, a referral to a specialist in this area is nearly always indicated. We recommend finding a psychologist, psychiatrist, or social worker with specific training and expertise in the treatment of sexual disorders who is willing to collaborate with the church in helping parishioners with sexual concerns. It is important to evaluate both the practitioner's expertise and his or her ability to remain respectful and supportive of the parishioner's faith.

Even minor pastoral interventions in this area may be profoundly helpful to men and women suffering from sexual disorders. For example, informing a young couple that premature ejaculation or lack of sexual interest are fairly common (and often quite treatable) problems for Christian couples may produce immense relief. Helping older male parishioners to appreciate the biological (especially vascular) changes that lead to erection problems and affirming the increasing normalcy of erection problems with age may alleviate anxiety and despair. Of course, such reassurance should be followed by referral to a medical provider. Finally, reassure parishioners that the sexual problems discussed in this chapter are among the most quickly and effectively treated of all mental health problems.

Chapter 4

Causing Distress in Others: Maladaptive Personalities

Every human being, including each parishioner, has a unique blend of behaviors, emotions, thought patterns, and relationship styles. Together, these components make up and define a person's *personality*. Each of us has consistent patterns of perceiving, relating to, and thinking about the environment and ourselves. These patterns, or *personality traits,* are fairly consistent across a wide range of important personal and social contexts. In combination, they make up our unique personalities. If a hidden camera were to record your behavior all day, everyday, it would not be long before even an untrained viewer could accurately predict your behavior in a range of personal and social situations. Your personality style would quickly become evident.

By the end of adolescence or early adulthood, a person's characteristic traits, interpersonal style, and broad coping techniques have crystallized into established patterns. These consistent and predictable patterns of behavior constitute the personality and they rarely change much after early adulthood. Although personality is rather firmly established by adulthood, one sign of psychological health is the ability to demonstrate occasional flexibility in behavior. Although most of us can modify our characteristic behaviors to meet specific environmental demands, some people are unable to do so. During the personality formation process, these individuals developed traits that are not only rigid and inflexible, but maladaptive because the person cannot appropriately adjust or perform in some important area of life. Persons with such inflexible personality styles have a *personality disorder.*

The DSM-IV describes personality disorders as enduring patterns of perceiving, relating to, and thinking about the environment and oneself that are exhibited in a wide range of important social and personal contexts.[1] These patterns are distinct from ordinary personality traits in that they are deeply etched, inflexible, and maladaptive. Like all personality styles, these maladaptive patterns are present from late adolescence or early adulthood. The presence of the disorder causes the person some distress or, more often, impairment in his or her social or occupational functioning.

In this chapter, we briefly discuss the ten major personality disorders. Each of these disorders shares some common criteria: (1) the person's inner experience and behavior deviates markedly from cultural norms and this deviation is evident in thinking, feeling, interpersonal relationships, or poor impulse control; (2) these consistent patterns are inflexible and present in a wide range of situations; (3) the disordered behavior leads to problems or distress in social or work-related functioning; (4) the pattern of behavior has been stable since late adolescence or early adulthood; and (5) the disordered behavior is not a product of one of the major psychiatric problems discussed in Chapters 2 and 3.

You may wonder why we decided to devote an entire chapter to personality disorders instead of lumping them with the other psychiatric disorders discussed in the previous chapters. We believe personality disorders are among the most problematic and vexing disorders the pastor is likely to face in his or her day-to-day life in the church. Why? Because parishioners with personality disorders are among the least likely of all to seek assistance or to recognize the maladaptiveness of their own behavior.[2] In fact, they will typically come to the pastor's attention only when they are in trouble, or when others in the church are angry at or concerned about them. Not only will most parishioners with personality disorders view themselves as no different from others, they will have little to no insight about how their behavior affects those around them. Although individuals with major psychiatric problems (see Chapters 2 and 3) view their symptoms as foreign or "outside" of themselves, those with personality disorders experience their pathological behavior as an integral and valued part of themselves. So, instead of saying, "Yes, I see why my behavior is causing problems and I really want to change it," this parishioner will say, "That's just the way I am." Personality-disordered parishioners are less accurate at describing their own interpersonal style than those around them.[3]

How prevalent are personality disorders? One major summary of epidemiologic studies on the topic indicated that between 10 and

13 percent of the population would meet criteria for a personality disorder at some point in their lives.[4] However, personality disorders are considerably more prevalent (perhaps as high as 50 percent) among those receiving professional mental health services—either by self-referral or (more often) referral by family members or third parties.[3] Although personality disorders develop gradually from childhood through early adulthood and become progressively more inflexible, they appear to be caused by both environmental (early experience) and genetic factors.[5]

Even though personality disorders are, by definition, distinct from other major psychiatric problems such as mood disorders, anxiety disorders, psychotic disorders, substance abuse, and sexual disorders, personality-disordered parishioners are considerably more likely to develop these psychiatric problems during their lifetimes. For example, a man with an antisocial personality disorder stands a greater risk for substance dependence or depression than a male parishioner who is not antisocial.

There are ten distinct personality disorders that can be subdivided into three diagnostic *clusters* based on similarities among the essential symptoms.

Cluster A: Parishioners with *paranoid, schizoid,* and *schizotypal* personality disorders generally lack relationships, have a restricted range of emotional expression, and have peculiar ideas. They are considered odd and eccentric by others. Their behavior may range from aloof and detached to suspicious and distrustful.

Cluster B: Parishioners with *histrionic, narcissistic, borderline,* and *antisocial* personality disorders tend to be dramatic, emotional, and erratic. They have little insight about their behavior and are extremely impulsive and manipulative. They tend to have chronic interpersonal problems and to use speech to influence, persuade, or threaten others. Cluster B personality-disordered people are more likely to come to the attention of legal authorities and mental health professionals than other people.

Cluster C: Parishioners with *avoidant, dependent,* and *obsessive-compulsive* personality disorders are generally the least disruptive and problematic of the three cluster types. Cluster C personality-disordered persons are driven by anxiety and fearfulness. They attempt to meet all demands placed on them by passively enduring, changing themselves, or withdrawing. They are sometimes difficult to distinguish from persons with anxiety disorders. Although they are more likely to seek treatment than cluster A or B types, they may respond to pastoral suggestions with anxiety, passivity, and initial compliance without ever actually altering their fundamental personality style.

A word of warning to pastors regarding the perils of diagnosing personality disorders. We recommend that you *not* suggest to parishioners that they suffer from a specific personality disorder. Psychiatrists, psychologists, clinical social workers, and other professionals with considerable experience in diagnosing these disorders will be the first to acknowledge that accurate diagnosis of a personality disorder takes considerable time and plentiful data from multiple sources (e.g., parishioner, spouse, parents, friends, employer, and various records and documents). Not only might the pastor inadvertently label a parishioner inaccurately, but personality disorder diagnoses can also be quite stigmatizing.[2] Even mental health professionals may unintentionally "write off" or discount a new client referred with a personality disorder diagnosis. We think it best for the pastor to be alert to clear signs of personality disorder patterns without formally attempting to diagnose parishioners. So, instead of saying, "Your behavior indicates you may suffer from a borderline personality disorder," it would be more helpful to say, "I've noticed a pattern of erratic mood swings and even rage from you at times. Have you ever considered seeing a professional about those concerns?" It is also important to keep in mind that persons with personality disorders do not generally respond quickly to treatment. Given the chronic and permanent nature of personality development (normal and abnormal), it makes sense that personality-based behaviors would be slow to change. Referrals to professionals for treatment of personality disorders should be made with an appropriate amount of guarded optimism.

As we briefly detail each of the ten major personality disorders, we will begin with a *presenting complaint* section, which provides a fictitious case example of what the disorder might "look like" in a particular parishioner. We then discuss the common features and symptoms of each disorder and provide a key indicators box highlighting some of the primary indications for the disorder. We conclude our discussion of each disorder with a very brief summary and guidelines section in which we discuss why such a person may come to the pastor's attention and how the pastor might most effectively and lovingly manage a parishioner with this personality disorder.

PARANOID PERSONALITY DISORDER

Presenting Complaint

Duane is a twenty-nine-year-old who works as a laborer in a textile factory. He requests an appointment with you, but insists on "complete" confidentiality and will only agree to see you when no other church office personnel are present. Duane appears agitated and uncomfortable during your meeting and he frequently scans the environment while speaking with you. Duane believes he is being "persecuted" by co-workers because of his Christian faith and his excellent work performance. He believes (although he has no evidence to corroborate his concerns) that co-workers are conspiring to get him fired. He frequently hears them talking and laughing and is convinced they are talking about him. He interprets maliciousness in seemingly benign comments and is certain these men are planning to "destroy" his career. He also notes being recently divorced due to his wife's infidelity. Although he admits there was never "hard evidence," he is certain she was cheating on him throughout their marriage. Duane then questions you in detail about your record-keeping practices and emphasizes again that he needs utmost confidentiality, as those who intend to harm his career may "pursue all leads . . ."

Common Features and Symptoms

The primary feature of paranoid personality disorder is a chronic pattern of distrust and suspiciousness of others such that others' motives are interpreted as intending harm.[1] This pattern begins early in life and remains rigid and consistent. Basically, persons with this disorder are mistrustful of others, always vigilant and defensive, fearful of losing independence, and chronically fearful and hostile in response. They will nearly always resist external influence and control—assuming that others mean them harm. Persons with paranoid personality disorder assume other people will exploit, harm, or deceive them. They become preoccupied with the supposedly malevolent intentions of others and the loyalty of friends and associates. They tend to view themselves as blameless and find fault, for their own mistakes and failures, in others. Persons with this disorder are considered hypersensitive and they constantly read hidden meanings or threats into the everyday conversations they hear. Paranoid personality disorder differs from paranoid schizophrenia or paranoid delusional disorder in that the person does not experience psychotic symptoms (hallucinations, delusions, or disorganization; see Psychotic Disorders in Chapter 2).

Paranoid Personality Disorder: Key Indicators

- Chronic and consistent distrust and suspiciousness of others, including a tendency to interpret the motives of others as malevolent.
- Specific indications of this paranoia may include the following: (1) suspicion that others are exploiting, harming, or deceiving the person; (2) preoccupation and doubt regarding the loyalty of others; (3) fear-based refusal to confide in or disclose to others; (4) perception of demeaning or threatening messages in benign remarks by others; (5) tendency to bear grudges against others for perceived wrongs; (6) suspiciousness regarding the fidelity of spouse or sexual partner.

Summary and Guidelines

The paranoid parishioner is unlikely to approach the pastor for assistance with his or her disorder. Instead, the paranoid person will complain about other parishioners, a spouse, family members, or co-workers and may even vent anger at the pastor. This person tends to view others as "against" him or her and will be extremely distrustful of the pastor and most others in the church. Religiously, a paranoid person may be among the most rigid and dogmatic in the church, yet his or her faith tends to be legalistic, formalized, and lacking in depth. The pastor may be shocked by this parishioner's apparent lack of insight as he or she tends to be extremely critical of others, but sees no fault in himself or herself. He or she may become angry and blame others in the church—perhaps engaging in angry outbursts that are disturbing to others. The parishioner will view his or her behavior as justified and interpret concern or correction from the pastor as evidence that he or she is also "against" the paranoid person. The religiously paranoid person is characteristically self-righteous and has tremendous difficulty with truly forgiving others for perceived wrongs or slights.

As you might surmise, the paranoid person is exceptionally difficult to manage and seemingly impossible to help. The pastor should remain honest (trustworthy), consistent, and should avoid criticism as much as possible. Still, the pastor should recognize that establishing a relationship with a paranoid person is extremely difficult and takes a significant amount of time. Very often, a paranoid person will terminate the relationship or leave the church altogether before the pastor senses that any real change has occurred. Referring the paranoid personality-disordered person for professional therapy must be done cautiously and with an emphasis on how the professional may be able to "help with the situation" rather than treating the parishioner's disorder. Paranoid parishioners may function best in the church if placed in roles and jobs that require minimal social interaction. As long as they can work independently, there may be fewer social exchanges for them to interpret as hostile or dangerous.

SCHIZOID PERSONALITY DISORDER

Presenting Complaint

Don is a fifty-one-year-old janitor at the church. Before beginning this job a year ago, Don had been at a previous janitorial job for thirty years, until the business closed. Don is very soft-spoken and never initiates conversation with others. He works slowly but steadily and prefers to work at night when no one else is in the church. Two church secretaries approach you to express strong concern that Don is a "psycho" and "demon-possessed." They cite his cold, emotionless demeanor and his active avoidance of all interaction with others as evidence. You visit Don and find that he has very poor social skills and an apparent disinterest in conversation or relationships. He tells you he prefers to be alone and that he has "always been that way." Don has no record of mental health or legal problems and he appears to be in no distress.

Common Features and Symptoms

The primary feature of persons with a schizoid personality disorder is an inability to form attachments to other people. They lack the normal human needs for love, approval, and belonging and have very few interpersonal experiences compared to their peers. As a result of their inability to form social relationships (and their clear disinterest in relationships in general), schizoids do not have close friends. They may have very few social connections except for primary relatives. Schizoid parishioners will appear apathetic, with a diminished capacity to experience emotional pleasure or pain. They do not usually experience pleasure in social activity—including sexual relations. They are often listless, distant, and socially disinterested. When it comes to social relationships, they are passive observers and are usually described as "loners" with solitary occupations and interests. To observers or co-workers, the schizoid person may be "weird," lacking any social savvy and sometimes even lacking attention to personal hygiene. Schizoid persons are no more likely to be dangerous than anyone else, though their odd behavior and extreme aloofness often create uneasiness or fear in others. When placed in a generally solitary living and employment environment, the schizoid person can be quite content and reasonably productive. Requiring social interaction of the schizoid person will be counterproductive.

Schizoid Personality Disorder: Key Indicators

- A consistent pattern of social detachment and a restricted range of emotional expression in interpersonal situations.
- Specific indications of this detachment and emotional restriction may include: (1) neither desires nor enjoys close relationships; (2) consistently chooses solitary activities; (3) little to no interest in sexual activity with another person; (4) takes pleasure in few, if any, activities; (5) lacks close friends; (6) is indifferent to praise or criticism; (7) shows emotional coldness or detachment.

Summary and Guidelines

Schizoid persons rarely seek professional or pastoral assistance. They are likely to come to the pastor's attention only if others complain about them or if they experience a major life crisis that requires some immediate assistance. In Don's case, the pastor may spend most of his or her time helping others adapt to Don. Don himself is probably oblivious to the concerns of others and would probably be disinterested even if he became aware of those concerns. Schizoid personality disorders are unlikely to change in adulthood. Psychotherapy and other interventions are not likely to be helpful. Unless the person is severely depressed (which is rare), referrals to mental health professionals are not indicated.

When the pastor becomes involved with schizoid parishioners, he or she should expect to be very direct and do most of the talking. Given the communication problems characteristic of schizoids, the parishioner may not have the social language necessary to communicate the primary concern or source of distress. Very often, a pragmatic change of the parishioner's role in the church (giving permission for him or her to miss meetings while focusing on solo tasks) or an adjustment at work, which allows the person to be free from most social demands, may work magic in reducing his or her concerns. Keep in mind that many schizoid persons would do fairly well in solitary research stations or as solo night security guards. Finding the right niche for these people—in life and in the church—is a critical challenge for the pastor.

SCHIZOTYPAL PERSONALITY DISORDER

Presenting Complaint

Larry is a thirty-one-year-old parishioner who rarely attends regular worship services. You notice that he occasionally comes to the less formal, and more sparsely attended, evening service. However, when he does attend, he sits near the back and appears uncomfortable. Larry's hygiene is poor and, based on your few interactions with him, you would concur with others who describe him as "weird." He has very poor social skills and appears quite uncomfortable interacting with others. Since leaving home, he has been employed only intermittently and cannot seem to keep a job. During your few conversations with him, Larry has been hard to follow. His speech rambles and he speaks in vague terms about seemingly unconnected and irrelevant things. He is preoccupied with "prophetic gifts" and thinks he may have received a "word" from God Himself. He has read everything he can find on the topic and frequently describes to you his latest prophetic experience. He is worried that others will reject him as a result.

Common Features and Symptoms

Persons with schizotypal personality disorder are among the most disturbed of the personality-disordered parishioners you may encounter. This personality disorder is often considered part of the "schizophrenic spectrum" of psychotic disorders (see Chapter 2). Although schizotypal personality disorder is a developmental disorder similar to the others discussed in this chapter, these individuals are sometimes initially misdiagnosed as schizophrenic. They may also have episodes of psychotic breakdown during which they do indeed manifest some signs of psychosis. However, for the most part, schizoptypal persons are odd, eccentric, and socially detached, not psychotic.

Similar to schizoids, schizotypal persons are chronically socially detached and have serious interpersonal skill deficits. They also have odd thinking patterns, perceptual distortions, and their behavior is considered eccentric or "weird" by others. Although they typically maintain contact with reality (in contrast to a truly schizophrenic or otherwise psychotic person), they engage in extremely superstitious, odd, or "autistic" thinking. Schizotypal persons communicate by mixing irrelevant, personalized, and circumstantial ideas into their speech. They will often ruminate about a specific fear or interest and engage in magical thinking about themselves and the world. For schizoptypal persons, the line between fantasy and reality is easily blurred. To others, these persons will appear confused, self-absorbed, emotionally detached, and unpleasant to interact with due to their extremely poor social skills and their very odd thought processes. Socially, schizotypal persons may indeed be anxious, often because they have experienced a great deal of ridicule and social rejection as they developed. They may be suspicious of others and have ideas of reference (the belief that others are referring to them in their conversations). About 3 percent of the general population may be schizotypal.[1]

If religious, a person with this disorder may be drawn to the most extreme or frankly bizarre religious beliefs and practices.[2] They may be inclined to believe they have exceptional or rare spiritual powers, psychic powers, or even the power to heal. Because they are socially uncomfortable and sensitized to ridicule and rejection, they often avoid crowded church services. If they do attend, they may sit in the back in order to avoid interaction with others.

Schizotypal Personality Disorder: Key Indicators

- A consistent pattern of social and interpersonal skill deficits including discomfort with and little capacity for close personal relationships, as well as distortions in thinking and perceiving and a pattern of eccentric or "odd" behavior.
- Specific indications of these deficits and eccentricities may include: (1) ideas that others are referring to them; (2) odd beliefs or magical thinking not shared by others; (3) unusual perceptual experiences; (4) odd or bizarre speech; (5) suspiciousness; (6) inappropriate or restricted emotional expression; (7) odd behavior; (8) few close friends; (9) excessive distrust of others and expectation of ridicule.

Summary and Guidelines

Although we emphasized at the outset that persons with personality disorders are not especially amenable to traditional forms of counseling and therapy, schizotypal persons may indeed require mental health intervention at some point. Like many of the other personality disorder types, they rarely seek mental health services on their own. They are inherently distrustful and wary of the motives of those who might wish to refer them for psychiatric assistance. Keep in mind that they have been ridiculed and rejected most of their lives.

In addition to his or her expectation of ridicule and malevolence from others, the schizotypal person has profound difficulty relating to others. He or she will ramble and speak in vague terms, have tremendous difficulty being specific about the problem at hand, and be unable to connect interpersonally as other parishioners do. As in the case of the schizoid parishioner, the pastor must go to great lengths to establish a trust-based working relationship. Kindness, consistency, and unconditional acceptance should be demonstrated. Using a kind but matter-of-fact approach to focusing and clarifying the person's thoughts and concerns is critical because schizotypal persons are highly prone to ramble.

Schizotypal parishioners may actually become looser in both their thinking and the ability to integrate all parts of themselves—in other words, they may become psychotic. In these cases (and ideally, prior to a full-blown psychotic episode), the pastor, hopefully in concert with the parishioner's family or employer, may make a referral to a psychiatrist or to an emergency room if needed. Hospitalization and medication may be indicated until the person is stabilized and capable of independent functioning once again.

HISTRIONIC PERSONALITY DISORDER

Presenting Complaint

Marla, twenty-six, is new to the community and the church. She is referred to the pastor by the layperson who oversees the singles ministry of the church. Although Marla has only attended the singles group for two months, she has wrought havoc in the group and created considerable tension among its members. Apparently Marla has kept the focus of the group almost exclusively on herself and her relationship problems. She has been extremely seductive with several of the male group members and has become sexually involved with two of them—creating a great deal of anger and conflict among all the members. In her session with the pastor she is tearful, yet there appears to be little depth to her grief. She fluctuates frequently from one emotional extreme to the other (usually anger to tears). Although she complains of being misunderstood and exploited, she is unable to be particularly specific about her concerns and the pastor cannot help but notice her very seductive manner of sitting and dressing. She appears desperate when their meeting time is up and pleads for another appointment. The pastor feels quite uncomfortable with Marla.

Common Features and Symptoms

Histrionic is the first of the "cluster B" personality disorders we will cover. Like the other disorders in the category, histrionic personality disorder is not easily treated and persons with the disorder typically leave a wake of chaos behind them. The essential feature of this disorder is excessive attention-seeking behavior as well as excessive and poorly regulated emotionality. Histrionic persons have a nearly insatiable need for attention and approval. When they are not the center of attention, they may become depressed or angry. Among the population, 2 or 3 percent meet the criteria for this disorder and women are diagnosed as histrionic more often than men.[1]

Although they often make positive initial impressions, appearing outgoing, friendly, talkative, and dramatic, they are gradually viewed as selfish, immature, unreliable, and demanding of attention. They are extremely superficial in their thought processes and emotional lives, which means that their relationships will tend to lack depth and be short term in nature. Quite often, histrionic persons are very seductive and relationships may begin with a primarily sexual focus. It is not unusual for these parishioners to dress very provocatively, wear excessive amounts of makeup, and become almost demandingly seductive. Relationships tend to be stormy as the histrionic person demands constant attention, and attempts to control and manipulate the partner.

Thought processes in histrionic persons can be described as "flighty." They have very little internal life and generally avoid blaming themselves for their own contributions to problems. Because of their cognitive and emotional superficiality, their involvement in religion and the church is often equally superficial, and driven primarily by social needs (attention). Once members of the church begin to lose interest in them, or become annoyed at their behavior, they often drop out.

Histrionic Personality Disorder: Key Indicators

- A consistent pattern of excessive attention-seeking behavior and emotionality in a range of contexts.
- Specific indications of attention-seeking behavior and extreme emotionality may include: (1) discomfort when not the center of attention; (2) interpersonal behavior characterized by sexual seductiveness; (3) rapidly changing and shallow emotional expression; (4) use of physical appearance to draw attention to self; (5) excessively impressionistic speech that lacks detail; (6) excessive dramatization and exaggeration in emotional expression; (7) highly suggestible; (8) considers relationships to be more intimate than they are.

Summary and Guidelines

Although the histrionic person will rarely approach the pastor for authentic feedback based on a desire for change, they may seek out the pastor as a potential source of attention. Their behavior may also generate enough conflict within the church that the pastor is compelled to respond. The pastor should exercise caution when working with the histrionic parishioner. Not only is the prognosis for real change poor, but the pastor is at high risk for becoming manipulated or, worse, seduced by this person. It would be common for the parishioner to attempt to elicit "special" attention from and time with the pastor—for example, meeting after hours or more frequently than is common.

When interacting with the histrionic person, it is important to remain very calm and measured. Because the parishioner will both think and respond emotionally in black and white extremes, it is often useful to get him or her to slow down and focus on the specifics of a given situation or relationship. Careful and repeated reality testing is necessary and the pastor must be consistently aware of not participating in the person's extreme thinking or emotional reacting. Above all, setting firm limits on meeting times, meeting parameters, and appropriate behavior is critical. Although histrionic persons are not generally very amenable to therapy, they may be referred for longer term personality-focused psychotherapy. Medications are unlikely to be useful; therefore the referral could be made to any seasoned psychologist, psychiatrist, or social worker with considerable experience in long-term therapy with personality-disordered clients.

NARCISSISTIC PERSONALITY DISORDER

Presenting Complaint

John is a twenty-four-year-old seminary student who has joined the church staff as an intern for the summer. John approaches the pastor with strong "concerns" about being assigned to work with young people for the summer. Although he says that youth work is important, John wonders if the pastor has overlooked his resume and letters of reference, and suggests they would indicate that he is "not your typical summer intern." John notes that he is considerably more advanced than most of his seminary peers and is ready to do some "serious preaching." He then subtly devalues the pastor's preaching and notes how he might have approached the previous week's message differently. He recommends that the pastor have him preach regularly and says, "I think it's safe to say you'll be impressed." He goes on to note that many of his seminary professors don't seem to understand his gifts and are probably jealous of his preaching talents. He seems oblivious to how his comments may be interpreted by the pastor.

Common Features and Symptoms

Narcissistic personality disorder has three essential features: (1) an exaggerated sense of self-importance, (2) a preoccupation with being admired, and (3) poor ability to empathize with or take the perspective of others. The term "narcissistic" comes from the Greek legend of Narcissus—a young man who fell in love with himself and pined for his own reflection in the water. Chances are, you know, or have known, a severely narcissistic person. The narcissist is so self-absorbed and preoccupied with garnering admiration from others that he or she can be an extremely unpleasant person to work with, let alone have a relationship with.

Narcissists possess a grandiose sense of their own importance and an inflated assessment of their abilities. They very frequently overestimate their abilities while simultaneously devaluing and underestimating the abilities of those around them. They will often make caustic or dismissing remarks about others (this can be subtle if the person is more sophisticated) while expecting that everyone else will recognize their unique or amazing talents. Parishioners with narcissism have a sense of entitlement. That is, they simply expect special recognition and privilege, whatever the context. They compare themselves favorably to famous or high-status persons, and expect others to see them as similarly entitled to special status. Other people view them as egotistical because they usually brag and make references to themselves and their talents. As a result of their inflated view of themselves, they often believe they can only be understood by other high-status people.

Another important feature of narcissistic personality disorder is an inability to take the perspective of others (egocentrism). Although most children slowly develop the capacity to take another perspective and empathize with the way others might feel, narcissists are generally unable to do this effectively. In addition to this empathy deficit, narcissists often take advantage of others, envy others, believe others envy them, and appear arrogant, snobbish, and exploitive to those who know them. Because their fantasy life is literally consumed with thoughts of unlimited success, power, beauty, ideal love, etc., they are often upset when others do not recognize their specialness. They are easily "wounded" when they do not receive the accolades and recognition they believe they deserve.

This personality disorder appears to be slightly more prevalent in men than women and it occurs in roughly 1 percent of the general population.[1] Although narcissistic and histrionic personality disorders share some features in common, the narcissist tends to be less dramatic and emotional than the histrionic person. In relationships, the narcissist may simply exploit out of a sense of entitlement, whereas the histrionic person is more needy. Finally, the narcissist seeks admiration while the histrionic person is desperate for attention.

In the church, narcissistic parishioners will be primarily motivated by self-aggrandizement. They will only be interested in positions and involvement that bring them notice and praise. Their internal spirituality may be dominated with expectations that God exists to meet their needs and kindly answer their prayers. When this does not appear to happen, they may quickly become disenchanted—feeling God has let them down. Narcissists in the church may view themselves as having special or unique spiritual gifts that deserve praise and recognition. They seek to be idealized and will delight in special recognition.

> ### Narcissistic Personality Disorder: Key Indicators
>
> - A consistent pattern of grandiosity, need for admiration, and lack of empathy for others.
> - Specific indications of grandiosity and need for affirmation may include: (1) a strong sense of self-importance; (2) preoccupation with fantasies of unlimited success, power, brilliance, beauty, etc.; (3) belief that one is special and unique and can only be understood by other special people; (4) requires excessive admiration; (5) has a sense of entitlement; (6) exploits others; (7) lacks empathy; (8) envies others and believes others envy him or her; (9) is arrogant and haughty.

Summary and Guidelines

The narcissistic parishioner will most likely be disliked by most people with whom he or she comes into contact. Although a favorable and even awe-inspiring first impression may be created, those who spend time with the narcissist begin to experience him or her as increasingly arrogant, obnoxiously self-focused, and egotistical. These parishioners will rarely seek treatment or pastoral counseling since they view themselves as perfect or nearly perfect. They tend to blame problems on others and view those around them as failing to understand their talents or as being jealous of them. They may come to the pastor's attention if their behavior, in some role within the church, begins to alienate others or if their spouse or supervisors require them to seek assistance.

The pastor should be wary of the narcissistic parishioner who wishes to have personal counseling. The biggest problem we see is that the pastor may intensely dislike the narcissist. Strong dislike for a parishioner may be distasteful for the pastor and may cause self-recrimination and personal distress. The narcissist may consistently devalue the pastor's credentials and performance and may suggest that the pastor really does not possess the credentials and/or experience to be maximally helpful. This parishioner may arrive late for appointments, discount the pastor's advice, and expect special treatment (for example, extra-long sessions or meeting times at odd hours). The narcissistic parishioner will be insulting and arrogant, and assume that rules which apply to others in the church do not apply to him or her.

Referrals for therapy are generally not likely to be helpful. Not only do narcissistic persons rarely follow through with treatment, there is no significant evidence that they benefit from any form of intervention. Firm limit setting, gentle but consistent feedback, and perhaps counseling for the narcissist's spouse and family may be useful.

BORDERLINE PERSONALITY DISORDER

Presenting Complaint

Tina is a twenty-five-year-old who requests "spiritual counseling" from her pastor. In her first session, she tearfully recounts a history of brief but intense relationships with men, which have all ended abruptly and angrily. Tina admits that she gets involved with the "wrong men" and that she is self-destructive when in relationships—abusing substances and engaging in sexual relations almost immediately. She initially believes that each of these men is "perfect" and "completely different," but quickly finds herself being exploited and sometimes abused. At the end of each relationship, Tina has become very depressed and even suicidal. When depressed, she has at times made lacerations on her arm "to stop the pain . . . and make sure I'm alive." Tina tells the pastor she feels "empty" inside and that she only feels like "somebody" when she is with a man. When Tina learns that the pastor will be on vacation for the following week, she appears very anxious and asks if there is a way she can reach him while he is away.

Common Features and Symptoms

Parishioners with borderline personality disorder have one of the most severe and disabling of the personality disorders. They will present with a history of unstable interpersonal relationships, an undefined self-image, chaotic emotional experiences, and notable impulsivity in more than one area. Friends or acquaintances may describe the borderline parishioner as moody, prone to extremes in emotion, and episodically depressed—sometimes even suicidal—though these episodes are interspersed with periods of anger, anxiety, or even euphoria. They are also interpersonally intense and prone to conflict with others, especially those with whom they become close. Their interests appear fickle and their attachments are intense but brief. They typically begin relation-ships by idealizing the other person, only to become quickly disap-pointed, rejected, and wounded by yet another person. They are fre-quently dissatisfied and unhappy with themselves and their lives, and are preoccupied with obtaining affection.

Parishioners with this disorder have an extremely unstable and frag-ile identity. For some reason, they have failed to complete the normal process of identity development that occurs in childhood and late adolescence. They are deeply fearful of abandonment and will spend a great deal of time trying to avoid this experience (even if it is imag-ined). Threat of abandonment may lead to angry outbursts (even physi-cal abuse) or suicidal gestures and self-mutilation. These parishioners may attempt to establish a relationship with the pastor (or others in the church) and then create substantial conflict when, inevitably, they find the pastor, too, is imperfect and they feel abandoned. They will report feeling chronically empty and bored and have a very low tolerance for being alone. Look for a history of intense and stormy relationships as well as a pattern of impulsive and destructive behaviors such as binges in gambling, sex, substance abuse, or reckless driving.

About 2 percent of the population may qualify for a diagnosis of borderline personality disorder[1] and 75 percent of those diagnosed are women. Borderline personalities are markedly overrepresented in psychiatric settings (inpatient and outpatient), suggesting they are a more volatile and service-intensive group.[6] Parishioners with borderline personality disorder will also be considerably more like-ly to have a major mood disorder (see Chapter 2). In general, they have an extremely poor ability to regulate themselves—both their moods and their basic identities.

Borderline Personality Disorder: Key Indicators

- A consistent pattern of unstable interpersonal relationships, self-image, and emotions as well as a pattern of impulsivity.
- Specific indications of this instability and impulsiveness are evident in: (1) frantic efforts to avoid real or imagined abandonment; (2) a pattern of unstable and intense relationships; (3) a persistently unstable sense of self; (4) impulsivity in at least two areas; (5) a pattern of self-harm or suicidal behavior; (6) chronic instability in emotions; (7) feelings of emp-tiness; (8) problems with intense anger.

Summary and Guidelines

Parishioners with borderline personality disorder may present the pastor with one of his or her greatest management challenges. Borderlines will think in rigid black and white terms, forcing extreme evaluations on life events, themselves, and those around them. Therefore, they will see the church and the pastor as all good (initially) or all bad (later). They will vacillate between a desire for intimacy (including safe dependence on others) and intense fear of getting close. They will see the pastor and the church community as a potentially hostile and dangerous place. They will likely arrange to be disappointed and abandoned by people in the church, including the pastor. Not only are they likely to see the world and others in all-or-nothing terms, their religious experience is likely to be much the same. They may be entirely active in the church or absent. They may see God as loving and kind or absent and rejecting, depending on their current emotional state.

For several reasons, we highly recommend that the pastor not attempt to do formal counseling with a parishioner who is clearly borderline in presentation. Borderline clients are among the most stressful for even seasoned clinicians to manage. They are difficult to help, minimally likely to benefit from most forms of therapy, and prone to create crisis after crisis for those treating them. In the same way, the pastor can expect to experience a good deal of chaos if he or she becomes involved in a close personal counseling relationship with a borderline parishioner. Even without a formal counseling component, the pastor should anticipate volatility, episodes of anger, and, possibly, threats of suicide. The pastor will initially be idealized and later may become the object of rage. The movie *Fatal Attraction* portrays a person with this sort of unpredictable borderline rage.

If the pastor attempts to refer the borderline parishioner for professional care, this may be experienced as yet another rejection (regardless of how it is conveyed). The parishioner may have a history of seeing multiple psychotherapists (without substantial benefit) and may also have a history of attending multiple churches. If a referral is made, we recommend that the pastor seek a seasoned professional with considerable experience in treating personality-disordered clients. Dialectical behavior therapy and other forms of cognitive-behavioral therapy show particular promise in helping these persons gain personal and interpersonal stability.

ANTISOCIAL PERSONALITY DISORDER

Presenting Complaint

Oscar, forty-eight, has begun dating a recently widowed woman in the church. He is polite and engaging in conversation and tends to make a very positive initial impression, especially on women. Oscar very quickly convinces his new female friend that she should allow him to move in with her. He is "between jobs" but insists this will not be for long. Oscar convinces the pastor to give him a "small loan" to help with food until he finds employment. Soon, the pastor learns that Oscar has secured similar loans from other parishioners. Alarmed, the pastor does some background checking and finds that Oscar has a long history of short-term relationships, usually with older women whom he exploits financially before abruptly moving on. He has never held a job for more than a few months due to his unreliability (and several instances of embezzlement). He has been in and out of jail and has a chronic history of alcohol abuse. When Oscar is confronted by the pastor, he insists he wants to change and commits to being accountable to the church. The following day, the pastor learns Oscar has disappeared.

Common Features and Symptoms

Persons with antisocial personality disorder are often initially charming and likable. However, others soon find them to be manipulative, deceitful, and willing to do almost anything to achieve their own ends. They are irresponsible and unreliable, highly impulsive, prone to illegal behavior, and sometimes vengeful regarding perceived injustices. They generally avoid attachments and their relationships are superficial and short-lived. They are disloyal, highly exploitive of others, insensitive, and even ruthless. They chronically disregard societal rules and believe that these rules do not apply to them.

Antisocials are distinct from the other personality disorder types in that a criterion for the diagnosis is the presence of the precursors to antisocial behavior in childhood and adolescence. Antisocial parishioners (men are considerably more likely to be diagnosed as antisocial) will always have a history of *conduct disorder* in adolescence (see Chapter 5). That is, they engaged in behaviors such as shoplifting, truancy, lying, cruelty to animals, fire setting, vandalism, and frequent fighting. The more conduct problems in adolescence, the more likely the development of antisocial personality disorder in adulthood. In the church, pastors should be alert to two major manifestations of this disorder. The first type of antisocial is the smooth, personable, charming person who manipulates and exploits others subtly—often without detection—for some time. The second type is the belligerent, antagonistic, and overtly criminal antisocial type. This parishioner will have a clear criminal history, arouse fear in others, and be viewed as unpredictable and dangerous. The difference between the two may be emotional intelligence or social polish. Both smooth and belligerent antisocials can be dangerous and they are unlikely to experience remorse following acts of harm and exploitation.

Key characteristics of parishioners with antisocial personality disorder include:

1. *Inadequate development of conscience.* Although his or her intelligence is often normally developed, the antisocial person appears unable to truly understand and accept ethical and moral values—even though he or she may claim to value these standards.
2. *Irresponsible and impulsive behavior.* Prone to thrill seeking and intense need for novelty, antisocials will impulsively break the law with little regard for the consequences of their behavior. They also callously disregard the needs and rights of others.
3. *Ability to impress and exploit others.* They are likable and disarming and can readily "read" the needs and vulnerabilities of those they exploit. Even when caught in a lie or criminal act, they can effectively rationalize their behavior or appear genuinely sorrowful.

4. *Rejection of authority.* Beginning in adolescence, antisocials act as though rules do not apply to them. Despite frequent contacts with authorities and various criminal convictions, they continue to act as though they are immune to the consequences.

5. *Inability to maintain good relationships.* Antisocials rarely have close friends. Instead, they have a long string of superficial acquaintances and appear incapable of truly bonding to another person. Not only are they exploitive and prone to extreme sexual promiscuity, they may additionally be violent in relationships, particularly when their immediate goals or desires are blocked.

Antisocial Personality Disorder: Key Indicators

- A consistent pattern of disregard for and violation of societal laws and the rights of others.
- This disregard and exploitation is evident in the following: (1) repeated criminal behavior; (2) deceitfulness (lying or conning others); (3) impulsivity; (4) irritability or aggressiveness; (5) disregard for the safety of self or others; (6) irresponsibility in work and relationships; (7) lack of remorse after harming or violating another.

Summary and Guidelines

If we can recommend only one thing to pastors when it comes to the antisocial personality, it is *be careful.* Although children of God, these men (and less frequently, women) have developed without a conscience and with a tendency to exploit without remorse. It is not unreasonable to assume that the faith of antisocial people will be limited in its overall impact on their lives. They will typically fail to practice what they say they believe, and they may relate to God as they relate to other people—in a superficial and pragmatic manner.[2]

The pastor must appreciate the significance of this parishioner's underdeveloped conscience. Because such people are really unable to grasp essential moral principles (though there may be an intellectual understanding), they will not be amenable to interventions focusing on the "wrongness" of their behavior. They will not experience guilt or remorse in a genuine way. The pastor can expect that they will only seek assistance to get something they want, such as money or assistance with convincing a spouse that they have changed this time, or when a temporary crisis ensues due to criminal behavior.

Referrals for treatment are not indicated as no single approach is likely to be helpful. True antisocial personality-disordered parishioners do not follow through or benefit much from mental health intervention. In the church, management of antisocial behavior should center on firm limit setting and clear, nonnegotiable consequences for inappropriate, exploitive, or illegal behavior. Good communication among pastoral staff can be crucial as the antisocial may attempt to manipulate several persons at once. Recognizing that this person has little capacity for conscience may help the pastor avoid anger and hostility toward the parishioner (which is often a natural reaction to the parishioner's exploitive behavior). Instead, the pastor can matter-of-factly confront the antisocial behavior, point out choices made, and the consequences that will follow.

AVOIDANT PERSONALITY DISORDER

Presenting Complaint

Glenna is an attractive and intelligent twenty-seven-year-old college administrator. She holds two master's degrees, one of which is in theology. Although she has attended the church for nearly three years, she has not become involved in any of the groups or forms of ministry. In fact, she appears aloof and avoids relationships. When the pastor tells Glenna she would like to meet with her to talk about her potential coleadership of the college-age ministry, Glenna appears startled and anxious. During their meeting, Glenna insists she has "nothing to offer" others and that she does not believe college students would enjoy having her lead the group. She says she "hates being up in front" of others and that it takes her quite a long time to feel comfortable with a group. She insists she would like to get to know some others in the church, but she says, "It always takes a long time with me."

Common Features and Symptoms

Unlike "cluster B" personality disorders, those in "cluster C" rarely become disruptive and thus often go unnoticed. Avoidant personality disorder is the first of the cluster C disorder types. Initially, the avoidant parishioner may appear schizoid because he or she is aloof, avoids interpersonal interaction, and has few friendships. However, in contrast to the schizoid who enjoys his or her aloneness, the avoidant person wants relationships but is too fearful of rejection to pursue them. While the schizoid is indifferent to criticism and interpersonally cold, the avoidant is shy, insecure, and hypersensitive to criticism. He or she usually has a lifelong pattern of avoiding social relationships and a reluctance to enter social situations. When it comes to relationships, avoidant parishioners are cautious, mistrustful, and fully expectant of ridicule or rejection. They experience anxiety symptoms in social situations and therefore work to reduce this discomfort through the well-learned mechanism of avoidance. They feel deeply inadequate and tend to read criticism into the behavior of others even when it is not present. Although they actively avoid others out of fear, they are often lonely, bored, and desire affection. Because they cannot face even the slightest risk of embarrassment or criticism, they will avoid social activities unless guaranteed acceptance. Thus, if the avoidant person has friends, they tend to be few and he or she may rely excessively on these limited friendships.

The avoidant parishioner will have recurring thoughts such as, "I am inadequate and have nothing to offer others," "There is nothing much about me to like," and "I am defective or obviously lacking." Their self-esteem is extremely poor. The irony is that, like Glenna in the case study, the avoidant person may actually have many desirable traits and be quite likeable. Finally, there is a strong correlation between avoidant personality disorder and social phobia (see Chapter 2). Whereas the avoidant person has a long-term personality style characterized in part by fear of humiliation and social rejection, the socially phobic person experiences extreme fear only in social situations in which he or she may be scrutinized. The socially phobic person may have little problem entering and enjoying relationships. Nonetheless, expect many of the symptoms of social phobia to be present in avoidant parishioners.

Avoidant Personality Disorder: Key Indicators

- A long-term pattern of social avoidance, feelings of inadequacy, and hypersensitivity to negative evaluation.
- This pattern of avoidance, inadequacy, and fear of evaluation is evident in the following: (1) avoids jobs that require significant interpersonal contact; (2) is unwilling to get involved with others unless certain of being liked; (3) avoids relationships due to fear of shame and ridicule; (4) is preoccupied with being socially rejected or ridiculed; (5) feels inadequate and therefore avoids social situations; (6) views self as inferior and unappealing socially; (7) is reluctant to explore new activities due to fear of embarrassment.

Summary and Guidelines

Of all the personality disorders we cover in this section, the avoidant type is among those with the best prognosis for change. Although these parishioners will respond to the pastor in much the same way they respond to others—with fear and avoidance—they desire connection and are quite lonely. This provides some strong motivation for change if the pastor and the church can offer and encourage gradually increasing social involvement. In fact, the church is perhaps the "ideal" location for the avoidant person to decrease his or her avoidance and develop some close friendships. When the pastor and other church members present a consistent, unconditionally accepting relational environment, the avoidant person stands the best chance of expanding his or her social risk taking.

Avoidant persons may see God in much the same way they see other people—as potentially threatening and rejecting. They may have difficulty accepting that God loves them without condition and they may expect God to be critical of them. They will expect the same thing from their pastors and may be shocked and distrusting if the pastor expresses interest or finds value in them. Avoidant parishioners will require the pastor to take a long-term incremental approach to establishing a relationship with them. They may avoid admitting even normal shortcomings for fear of disapproval. Modeling self-disclosure, admission of human weaknesses, and social connectedness may be very helpful.

Avoidant persons may benefit from counseling to address their avoidance and perhaps symptoms of social phobia as well. As long as making a referral does not communicate to these parishioners that the pastor finds fault with them, the pastor could consider referring to any mental health professional with experience in treating avoidant people in long-term therapy relationships. Medications are unlikely to be useful unless the parishioner is disabled by anxiety or depression connected to his or her personality disorder.

DEPENDENT PERSONALITY DISORDER

Presenting Complaint

Jenna, forty, has attended church all her life. Although she has never been a leader in the church, she has routinely served "behind the scenes," always saying "yes" to setting up for and cleaning up after church activities. In fact, the pastor has never known Jenna to say "no" to any request or to be anything but pleasant and accommodating. On many occasions, Jenna has apparently been exploited by others who know she will never object to being put out. At the same time, those who have worked with Jenna have sometimes expressed frustration at her lack of initiative because she requires specific direction and ample reassurance that she is doing things correctly. Recently, Jenna's physically and emotionally abusive husband, Tom, left her and her two children. Even though Tom had been very cruel to Jenna, she comes to the pastor in crisis and insists she simply "can't make it" without Tom "telling me what to do." She says she can't make decisions without him and that she is "not the kind of person who can just decide what to do or take care of myself."

Common Features and Symptoms

Parishioners with dependent personality disorder are extremely dependent on others and have strong needs to be taken care of by others—resulting in clinging and submissive behavior. These behaviors are designed to get others to care for them and arise from a core belief that they cannot adequately function alone. Dependent people have tremendous difficulty making even everyday decisions (e.g., what to wear, how to spend free time, etc.) without reassurance and advice from others. Adults with this disorder typically rely on a spouse while adolescents may rely on parents to determine most aspects of their daily routines.

Parishioners with dependent personality disorder will show discomfort and even panic at possibly having to be separated or alone for a time. They typically build their lives around another person (spouse or parent) and then work hard to keep them present by subordinating their own needs. Because they are fearful of being alone, they often fail to get appropriately angry when they are harmed or exploited. They will squelch their own reactions and rights rather than risk losing the person on whom they depend for guidance. They are markedly lacking in self-confidence and therefore do not initiate activities or projects without ample direction and reassurance from others. Because they are convinced they are incompetent, they present themselves to others as inept and requiring guidance. Dependent persons are preoccupied with fear of being alone and having to care for themselves. Therefore, when one relationship ends, they will often seek out a new one as quickly as possible and with great urgency. The few friends of the dependent person will describe him or her as bland, passive, needy, deferential, cooperative, and willing to do anything to help another—the primary motivation for this behavior is to maintain affection. The movie *What About Bob?* offers a fine example of this sort of clingy dependence.

Dependent Personality Disorder: Key Indicators

- A chronic and excessive need to be taken care of that leads to submissive and clinging behaviors, and fear of separation.
- This pattern of submissiveness and fear of separation is evident in the following: (1) difficulty making everyday decisions without advice and reassurance; (2) need for others to assume responsibility for this person; (3) difficulty expressing disagreement or anger for fear of losing approval and support; (4) difficulty initiating projects on own; (5) feels uncomfortable and helpless when alone; (6) goes to excessive lengths to obtain nurturance—even volunteering for demeaning tasks; (7) urgently seeks another relationship as a source of care when a close relationship ends.

Summary and Guidelines

Parishioners with dependent personality disorders rarely pose a "problem" for the pastor or the church in the same way that other personality disorders often do. They are not disruptive, demanding, or disturbing to others. In fact, they are often among the most quiet and service-focused members of a congregation. They may only come to the pastor's attention when a relationship ends and they are anxiety ridden about the possibility of being alone. Or they may be referred to the pastor by a friend or spouse upon whom they have been dependent for years. This person may be exasperated or preparing to terminate the relationship.

The dependent parishioner sees himself or herself as unable to handle the trials of life and, therefore, must attach to a stronger person in order to survive. He or she is essentially in search of a protecting nurturer to direct him or her in every area. The problem, of course, is that the pastor will be seen by the dependent parishioner as a particularly gifted expert with great potential for telling him or her precisely how to live—religiously and otherwise. These parishioners will be prone to become dependent on the pastor in the same way that they have depended upon others. They may praise the pastor profusely and follow each shred of the pastor's advice simply to please (not because they internalize the importance of changing their behavior). Additionally, they may see God as a great protector and rescuer who must take care of their every need.[2] However, when prayers are not answered, they will feel that God has abandoned them.

There are some specific risks for the pastor in caring for the dependent parishioner. First, some pastors are inclined to want to rescue dependent parishioners, particularly when the pastor is male and the parishioner female (more women than men are diagnosed with this disorder).[1] In this case, the pastor may be at risk for romantic involvement, which the dependent parishioner may foster as a means of securing caretaking. Another potential problem occurs when the pastor assumes an authoritative-directive stance, thus promoting a dependent stance on the part of the parishioner. In this case, the pastor will simply become the object of dependency. Instead, a peer relationship is recommended in which the pastor gradually gives less and less advice and pushes the parishioner to articulate his or her own feelings, needs, and agenda. Finally, the pastor may naturally respond with annoyance and irritation to the dependent person. Obviously, this is unlikely to be helpful. Instead, a kind but firm approach to encouragement mixed with limits on advice and direction giving is indicated.

Although dependent parishioners may benefit from a healthy counseling relationship, and such a referral may be indicated, be aware that the therapist will have to avoid the same dependent relational dynamics. Once again, we recommend finding a seasoned mental health professional with excellent personal boundaries and experience in treating persons with personality problems.

OBSESSIVE-COMPULSIVE PERSONALITY DISORDER

Presenting Complaint

Norman is a single, thirty-four-year-old technical writer for a publishing company and a parishioner in the church for several years. Since his appointment as the director of the Sunday school program two months ago, the other teachers have become increasingly unhappy and annoyed at what they consider "micromanagement" and "anal retentiveness." Norman has instituted many new regulations and tasks including mandatory weekly meetings with lengthy agendas, weekly inventories of all supplies, and step-by-step teacher guides for each lesson. Norman has gone to the pastor on several occasions asking about "denominational regulations" or "church bylaws" that might relate to Sunday school. He appears anxious and controlled, and rarely laughs. He seems driven to control the education process, yet shows little enjoyment of his new role. Finally, the high school class leader goes to the pastor in exasperation when Norman rejects his idea for taking the high schoolers to a water slide park. Norman insisted that such a trip was not part of the "accepted curriculum," and that any such deviation would need to be considered by the education committee, church board, and, possibly, the denomination headquarters.

Common Features and Symptoms

People with obsessive-compulsive personality disorders, OCD, (about 1 percent of the population) are excessively concerned with maintaining order and are extremely perfectionistic.[1] Although most successful people are well organized and attentive to detail, persons with OCD are dysfunctionally preoccupied with maintaining personal and interpersonal control via excessive attention to rules and schedules. They will be known for painstaking development and use of rules, procedures, and lists. They get so wrapped up in trivial details that they often lose sight of the ultimate goal or purpose for the activity. They may spend so much time on details that time is used poorly and they end up finishing projects late or at the last minute. They often have a poor sense of how annoyed others become about their obsessive perfectionism.

It is common for obsessive-compulsive parishioners to have trouble relaxing or enjoying leisure activities. They tend to focus on work and activity to the exclusion of recreation and friendships. Obsessive-compulsive persons will believe they do not have time to "waste" on such activities and they may take work along on vacations. They may also be excessively rigid and scrupulous when it comes to matters of ethics or values and may be highly inflexible with scriptural interpretation, changes to worship, etc. They adhere powerfully to dogma and have a low tolerance for deviation. Obsessive-compulsive individuals may also have difficulty getting rid of old and worn-out household items and may be quite miserly and stingy. Interpersonally, they are likely to be experienced as rigid and stubborn. They have great difficulty delegating tasks to others and are most comfortable having direct control over things. Other members of the community may experience them as rigid, stiff, and interpersonally cold.

Although certain jobs and situations require someone with obsessive-compulsive characteristics (e.g., airline pilot, nuclear power plant supervisor, etc.), those with the full-blown disorder are so excessively perfectionistic and detail oriented that they actually become dysfunctional and less able to successfully get the job done. A pastor with obsessive-compulsive personality disorder may languish for days on end with the original Greek and Hebrew translations of biblical texts for an upcoming sermon—spending so much time agonizing over precise definitions and textual meanings that he fails to actually write the sermon until late the night before.

Obsessive-Compulsive Personality Disorder: Key Indicators

- A consistent pattern of preoccupation with orderliness, perfectionism, and control, at the expense of flexibility, openness, and efficiency.
- Specific indications of this perfectionism and rigidity are evident in: (1) preoccupation with details, rules, lists, order, and schedules so that the major point of the activity is lost; (2) perfectionism that interferes with task completion; (3) excessive devotion to work and productivity and neglect of leisure activity and friendships; (4) unable to discard worn-out or worthless objects; (5) reluctance to delegate tasks; (6) adopts a miserly spending style toward both self and others; (7) demonstrates rigidity and stubbornness.

Summary and Guidelines

As is the case with all the personality disorders, it is not realistic to expect that the obsessive-compulsive parishioner will make marked changes in his or her basic personality style. Rather than asking an obsessive-compulsive person to give up his or her compulsive behaviors, it may be most productive to emphasize those behavioral aspects that are positive and helpful, while simultaneously showing the person how some flexibility may actually increase and enhance productivity and effectiveness in accomplishing tasks.

In the church, it is recommended that obsessive-compulsive parishioners not be placed in direct supervisory positions—particularly if their preoccupation with rules and order has negative effects on the performance of others. Instead, they may be given jobs that are fairly independent and routine. For example, organizing and keeping track of church supplies may be an ideal match. It is also recommended that the assignments of obsessive-compulsive people seldom be changed as they tend to have tremendous difficulty with change and readjustment to new tasks and novel situations.

The obsessive-compulsive parishioner's faith may be based primarily on dogma, principles, and rules rather than a relationship with God. He or she is likely to show little spontaneous expression of faith and is likely to prefer more structured prayer and ritual. On occasion, the parishioner will be consumed with fear of committing or preoccupation with avoiding a grievous sin. He or she may be rigid in making moral judgments about himself or herself and others. It is often difficult for the pastor to develop much of a relationship with these parishioners and they may only seek the pastor out when looking for correct or certain solutions to theological or task-focused questions. They may be very disappointed or even agitated if certainty is not offered. If a relationship can be established, the pastor might help the parishioner to slowly begin to appreciate the fact that perfection is not a realistic goal and that the obsessive-compulsive person's constricted way of navigating life is actually lessening the probability that he or she will efficiently and successfully "get the job done." Psychotherapy and counseling are not typically sought out or continued by the obsessive-compulsive person and prognosis for change is guarded at best. However, as is the case with obsessive-compulsive disorder (see Chapter 2), cognitive-behavioral treatments may be helpful for challenging at least some of the obsessive-compulsive person's erroneous beliefs and decreasing some compulsive behaviors.

Chapter 5

The Family in Distress: Childhood and Relationship Problems

Between 12 and 17 percent of American children have psychological disorders at any given time.[1-3] Among the childhood disorders, *attention deficit hyperactivity disorder* (ADHD) is the most common. Throughout childhood and adolescence, boys are diagnosed with psychological disorders at higher rates than girls for all of the established DSM-IV disorders except eating disorders.[4] In this chapter, we present the essential features of the most commonly confronted disorders of childhood and adolescence. We have selected disorders that are most likely to impact children and families in the church.

In contrast to psychological problems in adults, many problems in children are short-lived and resolve rather easily in the course of normal development. Because normal development in childhood and adolescence is rapid (and sometimes tumultuous), episodes of mood disturbance, anxiety, and even some behavioral acting out are considered somewhat normal—as long as they do not persist or become disabling. At the same time, however, children have a less stable and secure sense of identity and are therefore more vulnerable to the impact of immediate change or perceived threats. This normal vulnerability leaves them more exposed than adults to experiences of rejection, failure, and disappointment.

In this chapter, we will highlight ADHD, *oppositional-defiant disorder, conduct disorder, separation anxiety disorder* (disorders prevalent in childhood), and *eating disorders,* which are most prevalent in adolescence and early adulthood. We also cover *child and spouse abuse* as a pervasive problem that may impact families with or without children. Although depression and psychosis are problems affecting both children and adolescents, we refer the reader to Chapter 2 for descriptions of those disorders. It is worth noting that depression in children and adolescents can be quite serious; a referral to a mental health professional is strongly recommended when depression appears to be consistent or severe.

You may wonder why we have chosen to include abuse in this chapter. With over two million cases of child abuse reported annually in the United States,[5] and many more cases not reported, it is clear that pastors in all sectors of society are likely to encounter evidence of abuse or neglect at some point. Abused children are at increased risk for a number of the childhood and adult disorders discussed in this book, as well as permanent physical and social impairment. Similarly, violence aimed at adult women in families is a significant societal problem. One study found that about 3 percent of women in a large sample had been severely assaulted (punched, kicked, choked, beaten, threatened with a knife or gun, or had a knife or gun used on them) in the preceding twelve months.[6] We hope that the information on child and spouse abuse will be useful to pastors who may be among the first in their communities to become aware of abusive relationships.

As in the previous two chapters, we include a presenting complaint section that offers a look at each disorder in a fictitious case. We then cover the common features and symptoms, subtypes (when applicable), key indicators, and conclude with a summary and guidelines section that offers the pastor a brief recap and some recommendations regarding referrals and pastoral management.

ATTENTION DEFICIT HYPERACTIVITY DISORDER

Presenting Complaint

Alfred is a nine-year-old Sunday school student who is causing havoc in his class. His Sunday school teacher describes him as "out of control" and "completely hyper." He has been a problem for the teacher and the other students because of his impulsiveness and inability to control his motor behavior. You learn that, in his regular third grade classroom and Sunday school, Alfred will impulsively hit other children, knock things off their desks, erase material on the blackboard, and damage books and other school property. Alfred's regular teacher likes him, but says she is "worn out" and that Alfred is the closest thing she has seen to the "Tasmanian Devil" cartoon character. Alfred demands an excessive amount of attention from both his teachers and parents. In the classroom, he is in perpetual motion, darting about, talking excessively, and unable to focus on the task at hand. In spite of his behavior problems and poor self-esteem, Alfred is very intelligent. Nonetheless, he feels "stupid." A recent physical exam shows him to be healthy. His parents are "at wits' end" and wonder what to do.

Common Features and Symptoms

The essential features of ADHD are hyperactivity, short attention span, and developmentally inappropriate impulsiveness.[4] Attention deficit hyperactivity disorder is typically diagnosed prior to or during early elementary school as the symptoms tend to be present and problematic by early childhood. In the church, these children will be recognized by their physical overactivity, inattention, impulsiveness, and seemingly constant distractedness. They are often the bane of Sunday school teachers and, in the worship service, they tend to fidget, fuss, and fall off chairs. They are unable to wait their turn, interrupt conversations, and constantly talk or physically provoke others. When they burst into a room, they are noticed.

Many ADHD children are socially very immature. They are often of normal intelligence, but may have impaired math and reading skills. They hear well but listen poorly. They are generally physically healthy but very difficult to manage behaviorally. When ADHD symptoms are present in infancy, they most often include overactivity to stimuli such as noise, light, and temperature, as well as agitation, constant crying, and sleeplessness.[7] Roughly 50 percent of those diagnosed with ADHD present some clear symptoms by the age of four. In the United States, the incidence of ADHD is estimated to be about 4 percent of the child population, and boys are diagnosed with the disorder six times more often than girls. Firstborn boys are at higher risk for ADHD and about 50 percent of those with this disorder will also have problems with conduct disorder.

Although the specific causes of ADHD are still unclear, most mental health professionals see the disorder as having a strong biological component. Genetic influences are supported by the finding that ADHD children are three times more likely to have a sibling with the disorder. Also, families with ADHD children are considerably more likely to have histories of other psychiatric problems. Possible fetal and perinatal causes of ADHD include poor maternal nutrition, substance abuse, viral infection, and exposure to toxins. Abusive or chaotic family environments are known to exacerbate ADHD symptoms.

ADHD: Key Indicators

- Consistent signs of inattention, hyperactivity, and impulsiveness, which have persisted for at least six months, and are present by the age of seven. These symptoms cause problems for the child educationally and/or socially.
- Symptoms may include the following:

  1. *inattention* (a) fails to pay attention or makes careless mistakes in schoolwork; (b) has difficulty sustaining attention to tasks or play; (c) does not listen when spoken to directly; (d) does not follow through on instructions and fails to finish tasks; (e) has difficulty organizing tasks or activities; (f) avoids or dislikes tasks that require mental effort; (g) loses necessary items (e.g., pencils, paper, etc.); (h) is forgetful of daily activities.
  2. *hyperactivity* (a) fools with hands or feet or squirms in seat; (b) leaves seat when staying in seat is expected; (c) runs or climbs in situations where it is inappropriate; (d) has difficulty playing quietly; (e) constantly "on the go"; (f) talks excessively.
  3. *impulsivity* (a) blurts out answers before questions are completed; (b) has difficulty waiting turn; (c) interrupts or intrudes on others.

Summary and Guidelines

Children with ADHD are not uncommon in the church. They may range from the severely hyperactive and hard to manage child to the more reserved but extremely inattentive child. When parents have concerns about their children's behavior, or the pastor or other professionals (e.g., experienced teachers) believe a child may have ADHD, it is important for the pastor to encourage a referral to a qualified mental health practitioner. At the same time, it is critical for the pastor not to label normal overactivity and intensity in children as pathologic. The pastor should look for signs of actual relational and educational impairment before assuming that a child may have ADHD. It is also important to distinguish between ADHD and conduct disorder (covered in this chapter). In the case of conduct disorder, the child will engage in criminal behavior.

The treatment of choice for ADHD is stimulant medication. The two most commonly used medications are Ritalin (methylphenidate) and Dexedrine (dextroamphetamine). Stimulant medications appear to effectively diminish ADHD symptoms while increasing attentiveness, vigilance, and appropriate social interaction. These medications do not facilitate learning, but make the child more capable of paying attention and therefore more likely to learn. Although most pediatricians and family physicians will prescribe medications for ADHD, a psychiatrist or pediatrician with considerable experience in managing ADHD children is preferred. If a pediatrician or family doctor provides medication, the family may benefit from an additional referral to a mental health professional who can provide behavioral and family-oriented strategies for helping the child. For example, family counseling, group therapy, social skills training, and parent behavior coaching have been shown to be very helpful in treating ADHD.[7] While on medications, children must be monitored routinely by the prescribing doctor as the medications produce some side effects.

Parental guilt may be one of the major issues the pastor will have to address when dealing with ADHD, and it is one of the barriers to effective treatment. By providing support and accurate information to parents of ADHD children, the pastor will increase the probability that these children will be effectively treated and will become more adaptive in behavior. In larger churches, support groups for parents of ADHD children may be helpful.

OPPOSITIONAL DEFIANT DISORDER

Presenting Complaint

Ten-year-old Ryan's parents come to you and begin to describe Ryan's behavioral problems, which are so severe, you find it hard to believe that he is the same ten-year-old you see at the church. Ryan begins each day arguing with his mother about what to wear and what to eat. He typically has a tantrum at least once before school. He is banned from riding the bus due to his retaliations against children who tease him and his episodes of cursing at the bus driver. During the school day, Ryan may curse at his teacher if she asks him to stop doing something. He may overturn his desk and stomp out of the room if not allowed to use the bathroom on demand. When not in conflict with his teacher or principal, Ryan usually plays alone. After school, he battles his mother over homework, often breaking pencils and refusing to work altogether. When his mother restricts him to his room until he completes his homework, Ryan screams, slams his door, and turns up his music as loud as he can. Although Ryan calms down somewhat when his father comes home, he usually has a few more tantrums before bedtime. His parents are at their "wits' end."

Common Features and Symptoms

Children with oppositional defiant disorder (ODD) are chronically aggressive, argumentative, volatile, spiteful, and vindictive. They openly defy rules and requests and often go out of their way to annoy others (especially those they know well); this is usually the reason they are brought to the attention of a pastor or mental health professional. Lying is a way of life for these children and getting a reaction from others is a primary objective. They are rarely sorry for their defiant behavior and believe that fault lies with others (usually parents). Children with ODD are distinct from ADHD children in that they are chronically defiant and argumentative but not hyperactive or inattentive (although some children have both ODD and ADHD, which certainly makes them more difficult to manage). Oppositional defiant disorder is among the most common of all childhood psychiatric disorders, occurring in about 5 percent of all children.[4] Although ODD is more common in boys than girls prior to puberty, the rates are about the same following puberty. Symptoms of ODD typically become evident between the ages of one and three, and are nearly always present by age six.

Oppositional defiant disorder, characterized by negative, disobedient, and defiant behavior toward authority figures, may be a prelude to a much more serious disorder—conduct disorder. Conduct disorder involves violations of the rights of others (e.g., stealing, destroying property, coercing others, etc.). While ODD is typically present by age six, conduct disorder is not usually evident until age nine. Research has shown that ODD is nearly always present in children and adolescents who develop conduct disorder.[8] However, only about 25 percent of all children with ODD will go on to develop conduct disorder.

Oppositional Defiant Disorder: Key Indicators

- A consistent pattern of negative, hostile, and defiant behavior which is indicated by several of the following: (1) often loses temper; (2) often argues with adults; (3) often actively defies or refuses to comply with adult's requests or rules; (4) often deliberately annoys people; (5) often blames others for his or her mistakes or misbehavior; (6) often "touchy" or easily annoyed by others; (7) often angry and resentful; (8) often spiteful and vindictive.

Summary and Guidelines

Parents with ODD children could benefit from a high level of pastoral support. This may be difficult for two reasons. First, because ODD children usually reserve their obnoxious and overtly defiant behavior for their parents (and others they feel especially close to), and because they often display better behavior in front of people they see less often, the pastor may have difficulty believing that they are as difficult to manage as the parents report. Second, the pastor may view the ODD behavior exclusively as the result of poor or inadequate parenting. Although poor parenting skills or inconsistent delivery of discipline may contribute to ODD behavior in children, parenting style may not always be the primary problem, since some children appear to be inherently oppositional and defiant in their behavior—even in the face of competent parenting.

For these reasons, it is recommended that the pastor offer the parents encouragement and, if the parents are willing, refer them to a mental health professional with expertise in treating child behavior disorders. Because ODD children may be masters at creating conflict between caretaking adults—sometimes creating conflict between parents, teachers, and relatives—it is important that a neutral party with expertise in managing ODD behavior be consulted. Unfortunately, little is known about the most effective treatments for ODD,[9] except that the prognosis is usually guarded as a percentage will go on to demonstrate conduct disorder in adolescence and antisocial behavior in adulthood. Among the available treatments, systematic training of parents in the use of behavioral techniques (consequences and reinforcements) with their children is generally more effective than other kinds of therapy, including family therapy.

CONDUCT DISORDER

Presenting Complaint

Adam is an eleven-year-old who seems "headed for trouble." His mother, who is a single parent, approaches you and appears anxious and overwhelmed by her son's incorrigible behavior. Adam has been stealing money from his mother and has been constantly fist fighting with his two brothers and peers at school. Although he is supposed to go directly home from school, he refuses to comply with his mother's rules and routinely wanders the streets alone, breaking windows, vandalizing property, and smoking cigarettes. He has been arrested once for shoplifting and has been expelled from school for stealing and fighting. Adam appears to have little regard for authority and pays almost no attention to his mother's attempts to discipline him. He lies frequently and shows little remorse for his behavior. Adam's father has almost no contact with the family. His mother works long hours and is rarely effective in monitoring, let alone controlling, Adam's behavior or whereabouts.

Common Features and Symptoms

The key features of conduct disorder are a persistent, repetitive violation of rules and a disregard for the rights of others. It is as though the conduct-disordered child or adolescent specializes in "bad" behavior. These behaviors are often criminal in nature, violate social norms, and often violate or exploit others. Conduct disorder is considerably more prevalent in boys (9 percent) than girls (2 percent),[4] and it is often the precursor to adult antisocial personality disorder (see Chapter 4). Children who develop conduct disorder by age ten are considerably more likely to become antisocial adults than children who develop this disorder in adolescence. Characteristic conduct-disordered behaviors include lying, stealing, truancy, physical aggression, cruelty to animals and other people, and destruction of property. These children often run away from home, abuse substances, and engage in sexual activity. They may also be irritable, impulsive, and prone to angry outbursts. They typically come to the attention of the church and various mental health professionals via their distraught parents or the juvenile court system.

Risk factors for conduct disorder include a family history of anti-social personality disorder, substance abuse, child abuse (physical, emotional, or sexual), and learning disabilities that interfere with school success. Evidence for a genetic predisposition comes from the finding that adopted children whose biological fathers have criminal records have higher rates of conduct disorder.[8] Conduct disorder is considerably more common in families where there is marital conflict, divorce, father absence, and authoritarian parenting. Although conduct-disordered children are quite manipulative and socially savvy ("street smart"), they tend to be delayed with respect to verbal intelligence and academic achievement—often because they have been unable to learn (learning disability) or unavailable for education due to their behavior and home situation.

Conduct Disorder: Key Indicators

- Persistent and repetitive behaviors that violate the rights of others and major societal norms, as indicated by several of the following: (1) aggression toward and cruelty to people or animals; (2) bullying, threatening, and initiating fights; (3) stealing with or without confronting the victim; (4) forcing someone into sexual activity; (5) destruction of property; (6) setting fires; (7) lying and deceitfulness; (8) violation of parental rules; (9) truancy; (10) use of a weapon to steal from or harm another person; (11) running away.

Summary and Guidelines

The conduct-disordered child or adolescent presents a troubling picture to the pastor. These children are often quite resistant to rebuke or correction. Their lack of remorse or regard for authority, or the suffering of others, makes most interventions ineffective. When there are clear signs of conduct disorder, it is important for the pastor to encourage parents to have the child evaluated by a professional with expertise in this disorder. Although no specific treatment is nearly always recommended or likely to be effective (as in the case of stimulant medication for ADHD), most professionals agree that one key to a positive prognosis in treating conduct disorder is early intervention.

A psychologist who treats childhood disorders may be an especially good referral, as commonly coexisting disorders such as learning disabilities, mood problems, ADHD, and substance abuse will require careful assessment and, if present, simultaneous treatment. In some cases, medications that reduce arousal, impulsivity, and aggression have been helpful. Other common interventions include removing children from abusive homes, parent coaching to both reduce the frequency of authoritarian parenting behaviors and increase effective behavior management, and teaching limit-setting skills. Most often, parents of conduct-disordered children are too permissive or too authoritarian. The church may be especially helpful by providing parenting resources, educational materials, and peer support. Because many conduct-disordered children have learning/academic problems, the church may also consider tutorial help as an outreach of the deacon's or children's ministry. Finally, the pastor can be a source of hope to both parents and children by conveying God's promise that if they "train up the child in the way that he should go, and when he is old, he won't depart from it" (Proverbs 22:6, RSV).

SEPARATION ANXIETY DISORDER

Presenting Complaint

At an evening adults-only meeting at the church, you are surprised to see Mary's eleven-year-old daughter, Diana, sitting in the hallway outside the church meeting room. When you ask Mary if everything is okay, she rolls her eyes in exasperation and explains that Diana refuses to allow Mary to go out without her. In fact, Diana will have a tantrum, scream, and even threaten to kill herself if her mother attempts to leave her with a babysitter, or alone for any period of time. Mary says she has had to home school Diana, not because Mary values home schooling, but because Diana refused to attend school if it meant being away from her mother. Diana is obsessed with concerns that her mother will be killed if the two are apart or that Diana will be kidnapped and unable to see her mother again. You are particularly surprised to learn that Diana refuses to go to sleep without Mary in the room and that, as a result, Mary now sleeps in the same room with her daughter.

Common Features and Symptoms

Children with separation anxiety disorder live in constant fear of separation from their major "attachment figure" (usually a parent). They fear that their caregiver will die or that they (the child) will be lost, kidnapped, or otherwise permanently separated from the parent. They continually cling to or shadow their caregiver and are miserable, anxious, and depressed when separated from them. Going to a friend's house or staying with a babysitter may be a substantial ordeal and these children often refuse to attend school. If they are forced to attend school, they may attempt to sneak away or may remain sullen, withdrawn, and refuse to complete work. Children with this disorder often have a number of other fears—especially fear of the dark. Although they may have some legitimate physical symptoms of anxiety when threatened with separation from their parents (e.g., nausea, headaches, vomiting), they may quickly learn to manufacture these as a means of keeping their caregiver from leaving.

While children may be truly afraid of being separated from their primary parent, their clinging behaviors are often inadvertently strengthened by parents who habitually "give in" and remain with or rescue these children. Parents of children with separation anxiety disorder are frequently called out of church services by Sunday school teachers to retrieve their children who are having tantrums. Very often, parents of these children will only seek professional help or approach their pastors about the problem when the children reach school age and refuse to attend.

Although most children go through a time of anxiety about separation from their parents in early childhood and again around the time school starts, children with separation anxiety disorder do not outgrow this transitional phase. Instead, their anxiety can become overwhelming and prevent them from learning, developing relationships, and enjoying any independence. Boys and girls are equally likely to have this disorder, and it is present in about 4 percent of children and adolescents.[4] The initial symptoms of this disorder often emerge following a significant trauma (e.g., loss of a family member, serious illness, or a family move), and they almost always occur before adolescence. The symptoms may fluctuate for years, and children who struggle with this anxiety problem are considerably more likely to develop anxiety disorders, particularly panic disorder (see Chapter 2), in adulthood.

Separation Anxiety Disorder: Key Indicators

- Age-inappropriate and excessive anxiety about separation from home or one's primary caregiver.
- Signs of this inappropriate and excessive anxiety include: (1) consistent excessive distress when the child anticipates being separated from home or parent; (2) ongoing worry about losing, or possible harm befalling, major caregiver; (3) ongoing worry that a major event (kidnapping or getting lost) will separate him or her from the caregiver; (4) persistent reluctance to attend school due to fear of separation; (5) excessive fear about being alone; (6) refusal to go to sleep without being nearby a caregiver; (7) repeated nightmares involving separation; (8) repeated physical complaints (e.g., headaches, stomachaches, nausea, or vomiting) when separation occurs or is anticipated.

Summary and Guidelines

A general rule of thumb among professionals working with children diagnosed with separation anxiety disorder is that both the child and the primary caregiver contribute to the anxiety. Although the child often comes from a family that seems very close-knit and caring, closer examination will often reveal a parent with profound difficulty letting go of the child and experiencing great distress at leaving the child. The pastor may have to balance sensitivity to the parent's well-intentioned zeal about caretaking with gentle suggestions that perhaps the parent contributes to the child's anxiety and avoidance behavior by not allowing him or her to experience the normal distress that comes with separation and healthy individuation. In other words, these parents can be viewed as giving their child "too much of a good thing." Of course, many parents of children with this disorder will be quite defensive regarding their role in perpetuating their children's behavior. The pastor would be wise to make an appropriate mental health service referral if this is the case.

Although a number of different treatment approaches have proven helpful with separation anxiety disorder, all of them require full parental compliance to be effective. *Transitional objects* such as blankets, stuffed animals, and pictures of family members can be helpful for the child learning to tolerate parental absence. Helping a parent to reduce his or her own anxiety about a child's distress is also helpful since a child often becomes most upset when he or she senses a parent's anxiety. Finally, grief work may be necessary for children whose separation anxiety is the result of the death or loss of a major attachment figure. Again, we recommend a mental health practitioner experienced in working with children who understands normal and abnormal child development.

EATING DISORDERS

Presenting Complaint

The church youth pastor phones you and reports "a little problem" at the church summer camp. One of the counselors, a nineteen-year-old college sophomore named Tammy, has been discovered forcing herself to vomit on several occasions after meals and at least two times late at night. This has been a problem because several junior high school girls in Tammy's cabin are aware of this and have made worried comments to other counselors. When confronted, Tammy "broke down" and admitted that she began binging and purging during her freshman year in college. Tammy comes to see you the following week and describes the onset of bouts of excessive eating followed by forced vomiting. These bouts began during the previous fall when her first "serious" college boyfriend ended their brief but intense relationship. Tammy describes becoming very depressed and anxious about whether or not she was attractive. She describes binges late at night that can include an entire pizza and a two-pound bag of cookies. Although she has felt quite depressed after her purging, she admits, "I just can't seem to stop on my own."

Common Features and Symptoms

Anorexia nervosa and *bulimia nervosa* are the two most prevalent eating disorders. Both involve a preoccupation with weight and unhealthy (potentially lethal) approaches to losing weight. The frequency of these disorders is escalating in the highest risk group—middle-class adolescent girls and young adult women. These disorders are among the most distressing to parents and the pastor may be called upon to provide support as well as referrals for assistance. It is important to be aware that anorexia can quickly become life threatening if not actively treated.

Subtypes

Anorexia Nervosa

First documented in 1689 and labeled in 1874, anorexia is characterized by an irrational fear of becoming fat, an obsessive pursuit of thinness, excessive weight loss, a distorted body image, and the distorted belief that one is too fat. Between 1950 and 1980, the incidence of anorexia among adolescent girls increased more than 300 percent. The average age at which anorexia begins is seventeen, although it can begin even before adolescence. About 1 percent of women meet criteria for this disorder, and it is considerably less common in males. Among those diagnosed with the disorder, about 5 percent can be expected to die as a direct result (the most prominent example is the anorexia-related death of singer Karen Carpenter).

More serious cases of anorexia are usually easy to spot. Anorectic persons will appear cheerful and energetic, yet very emaciated, and even skeleton-like in appearance. Anorectic men and women often begin as model children who subsequently begin dieting because of concern that they are slightly overweight. The initial diet often begins after the anorectic has experienced a life stressor (e.g., parents' divorce or a failed romantic relationship). After losing some weight, the person will often decide to continue weight reduction until she or he nearly stops eating altogether. Except for the most advanced cases, anorectic persons think about food almost constantly. They enjoy cooking for others, memorize their caloric intake, hoard food, and often eat alone. To accelerate weight loss, they may exercise excessively, abstain from fats or carbohydrates, use laxatives, or induce vomiting (although this is more common in bulimia).

Anorexia is a very serious disorder that can last for years. It can be cyclical, with periods of remission, or it can be persistent and uninterrupted. Although nutritional recovery may occur within a few years, abnormal eating patterns and preoccupation with weight and body shape may last much longer. About 40 percent of anorectics recover fully. Another 30 percent show significant improvement and 30 percent remain severely impaired by the disorder. The typical anorectic person is a white, college-bound, teenage girl from the middle to upper classes. Although men can be diagnosed with anorexia, this is less often the case, and research on men with eating disorders is sparse.

Anorexia Nervosa: Key Indicators

- Refusal to maintain body weight at or above a minimally normal weight for age and height (weight loss leading to total weight less than 85 percent of what would be expected).
- Intense fear of gaining weight or becoming fat (even though the person is underweight).
- Distorted perception of one's own body weight or shape (sees himself or herself as overweight or fat when this is not the case, or denies the seriousness of his or her low body weight).
- If the person is a postpuberty female, she has missed three consecutive menstrual cycles.

Bulimia Nervosa

First recognized in the 1950s, this disorder is characterized by periods of binge eating followed by self-induced vomiting or other compensatory behaviors. The term bulimia means "hunger of an ox," and aptly describes the prodigious quantities of food consumed (as many as 11,500 calories) during a single binge episode. Bulimic persons describe being driven to consume huge amounts of unhealthy food (binge) and have been known to do so as many as nine times per day. The binge may last for an hour and the bulimic will typically "gobble," instead of chew, a substantial volume of high-calorie foods. The person may spend $100 or more on food binges in a day. They may also steal food for binges, and they almost always engage in binge eating while alone. The binge will end when the person is discovered, falls asleep, develops stomach pain, or forces himself or herself to vomit (approximately 88 percent of bulimics self-induce vomiting). After vomiting, the bulimic may or may not continue to binge.

Prevalence rates for bulimia are about 0.5 percent for the general population and as high as 4 percent for the college student population.

Like the anorectic, the bulimic will most often be a white, middle- to upper-class female (90 to 95 percent of those with bulimia are women) college student. She is likely to view her binge eating as abnormal and may despise and fear her inability to control it. She is likely to be unhappy, self-deprecating, and preoccupied with appearance, body image, and sexual attractiveness (in contrast to the anorectic, who has less concern about sex appeal). A period of mild to serious depression often precedes a binge. Although the binge may provide temporary mood relief, postbinge experiences of depression are also common—thus creating a vicious mood-related cycle. Bulimic persons often have impulse control problems in other areas. Approximately one-third have abused alcohol or drugs, engaged in shopping sprees, or been promiscuous.

Bulimia usually begins later than anorexia, but it too may follow some difficult loss or life event. It is often a chronic disorder with alternating periods of normal and binge eating. Bulimics generally improve and recover completely. Although death related to this disorder is relatively rare (usually linked to deficiencies in potassium due to frequent vomiting), many bulimic persons suffer from electrolyte imbalance, dehydration, cardiac problems, intestinal damage, and dental problems. Many individuals with bulimia have other psychiatric disorders such as depression (75 percent), anxiety disorders (43 percent), substance disorders (49 percent), and cluster B personality disorders (50 percent).

Bulimia Nervosa: Key Indicators

- Consistent episodes of binge eating (eating, in a discrete period of time, an amount of food larger than most people would eat during a similar time period and under similar circumstances) and a sense of lack of control over the binge eating.
- Recurrent inappropriate compensatory behavior following a binge such as: (1) self-induced vomiting; (2) laxative use; (3) diet pill use; (4) enemas; (5) fasting; or (6) excessive exercise to prevent weight gain.
- The binging and compensatory behavior occur at least twice a week for at least three months.
- The person's evaluation of himself or herself is based excessively on body shape or weight.

Summary and Guidelines

The pastor's role in assisting parishioners (and their family members) who suffer with eating disorders can be very significant. In most cases, stress on the family as a result of this unremitting condition is enormous. Few things are as distressing to a family as a child who begins to systematically starve himself or herself, or one who engages in repeated episodes of dangerous compensatory behavior (e.g., vomiting). The pastor may provide a critically important listening ear. He or she may also be the first to recognize the signs of an eating disorder and may provide the vital function of recommending immediate intervention with a qualified professional. Among parishioners with eating disorders, it is wise to expect a high degree of denial that any problem exists. The pastor may be called to participate, with the family or others, in a loving but tough confrontation of the sufferer in order to break through denial and leverage him or her into treatment. Given the severity of these disorders, it would be unwise for the pastor to attempt an intervention on his or her own.

Psychiatrists, psychologists, or social workers with expertise in treating eating disorders are highly recommended in nearly every case. In the most severe cases, merely getting the person transported to a hospital may be critical. Considering the potentially fatal consequences of anorexia, the initial treatment goal is always to simply keep the person alive and stabilize him or her medically (stop weight loss and balance internal systems). When weight loss has made the parishioner medically unstable, he or she may be involuntarily hospitalized. Once stabilization has been achieved, treatment typically focuses on treating medical complications, modifying unhealthy eating habits, improving family relationship patterns, enhancing self-control and self-concept, and correcting distorted thoughts, which often precipitate self-starvation.

Most bulimic parishioners can be treated as outpatients. Exceptions include those who have medical complications, a severe binge-purge cycle, sudden weight loss, or a family crisis (leading to a psychiatric admission). Cognitive-behavioral therapies, interpersonal therapy, and antidepressant medications have all been used with success in helping bulimic persons. Treatment typically includes two phases: (1) breaking the binge-purge cycle with behavioral techniques and (2) modifying disturbed attitudes and beliefs about body shape, weight, and dieting using cognitive-behavioral interventions.

CHILD AND SPOUSE ABUSE

Presenting Complaint

The Jenkins family has attended your church for several years. Tom is a night security guard at a local college and Jennifer works as a teaching assistant in the elementary school. Another parishioner comes to you and expresses concern that Tom may be abusing his wife. She notes that Jennifer sometimes has marks around her face that she refuses to discuss or insists are related to a recent fall or other accident. You have known Tom to be very short-tempered and "uptight." He has also been threatened with unemployment lately and the family is under a good deal of stress. At church, you notice that the couple's two young children appear sullen and frightened around their father. You wonder how to respond to this situation and if it is really possible that Tom could be abusing his wife or perhaps even his children.

Common Features and Symptoms

Child and spouse abuse affect millions of families each year. Both forms of domestic violence are almost certain to occur within some families in most congregations. The pastor should anticipate that a percentage of his or her congregation will be impacted by the effects of violence or neglect. In this section, we highlight the essential characteristics of both child abuse and spouse abuse with an emphasis on characteristics of abusers, causes of abuse, and effects or outcomes. We also offer some recommendations for ways the church might work to reduce violence in the home. We do not provide a key indicators box since abuse and neglect can vary widely and the specific impact on a child or spouse may depend on a host of factors. Our primary recommendation is that pastors accept the fact that abuse of children and spouses is probably occurring in some church members' homes.

Subtypes

Child Abuse

Although child abuse and neglect can be defined in a multitude of ways, Public Law 104-235 defines child abuse and neglect as, at a minimum, any recent act or failure to act on the part of a parent or caretaker resulting in death, serious physical or emotional harm, sexual abuse or exploitation, or an act or failure to act which presents an imminent risk of serious harm. A child is anyone under the age of eighteen. The National Clearinghouse on Child Abuse and Neglect has identified four primary types of child maltreatment: emotional abuse, neglect, physical abuse, and sexual abuse.[10]

Emotional abuse. Emotional abuse includes acts or failures to act that cause or could cause serious distress or disorder in children. This may include a range of behaviors including bizarre forms of punishment (e.g., confinement to a closet), rejecting or belittling treatment, use of derogatory terms, and habitual scapegoating or blaming. Emotional abuse is sometimes referred to as verbal abuse and mental abuse.

Neglect. Neglect is the failure to provide for a child's basic needs. Neglect can be physical, educational, or emotional. Examples include failing to provide adequate food, clothing, or medical attention, allowing children to be consistently truant from school, or withholding emotional support or attention from a child.

Physical abuse. Physical abuse is most simply the infliction of physical injury upon a child. Physical abuse may include burning, hitting, punching, shaking, kicking, beating, or otherwise harming a child. Although the parent may not have intended to harm the child, the injury is not an accident. Parents who harm their children during the course of "discipline" are also guilty of physical abuse.

Sexual abuse. Sexual abuse may be defined as any inappropriate sexual behavior with a child. It includes fondling a child's genitals, making the child fondle the adult's genitals, intercourse, rape, sodomy, exhibitionism, and sexual exploitation. To be considered child abuse, these acts must be committed by a person responsible for the child's care or a person related to the child. If a stranger commits these acts, it would be considered sexual assault and handled solely by the police or criminal courts.

Of concern is the fact that the rate of child abuse in the United States appears to be moving upward. The number of children reported abused and neglected rose 64 percent between 1980 and 1988, for a total of 2.2 million cases reported in 1988.[5] In 1996, an estimated 3.1 million children were reported to child protective agencies as victims of abuse or neglect.[11] Between 1986 and 1993, the number of children seriously injured by all forms of child maltreatment quadrupled, and the number of children sexually abused increased 83 percent. Ample data suggests that child maltreatment is pervasive enough to be an issue at the local church level. Pastors and education staff should be vigilant for signs of abuse and neglect among children in the congregation.

Although boys are more often physically abused than girls, girls are three times more likely to become victims of sexual abuse. Research has consistently demonstrated that children who are abused and neglected are at increased risk for a host of childhood and adult psychological problems. These include impaired intellectual functioning and memory difficulties, problems with relationships, depression, antisocial personality traits, and self-destructive behaviors. Children who are sexually abused can be expected to have poorer social adjustment, relationship and sexual problems, guilt and shame regarding the abuse, and a range of psychiatric problems as adults (mood disorders are particularly common).

What kinds of parents are likely to abuse? Overall, abusive parents tend to be younger (under thirty), lower in socioeconomic status, prone to psychological problems of their own, and suffering from a range of stressors (e.g., marital discord, unemployment). The pastor should remain watchful for these risk factors as well as impulse control problems, anger management difficulties, alcohol or drug abuse, and obvious signs of abuse or trauma in children. The vast majority of child abuse perpetrators are the parents of the children. It is important to keep in mind that any parent can abuse a child under the right circumstances or in a stressful situation. Belsky noted, "There is no one pathway to these disturbances in parenting; rather, maltreatment seems to arise when stressors outweigh supports and risks are greater than protective factors."[12]

Although no single behavior or behavior pattern reliably identifies children who are being abused, there are some common physical and behavioral signs for which mental health professionals remain vigilant when assessing children. These include external marks (bruises and scars), depressed mood, anger problems, poor self-esteem, sexual acting out or sexually laden speech, interpersonal detachment or interpersonal "clinging," and an exaggerated startle response (flinches or cowers). Of course, children may simply disclose abuse to the pastor or Sunday school teacher. Since children rarely fabricate stories of abuse, their comments should be taken very seriously.

In most states, pastors and other professionals are required to report cases of known or reasonably suspected child abuse. This means that pastors may at times be required to do something which precipitates a substantial crisis in the lives of some parishioners. Informing these parishioners of this obligation prior to any sort of formal pastoral counseling is wise. Beyond reporting cases of abuse and attempting to support children and families in the wake of the ensuing intervention by authorities, the church might be proactive in preventing child abuse and supporting parents at risk. Specifically, the church might consider educationally focused programs that increase awareness of abuse—both for parents and youth workers. Parent preparation training for soon-to-be-married couples or couples preparing to have their first child might also incorporate training in risk factors for abuse and strategies for reducing this risk. Support groups for parents who have had trouble with abuse or anger control might also be useful, and could focus on development of adaptive and effective parenting skills.

Spouse Abuse

Violence within marriage is now recognized as a considerable social problem in the United States. According to various surveys, about 2 million women are assaulted by male partners each year.[6,13] If about one in eight husbands is physically violent with his spouse each year, it is reasonable to assume that some of these couples will be involved with the church. Yet, admission of violence in the home can be quite stigmatizing and shaming for both partners. It will be a challenge for most churches to create an environment in which admission of a range of problems—including violence—is acceptable.

The most obvious concern related to domestic violence is the risk of serious injury or death. Up to 25 percent of all homicides committed in the United States each year are committed by a husband or wife.[13] Violence from husbands to wives is the primary pattern in over 90 percent of cases of domestic violence. Marital violence is also strongly linked to psychological problems and major disorders, including depression, alcohol abuse, and PTSD (see Chapters 2 and 3). We know that violence between adult partners is linked to higher rates of child abuse as well. Even when children are not physically abused, they tend to be traumatized and disturbed by watching violence between parents.

Why do marriage partners batter one another? Although many factors help explain the problem of battering in marriage, most violent men have learned this approach to handling stress, anger, or conflict—typically from their own fathers or other male models. Violent men are quite likely to have come from violent homes as children. They often have a restricted range of appropriate responses when it comes to managing their own anger or negotiating disagreement with their partners. Very often, they have impulsive personality features, personal rigidity, and poor communication skills. These men are also more likely to believe strongly that they should have control over their wives and that their wives should submit without condition. The pastor may need to be particularly vigilant for male parishioners' selective use of scripture to support highly controlling and violent behavior. For example, some men may focus exclusively on verses such as "Wives, be subject to your husbands as you are to the Lord" (Ephesians 5:22, RSV), while ignoring related versus such as "Be subject to one another out of reverence for Christ" (Ephesians 5:21, RSV).

It is critically important that pastors be vigilant regarding the possibility of marital violence among parishioners—particularly those who seek counseling from the pastor. One reason is that, among couples seeking counseling, studies show that as many as half have experienced marital violence (most often perpetrated by the husband). Although most abused women will not spontaneously offer this information, research suggests that when specifically asked about violence, over 50 percent will acknowledge it.[13] Therefore, the pastor should remain aware of the potential for violence in all marriages and not hesitate to matter-of-factly inquire as to whether this has been a problem for any couple that he or she is counseling.

As in the case of child abuse, a church congregation that offers support to couples and individual victims of violence is likely to be most helpful. Beyond support groups, however, the pastor must be willing to intervene in cases where violence appears serious and likely to be repeated. Although states do not generally mandate reporting of partner abuse (as is nearly always the case with child abuse), victims of domestic violence are sometimes murdered or permanently injured by spouses when they attempt to leave an abusive marriage. Pastors and church bodies are encouraged to have a clear plan for responding to these cases. This may involve contact with the police and immediate referral to a shelter for battered women in the community, or an equivalent service offered via the church.

Chapter 6

Selecting a Mental Health Professional

For many pastors, especially those with limited training in counseling, the task of selecting a mental health professional (MHP) for parishioners can be daunting. In cities of even modest size, the Yellow Pages are often filled with a range of individuals advertising themselves as people helpers of one kind or another. A wide range of titles, credentials, and specialties are typically highlighted. Sometimes, the ads strongly imply guarantees of help for nearly any psychological problem. How do you choose MHPs who are right for your parishioners? How do you go about building a referral list of competent MHPs to help with the variety of people and problems you will encounter in your congregation?

In building a referral list for use in your church, we strongly recommend carefully evaluating MHPs in your community *before* you refer a parishioner to one of them for help. It is customary for MHPs of every sort to grant thirty-minute complementary sessions to prospective referral sources. These sessions will allow you to gather important information about each provider's background (personal and professional), experience, qualifications, and specialization. It will also allow you to get a "sense" of providers, how skilled they seem to be, and how sensitive they appear regarding issues of faith. We believe getting to know mental health practitioners on this more personal level is critical in helping you determine whether you would feel confident referring your church members to them. If a prospective MHP refuses such a complementary session, we recommend against including them on your referral list.

TYPES OF MENTAL HEALTH PROFESSIONALS

In this section, we describe the different kinds of MHPs, including their training, general areas of expertise, and credentialing.

Clinical or Counseling Psychologist (PhD, PsyD)

Psychologists are trained in psychology doctoral programs, which involve four to six years of education at the graduate level. The final year is devoted to a full-time supervised internship, preferably at a site approved by the American Psychological Association (APA). Psychologists receive extensive academic training in human development, personality, pathology, assessment, and treatment interventions. They also undergo a great deal of practical training with a range of clients and problems. Psychologists have expertise in assessment and treatment of disorders ranging from the most mild adjustment problems to the most severe organic and psychotic disorders. They are qualified to administer psychological tests as part of their assessment of clients and use a range of behavioral strategies and counseling or psychotherapy approaches to resolve problems. They are considered expert witnesses in court.

Psychologists are required to be licensed in all fifty states and usually undergo written and oral examinations to become licensed. They are required to adhere to the APA ethics code and are subject to disciplinary procedures for unethical conduct. Maintenance of licensure typically requires ongoing education in the field. Psychologists do not prescribe medications, and only licensed clinical and counseling psychologists are qualified to provide assessment and treatment services.

Psychiatrist (MD, DO)

Psychiatrists complete medical school to become physicians prior to completing a three-to-four-year residency in psychiatry. Following the residency, psychiatrists may become board certified in this specialty, and board certification is an important indication of competence to practice. Psychiatrists have extensive medical training and expertise in biologically and psychologically based disorders. They are able to prescribe psychiatric medications and, in fact, are known for frequently prescribing medication such as antidepressants to treat serious depression or antianxiety medications to treat severe anxiety. Psychiatrists often have admitting privileges at local hospitals and may facilitate a parishioner's inpatient hospitalization, if necessary, in the case of a serious psychiatric disorder. Also, some psychiatrists practice electroconvulsive therapy (ECT) for severe depression.

Psychiatrists may employ a great variety of interventions. Many psychiatrists rely rather exclusively on medications and may only meet with patients briefly to check on the success of certain medications and dosages. A smaller number of psychiatrists also practice talking therapies with clients and, in fact, may be quite skilled at this. It is imperative to know in advance whether a psychiatrist has much training in psychotherapy and, if so, whether he or she actually uses this training in practice. Psychiatrists may be designated as expert witnesses in court and are typically the most expensive mental health providers.

Social Worker (MSW)

Social workers complete a two-year master's degree in social work followed by a year of full-time postgraduate supervised experience. These practitioners receive training in the diagnosis and treatment of individual and family problems, social work techniques, and focused skills in linking people with community resources. Many states allow social workers to become licensed clinical social workers (LCSW) and this should be an important selection criterion in those states. Licensed clinical social workers may collect third party reimbursement similar to psychologists and psychiatrists. About 50 percent of social workers have been admitted to the Academy of Clinical Social Workers (ACSW). Social workers have clear expertise at troubleshooting complex system problems and linking clients to services in the community. Many of them are also quite skilled in the practice of therapy for various problems.

Counselor (MA, MEd, MFCC)

Counselors typically have a BA and two to three years of graduate training in counseling, psychology, marriage and family therapy, or pastoral counseling. These degrees may be offered in secular universities or religious colleges and seminaries. The academic requirements of such degree programs vary widely and it is possible that such practitioners have a great deal of supervised clinical experience, or nearly none at all. Counselors are generally trained to help with areas such as careers, adjustment issues, relationships, or general mental health difficulties. Marriage and family therapists are especially well trained for management of relationship problems. They neither have extensive training in diagnosis and treatment of more serious disorders, nor are they qualified to administer or interpret psychological tests, or prescribe medications. The primary concern with this category of MHPs is the wide variability in training and expertise.

Although many states require counselors to be registered or certified, only a few states allow counselors to be licensed. Registration ensures only that the counselor has obtained a master's degree in counseling from an accredited program. Certification indicates that, in addition to the degree, the counselor has accumulated a specified number of hours of supervised practice and has passed a written state board exam. Licensed professional counselors (LPCs), and sometimes marriage and family therapists (MFTs), can receive direct third party reimbursement for services rendered; however, this varies widely across states. Most counselors belong to national organizations such as the American Counseling Association (ACA), the American Association of Marriage and Family Therapists (AAMFT), the National Board for Certified Counselors (NCC), and the American Association of Pastoral Counselors (AAPC).

VALUES AND FAITH COMMITMENT

In the same way that you would be cautious about placing a parishioner with emotional problems in the hands of someone who is inexperienced or ineffective, it is unlikely that you would send him or her to a therapist who is openly or subtly antagonistic toward the parishioner's religious faith and values. Although licensure or certification indicate that the MHP has passed certain educational and training milestones, and (probably) does not have obvious character defects, it does not ensure that the therapist will be either effective or respectful of the client's faith and values. In fact, many MHPs have been historically antireligious in their practices and some of them work to convince clients that religious beliefs are highly correlated with mental illness. Because the process of therapeutic change is often painful and threatening to a client, it is essential that the pastor match the parishioner with an MHP who will be both effective and respectful of the client's faith.

Research shows that, during the course of counseling, a client's personal values (including those related to faith) are likely to change in the direction of the counselor's. This means that effective therapy often involves some adoption or acceptance of the counselor's values. For this reason, we recommend considerable care in selecting MHPs who will at least be very sensitive to and respectful of Christian beliefs and values. Better yet, you may find MHPs who are explicitly Christian in their own lives and who will not only honor, but actively promote a client's faith-based lifestyle and find ways to use the client's faith to overcome difficulties. During your interview with a prospective MHP, we highly recommend asking some very direct questions about the practitioner's own religious beliefs, the extent to which he or she feels comfortable working with religious clients, and the manner in which he or she might respond to a few common problems that may have clear connections to the client's beliefs. For example, how would he or she typically respond to crises of faith, marital difficulties, gender orientation concerns, etc.?

EXPERIENCE AND SPECIALTIES

As previously noted, having a graduate degree does not ensure that a particular provider will be even minimally competent to treat a specific mental health disorder or problem. For example, a psychiatrist may have tremendous expertise when it comes to managing serious psychotic and depressive disorders with elaborate combinations of psychotropic medication, yet know almost nothing about how to help couples with marital problems. A psychologist may have remarkable experience in treating adults with a range of problems, yet may never have worked with a child client. A newly minted counseling program graduate may have far less experience than you, the pastor, in providing counseling for the specific problem that you may want to refer to them.

The point here is that, as a referral source, it is important for you to glean information about each MHP's actual experience in the field. How much practical training have they had? To what degree are they competent to work with adults, children, couples, and families? Would they prefer not to work with specific groups of people or types of problems? Do they have focused expertise in working with certain problems or kinds of clients? If so, is this expertise recognized by others in the field or other pastors who routinely refer parishioners to them? In our experience, MHPs who are the most "expert" and competent are those who are open and clear about areas in which they are not well trained. They frequently set limits and recommend other providers when asked to practice outside their areas of competence. Furthermore, when asked about these relative weaknesses in preparation or preference, they are nondefensive. Be wary if an MHP suggests to you that he or she can work equally well with almost any kind of client and any sort of difficulty.

PERSONAL TRAITS

Is this person kind, competent, and fun to be around? This may sound like an odd question, but we take it seriously when it comes to evaluating individuals who are likely to be helpful or "therapeutic" to those they serve. Mental health professionals can have remarkable IQs, top-notch academic credentials, and advanced specialties in several areas, yet be utterly unhelpful. If they lack excellent interpersonal skills, be suspicious. In our experience, the best therapists are those with great training, extensive experience, and a "knack" for knowing how to convey warmth, unconditional regard, and kindness to clients. Excellent therapists are personable. They often have a wonderful sense of humor, yet know when to use this without offending their clients. They are gentle, yet willing to set boundaries and clearly confront clients when needed. Their clients look forward to seeing them, and feel genuinely cared for and respected by them regardless of the problem(s) with which they present. In essence, we are recommending that you seek out men and women who are interpersonally gifted and obviously healthy. How *you* feel when you interact with them may be a strong indicator of how your parishioners will feel.

OTHER DETAILS

It is important, in your assessment of a prospective MHP, to inquire about his or her fee structure and approach to handling finances with clients. For instance, it is helpful to know if insurance is accepted, what the provider's standard hourly fee is, and whether the provider employs a sliding scale to assist clients with few financial resources. Additionally, it would be helpful to know if the provider ever sees clients "pro bono" (without charge). Psychologists, for example, are encouraged by their ethical code to provide some service without charge to those in need.

Another important issue concerns the extent to which an MHP is comfortable working with you, the pastor, in helping parishioners. Specifically, if your parishioner signs an appropriate release of information and prefers to have you speak to his or her MHP, is the provider open to this sort of liaison work? Of course, it is important that both you and the MHP minimize unnecessary violations of the parishioner's privacy, but sometimes coordinating counseling or other services will substantially benefit the parishioner. For example, following an inpatient period of treatment for alcohol dependency, a parishioner may continue in outpatient substance abuse therapy and come to see you to address spiritual and/or marital concerns. If requested by the parishioner, is the provider willing to discuss the treatment with you and recommend certain topics or approaches? We think a good provider should be willing to do this.

Although it is important to respect the MHP's right to privacy, it may be important in some cases to ask more detailed questions about his or her beliefs or practices related to certain kinds of clients or client problems. For example, you may be a pastor who refers a good number of women who have had or who are considering abortion. How does the MHP approach this issue and is his or her approach congruent with the church's doctrine? Related issues of concern may include homosexuality, marital discord, parent-child conflict, and premarital or extramarital sexual relationships.

Chapter 7

Types of Mental Health Treatment

In this chapter, we will attempt a most ambitious task—to briefly and succinctly summarize the major mental health treatments. We begin by defining the essential characteristics of counseling and psychotherapy. We then explore the important issue of treatment "efficacy" (i.e., does therapy actually work?). We consider the importance of referring parishioners to "Christian" or religious providers. We then summarize the essentials of psychological testing—including suicide risk assessment. The bulk of this chapter is devoted to summarizing each of the major types of mental health intervention. Specifically, we will present the basics of individual, marital, family, and group therapy, psychiatric medication, inpatient hospitalization, drug and alcohol treatment, eating disorder programs, hypnosis, and electroconvulsive therapy. We conclude with a brief warning about "fads" in mental health treatment.

WHAT ARE COUNSELING AND PSYCHOTHERAPY?

Counseling and psychotherapy are interchangeable terms that describe the process of helping another person make some psychological change—typically from a less adaptive state to a more adaptive state. In the mental health field, counseling is generally considered less formal, directed toward less severe forms of client disturbance, or treatment conducted by a nondoctoral-level practitioner. Counseling may also be focused on adjustment problems, career choices, and relationship issues, while psychotherapy is generally thought to focus on more serious personality or psychiatric disorders. In our experience, these distinctions are not very useful. In this chapter, we use the term "psychotherapy" to encompass all approaches to helping people that are rooted in verbal interaction and a good working relationship. At times, skilled practitioners will engage in systematic treatment of serious pathology, while at other times they will simply help a client explore life options or process a stressful event. We refer to all of these approaches as psychotherapy.

In psychotherapy, a mental health professional (MHP) applies specific interventions designed to promote new understandings, behaviors, and emotions on the part of the client. The fact that these interventions are deliberately planned and systematically guided by both theory and (ideally) research findings, makes them psychotherapy and not some less formal approach to helping. All psychotherapy is rooted in a relationship between the MHP and client. Although the relationship is often formed very quickly (in the first session or two), a good therapy relationship is characterized by listening, receptiveness, warmth, empathy, and a lack of negative evaluation on the part of the therapist. Undergirding all effective psychotherapy is an assumption by the therapist that people have the capacity for change. That is, clients can learn more adaptive ways of perceiving, evaluating, and responding to themselves, others, and the world around them.

Psychotherapy first emerged only a century ago with the development of psychoanalysis in the late 1800s. Prior to this, approaches to helping people overcome psychiatric disorders ranged from the barbaric to the bizarre. For example, beginning in the Stone Age, *trephining*—the practice of drilling holes in the skull to release evil spirits—was used to reduce abnormal behavior. As late as the 1800s, staff at insane asylums would spin psychotic patients in chairs, dip them in ice baths, or lock them in cages to control aberrant behavior. Today, psychotherapy is typically practiced in the MHP's office and is centered on verbal exchange regarding the client's symptoms and concerns.

Mental health professionals may focus on a wide range of interventions that are selected in light of the specific client's strengths, deficits, and symptoms. In psychotherapy, the therapist may attempt to (1) change maladaptive behavior patterns; (2) improve interpersonal skills; (3) resolve conflicts among various motives; (4) modify irrational or dysfunctional beliefs about self, others, and the world; (5) reduce problematic emotional responses; (6) enhance a clear-cut sense of identity;[1] and (7) facilitate mood change. Psychotherapy appointments are usually scheduled on a weekly basis. This allows for steady progress on the problem as well as adequate time between sessions for the client to work on issues discussed in the session, complete homework, or experiment with new behaviors and ways of thinking. Psychotherapy may or may not be reimbursed by insurance companies and, if coverage is available, it is usually incomplete.

Psychotherapy is not magic. Some parishioners will make no gains or show only modest improvement after therapy. This is due to the fact that psychiatric problems are often long-standing and extremely complicated. Some disorders begin in early childhood, become fixed patterns by adolescence, and are sustained in adulthood by disturbing or chaotic relationships and environments. For example, people with personality disorders (see Chapter 4) are especially resistant to change. Nonetheless, skillful psychotherapy can be helpful to most people suffering from a wide range of concerns and symptoms. For some, it may be the only real hope of achieving long-lasting change.

Although research in the field of psychotherapy suggests that young, attractive, verbal, and intelligent clients are most likely to make gains in therapy, in our experience, motivation for change is probably the most important determinant of outcome. In fact, we concur heartily with Albert Ellis, one of the greatest original psychotherapists. He argued strongly that for people to really improve in therapy, they had better be willing to work their rear ends off (our paraphrase) not only during the therapy sessions, but between sessions and after therapy is finished in order to sustain therapy gains.[2] Psychotherapy research has confirmed that client motivation and the severity of the disorder are two of the best predictors of a positive psychotherapy outcome.[3]

DOES PSYCHOTHERAPY REALLY WORK?

When you refer a troubled parishioner for psychotherapy, is he or she likely to actually improve? As previously noted, this may depend to a large extent on the client's motivation for change. Treatment outcome is also likely to depend on such critical factors as the therapist's technical skill and natural interpersonal gifts, the quality of the therapeutic relationship, accurate identification of the target problem, and the extent to which the treatment approach "matches" the client's problem.

In 1952, Hans Eysenck, a respected British psychologist, published an article that sparked a great deal of debate and research on the effectiveness of psychotherapy. Eysenck concluded that over half of all persons with psychiatric distress get better on their own—with no treatment at all. He called this *spontaneous remission*. Although some people do get better without professional help, it turned out that Eysenck grossly overestimated the number of impaired people who spontaneously improve. Today, hundreds of research studies on the effectiveness of psychotherapy have demonstrated unambiguously that those who have therapy improve more and improve more rapidly than those who have no therapy.[4] For example, an analysis of over 475 psychotherapy studies found that the typical psychotherapy client is better off than 80 percent of those with distress who remain untreated.[5] In addition, there was only minimal difference in outcome between different types of psychotherapy (most approaches to helping people change seemed to work well). So, the chances that a parishioner in distress will benefit from competent psychotherapy are quite strong. Furthermore, most of the improvement is likely to occur early in psychotherapy (most treatment gains occur during the first six months of any type of psychotherapy).

Not only is psychotherapy likely to produce significant reductions in distress, it is also evaluated quite positively by clients themselves. In 1995, *Consumer Reports* published results of a survey of the magazine's readership regarding satisfaction with and effectiveness of psychotherapy.[6] Among the 4,100 respondents who had undergone professional mental health treatment, 85 percent believed they had improved significantly as a result of their mental health treatment and most were also quite satisfied with their MHP. Those who continued longer in therapy reported the most gain, and there were no differences between psychiatrists, psychologists, or social workers when it came to satisfaction. Readers were less satisfied with counselors and family physicians than the other provider types.

Overall, findings from psychotherapy outcome research seem to support cautious optimism regarding the effectiveness and efficacy of psychotherapy. As a general rule, parishioners who are distressed or show evidence of any of the disorders covered in this guide are likely to improve with psychotherapy delivered by a competent MHP. They are also likely to be reasonably satisfied with their care. Having said this, we recommend that you reread Chapter 6. There is a wide range of practitioners. Although most are likely to be quite competent, others may be poorly suited to the profession, poorly trained, or incompetent to practice with the sorts of clients and client problems of concern to you. Again, it is critical that you carefully screen those MHPs to whom you plan to refer. Elicit recommendations from other clergy until you have a list of consistently recommended and highly respected MHPs to whom you may refer parishioners.

SHOULD THERAPY (AND THE THERAPIST) BE CHRISTIAN?

Pastor Jones lives in a community with very few Christian mental health practitioners. What is worse, the two Christian MHPs with whom Pastor Jones is familiar do not seem very competent. The few parishioners he has referred have reported little benefit from the therapy and have not remained in therapy long. Pastor Jones has heard from parishioners and friends that Dr. Hogan, an experienced psychologist (though not a Christian), is an exceptionally talented and seasoned psychotherapist. Although he does not share the faith of his religious clients, he is very sensitive to religious concerns and collaborates effectively with clergy.

Should Pastor Jones refer parishioners to Dr. Hogan? Our recommendation would be *yes.* Although it would certainly be ideal for pastors to have a number of competent Christian MHPs to whom to refer parishioners in distress, this is often not the case. If a qualified MHP is respectful of clients' faith and willing to see religious commitment as a strength in psychotherapy, then we see no reason why the MHP *must* be Christian or even religious for that matter.

For several reasons, we encourage you not to limit your referral list exclusively to Christian providers: (1) There may not be Christian MHPs in your community. Those who are Christian may not have a reputation for excellence (or even basic competence). (2) We believe God can use secular MHPs to the glory of His Kingdom in much the same way that He can use secular physicians and dentists. Although it is certainly true that the work of psychotherapy often intersects with the personal/spiritual side of a parishioner at deep levels,[7] kind and respectful (though secular) MHPs can be expected to help parishioners with their presenting problems. (3) Very few parishioners are referred to MHPs for spiritual concerns. Rather, they suffer primarily from psychiatric distress, which should be treated by competent MHPs. Whether these MHPs have a similar faith or theological savvy is probably less important in many cases of emotional disturbance. (4) We would strongly prefer a competent MHP to one that advertises himself or herself as a Christian, but is less effective. We have found that God uses the gifts of such excellent professionals to bring relief to His people.

If you are fortunate enough to have a good Christian MHP to whom you refer parishioners, you may wonder what is distinct or unique about Christian counseling and what to expect when the MHP indicates that he or she practices a Christian approach. Although there is certainly wide variability among individual MHPs, there are at least three distinct components you might expect to find.[8] First, Christian therapy is *psychologically sound*. Christian psychotherapists should be up-to-date with the latest research in their field and use cutting-edge and scientifically sound therapy techniques when these are appropriate with their clients and not at odds with clients' faith. Second, Christian counseling should be *scripturally congruent*. This means that the therapist carefully evaluates therapy techniques via the grid of a faith commitment to Jesus Christ. Third, Christian counseling is *Holy Spirit directed*, meaning that the Christian MHP submits to Christ and recognizes that the outcome of counseling rests on God's power.

Keep in mind that although many parishioners will strongly prefer a mental health professional of the same faith, others will be less concerned about this issue and some may even reject the notion of going to a Christian provider. Although in most cases a qualified MHP who also shares the parishioner's faith is likely to be an ideal referral, not all MHPs who advertise themselves as religious will necessarily be competent and effective. It is important that the pastor scrutinize all MHPs.

PSYCHOLOGICAL ASSESSMENT AND TESTING

Psychological Assessment

The initial contact between a parishioner and a mental health professional will typically set in motion a process called *assessment*. During the assessment phase of treatment, the MHP attempts to more clearly understand the nature and extent of the problem for which assistance is being sought. The goal of assessment is to identify the main dimensions of the client's problem, develop a diagnosis, and predict the client's likely response to various treatment options. The process of assessment is sometimes quite brief and may be completed during the initial portion of the first session. At other times, it may be lengthy and convoluted—especially when the client has many problems or when the source of his or her symptoms is unclear.

Although each type of MHP may approach assessment somewhat differently, assessment is an essential component of competent practice and, for most professionals, an ethical requirement. Why is assessment so important? Consider the following cases:

> A counselor begins "anger management" therapy for a young man who has recently developed sudden mood swings and out-bursts of anger and tearfulness that are uncharacteristic. The treatment is ineffective and only after his death from a hematoma does she learn about a recent head injury he suffered at work. Or, consider the psychologist who discharges a sixty-eight-year-old man from the hospital emergency room because the man appears happy and claims the police were mistaken in assuming he was walking in traffic in an attempt to kill himself. After this man's successful suicide the next day, the psychologist learns he had recently lost his spouse of forty years and had no other social support. Finally, imagine the pastoral counselor who immediately provides "biblical counseling" to a woman with depressive symptoms. When her symptoms do not improve, the woman feels even more depressed—assuming she has now failed spiritually as well. After she is hospitalized for severe depression and suicidal thoughts, it becomes evident that the woman has a long family history of biological depression. She improves rapidly when given the appropriate antidepressant medication.

Each of these cases offers an example of why careful assessment of each client is so important to most mental health practitioners. Appropriate treatment of a client cannot occur without an assessment of the causes and nature of his or her symptoms, environmental stresses and resources, and personality traits. Ideally, treatment will not proceed without a clear diagnosis of the client's problem.[9] Although there are concerns with "labeling" a client, we believe the benefits in terms of accurate treatment selection and case management outweigh the potential risks in this area. In fact, numerous malpractice lawsuits have been brought against MHPs who provided ineffective, or even harmful treatment due to lack of assessment or inaccurate assessment of the client's problem.

Although assessment and diagnosis are both ongoing processes, the MHP will be most concerned with these activities early in his or her relationship with a parishioner. Crucial decisions will stem directly from early assessment. These decisions may include which treatment(s), if any, will be prescribed, whether hospitalization is required, which medications, if any, should be offered, and whether various family members should be included in therapy along with the parishioner. During the initial assessment, the MHP will typically want to hear about the main problem or complaint, formulate an initial diagnosis, gain some sense of the person's history and development, develop a picture of his or her context (including stressors and supports), assess the person's primary personality features (especially any signs of a personality disorder; see Chapter 4), and develop hypotheses about how the person is likely to behave in the future.

Although many sources of information may be pursued during an assessment, the MHP will typically conduct a face-to-face interview with the parishioner to glean most of the information mentioned above. In addition, the parishioner may be referred for a physical examination (particularly when the primary symptoms could have a biological basis). The MHP may also engage in observation of the parishioner's behavior in his or her routine environment. For example, observing a child with behavioral problems at home or at school can be quite helpful in shedding light on the causes and reinforcers of his or her problem behavior. Assessment may also involve administration of standardized psychological instruments. *Psychological testing* is conducted by psychologists as part of the assessment process.

Psychological Testing

Psychologists use scientific approaches to developing standardized psychological tests.[10] These tests allow the psychologist to obtain a sample of the parishioner's behavior in response to a set of questions or other stimuli. The person's responses can then be compared to others in his or her age and gender group, which also allows comparison of the person's score(s) to others with or without mental health problems. Tests may provide important data regarding a parishioner's personality characteristics, motivations, values, experience of specific symptoms (e.g., depression), intellectual ability, relationship skills, etc. Good psychological tests are carefully developed and standardized to give both reliable (consistent) and valid (accurate) results, in contrast to the popular tests one may find in magazines. The content of these tests is usually protected by the companies that develop and publish them. Psychologists use tests in much the same way that physicians use laboratory findings—to gain better information about the nature of a patient's problem in order to select and deliver the most effective treatment. The following table highlights the major psychological tests for the assessment of intelligence, personality and psychopathology, and specific symptom distress.

Commonly Used Psychological Tests

Intelligence
Stanford-Binet Intelligence Test
Wechsler Adult Intelligence Scale (WAIS)
Wechsler Intelligence Scale for Children (WISC)

Personality and Psychopathology
Minnesota Multiphasic Personality Inventory (MMPI)
Millon Clinical Multiaxial Inventory (MCMI)
16 Personality Factor Inventory (16PF)
Myers-Briggs Type Indicator (MBTI)
Taylor-Johnson Temperament Analysis (T-JTA)
Rorschach Inkblot Test
Thematic Apperception Test (TAT)
Sentence Completion Test

Specific Symptom Distress
Symptom Checklist 90 (SCL-90)
Outcome Questionnaire (OQ-45)
Beck Depression Inventory (BDI)

Intelligence tests are carefully developed and standardized measures of the various facets of intellectual ability. They typically have multiple subtests designed to tap the different manifestations of intelligence. These tests must be administered and interpreted by a psychologist and usually require two or three hours to complete. The result is a standard score that compares a person's raw scores with his or her peers. Not only do intelligence tests give an accurate reading of a client's overall intellectual ability, they provide specific feedback regarding relative intellectual strength and weakness. They are also critical in detecting learning disabilities and neurological (brain) injuries or deficits.

Tests of personality and psychopathology attempt to measure personality characteristics and the extent to which a person shows evidence of one or more psychiatric disturbances. Personality tests are generally divided into *objective* and *projective* tests. Objective personality inventories are structured questionnaires, which the person completes independently, and he or she must choose between response alternatives. The results are carefully quantified and compared to standard norms as well as groups from selected clinical populations (e.g., depressed patients, anxious patients, traumatized patients, etc.). The most popular of the personality inventories is the Minnesota Multiphasic Personality Inventory (MMPI, now the MMPI2). It is the most frequently utilized personality inventory in the world. A psychologist with experience interpreting the MMPI will be able to draw conclusions about the person's approach to assessment (open or defensive) and the extent to which his or her responses are similar or dissimilar to normal and clinically disturbed groups. Other personality inventories such as the MCMI, 16PF, and Myers-Briggs are also useful for specific assessment purposes.

Projective personality tests are unstructured because they rely on pictures, incomplete sentences, inkblots, or other ambiguous stimuli to elicit responses. The most famous projective technique is the *Rorschach Inkblot Test*, which requires the person to tell the examiner what he or she sees in the various inkblot stimuli. Responses are then pooled and scored. Conclusions are made about the person's personality structure, thinking styles, primary concerns, and evidence of disturbance. Other commonly used projectives tests include the *Thematic Apperception Test* (TAT), in which the person makes up stories to go with pictures, and the *Sentence Completion Test*, which requires the person to finish incomplete sentences. The downside of projective techniques is their unstructured nature and the fact that different examiners sometimes arrive at very different conclusions using the same test results (unreliability). Projectives should only be used to augment findings from other sources such as clinical interviews and objective tests.

Some psychological tests are designed to tap the parishioner's functioning in a specific symptom area (or several areas). For example, the *Beck Depression Inventory* (BDI) is a pure measure of depression. In responding to this test, the client will help the examiner understand to what degree he or she experiences symptoms of depression. The score will become one factor in determining whether a diagnosis of depression is appropriate. The SCL-90 and OQ-45 are brief objective tests that tap several different symptom areas and provide the examiner with clues as to which symptoms are currently most problematic.

Most standardized psychological tests may be purchased and administered only by licensed psychologists or other MHPs with specific graduate training in the psychometric properties of tests and test interpretation. To find information on any psychological test, we recommend consulting either *Tests in Print* (TIP)[11] or the *Mental Measurements Yearbook* (MMY).[12]

Suicide Risk Assessment

Assessment of suicide risk is among the most vexing and difficult tasks faced by MHPs. Professionals must often decide whether to have suicidal clients admitted to a mental hospital or to send them home. They must decide whether to call the police, and even warn others about the client's condition, or whether to maintain confidentiality and attempt to provide outpatient treatment alone. Not only are the consequences of incorrect clinical decisions in the area of suicide assessment grave, matters are made worse by the fact that the decision to attempt suicide is often complex and due to multiple causes. Therefore, even the most seasoned and conservative MHPs may at times "miss" indicators of suicidal thinking in clients, or clients may kill themselves without giving their therapists any warning at all.

In evaluating a client's risk of suicide, MHPs will use multiple sources of data including psychological test results, the client's behavioral and verbal presentation, information about his or her history (especially previous episodes of suicidal behavior or impulsive acting out), an analysis of the client's environment, and input from significant others in the client's life.[13] The most common predictors of suicide are summarized in the following table.

Common Predictors of Suicide Risk

1. *Demographics*—Older white males are most likely to commit suicide, followed by inner-city African Americans. Women are 1.5 to 3 times more likely than men to attempt suicide while men are about 3 times more likely than women to complete suicide.
2. *Depression*—Depressed people are much more likely than others to kill themselves.
3. *Alcoholism and Drug Use*—Both are highly correlated with suicide.
4. *Suicidal Thoughts, Talk, and Preparation*—Those who actually kill themselves are likely to have contemplated it for some time, talked with someone about it, and even made plans.
5. *Previous Suicide Attempts*—A substantial proportion of those who kill themselves have attempted at least once before.
6. *Lethality of Method*—Overall, men choose more lethal methods and lethality predicts success.
7. *Isolation and Loss of Support*—Those with little social support and those who have recently lost a loved one or ended a relationship are at higher risk for suicide.
8. *Hopelessness*—This is one of the strongest predictors of suicide. Clinicians are most alarmed by clients who appear to have lost hope for change or improvement.
9. *Modeling*—A family history of suicide predicts higher risk.
10. *Life Stress*—Recent economic, employment, or relational stress as well as recent exposure to a trauma are all risk factors for suicide.
11. *Impulsivity*—Those with a history of impulsive behaviors (e.g., violence or substance abuse) are at increased risk of impulsive suicidal behavior.

It is important that pastors remain alert to signs of suicidal thinking and behavior among parishioners. If the pastor has referred a parishioner for evaluation of suicide risk, it is essential that he or she follow through to ensure that the parishioner has made contact with the provider. After this has occurred, it is important that the pastor contact the MHP to report new indications of suicide risk should they become evident. Of course, this is most helpful if the parishioner has signed a release allowing the MHP to talk with the pastor about the case. Keep in mind that MHPs are acutely concerned about suicide risk among their clients. They have clear moral, ethical, and professional responsibilities to place the life and welfare of their clients above all else. Most MHPs will be highly attuned to suicide risk factors.

INDIVIDUAL PSYCHOTHERAPY

At the start of this chapter, we defined and discussed counseling and psychotherapy. In this section, we briefly describe the major approaches MHPs might use to treat individual clients in psychotherapy. Unlike marital, family, or group psychotherapy, these interventions are focused on an individual client. The MHP will attempt to help the parishioner make some discernible change in line with his or her therapy goals. Changes might include reduction or elimination of distressing symptoms, development of new understandings of self or others, improvement in specific skills (e.g., assertiveness or interpersonal skills), and increased flexibility and adaptability. The therapist typically provides an environment in which the client can practice new ways of feeling and acting. Of course, the MHP brings much more than skills and techniques to the therapy enterprise. His or her personality (including empathy, warmth, and kindness) is a critical ingredient in creating a strong *therapeutic relationship* (sometimes called a good working alliance).

Although there are hundreds of "types" of psychotherapy,[5] in reality, most of these can be easily reduced to a handful of original and distinct "schools" of psychotherapy. In the subsections that follow, we summarize the four most common types of individual psychotherapy. These include *psychodynamic, behavioral, cognitive-behavioral,* and *humanistic* psychotherapies. Although each of these approaches to therapy can be tailored to the beliefs and concerns of religious clients, some may be more problematic for parishioners than others. For an excellent Christian critique of each approach, we recommend Jones and Butman's 1991 book, *Modern Psychotherapies.*[7]

Psychodynamic (Psychoanalytic) Psychotherapy

Psychodynamic therapy and *psychoanalysis* are related forms of psychotherapy that emphasize techniques rooted in the writings and practice of Sigmund Freud. We briefly describe both traditional psychoanalysis and the more recent development of this approach known as psychodynamic psychotherapy.

Psychoanalysis is based on Freud's view that people are often unaware of the factors that determine their emotions and behavior. These *unconscious* factors produce psychiatric symptoms, personality problems, occupational trouble, and relational difficulties. Psychoanalysis is a long-term and intensive procedure for helping a client uncover repressed memories, thoughts, and fears (frequently developed during childhood) and understand the role these factors play in causing the client's current problems. In traditional psychoanalysis, the client is often asked to attend hour-long sessions several times per week for several years. The therapist, called an *analyst,* asks the client to lie on a couch. The analyst sits behind the client to reduce distraction.

The primary techniques of psychoanalysis include: (1) *free association*—the client must say whatever comes to mind, regardless of how personal, painful, or even irrelevant it may seem; (2) *analysis of dreams*—the client is asked to remember and report content from dreams, allowing the analyst to interpret the unconscious or hidden meanings and conflicts evident in the dream content; (3) *analysis of resistance*—the analyst points out and interprets a client's unwillingness or inability to talk about certain thoughts, motives, or experiences (missing sessions is usually considered evidence of resistance); and (4) *analysis of transference*—because a client often reacts to the analyst in the same manner that he or she has reacted to significant others, the analyst may point out and interpret elements of the therapy relationship as a means of helping the client understand how he or she responds relationally.

Psychoanalysis is rarely practiced by therapists today. Experience and research have shown it to be long, very expensive, and less effective than many other forms of therapy. In fact, we can think of no client problem for which we would recommend psychoanalysis as the preferred treatment. Not only is this approach unnecessarily long and expensive, traditional psychoanalysts tend to be fairly inflexible in their approaches—using only psychoanalytic techniques. Some parishioners (with plenty of time and financial resources) may find psychoanalysis interesting and personally helpful as a means of learning more about themselves and their motives. Nonetheless, this would not be an appropriate referral for the typical parishioner seeking relief from distress.

Psychodynamic psychotherapy is the contemporary alternative to psychoanalysis. Although it utilizes many of the same principles and understandings pioneered by Freud, sessions tend to be weekly, the client and therapist sit face-to-face, the therapist is more verbal (compared to the silence of the psychoanalyst), and the treatment process is more interactive. Instead of several years, psychodynamic therapy may range from a few sessions to a year or more, but twenty sessions are not uncommon. Psychodynamic therapists do not focus so much on hidden drives and unconscious conflicts but tend to help clients correct distorted views of their interpersonal relationships through interaction with the therapist. Exploration of important early experiences may still be part of treatment, but this occurs in a much more active and abbreviated fashion.

Short-term approaches to psychodynamic psychotherapy may be useful for some parishioners—particularly those with strong verbal skills and a great deal of intellectual curiosity. They may be less helpful for parishioners in acute distress (depression or anxiety) and more useful for those with recurrent relationship problems. Although highly skilled psychodynamic therapists may help parishioners increase self-understanding and modify unhealthy patterns of responding to others, it is important that treatment be clearly problem focused and not unnecessarily long.

Behavior Therapy

Behavior therapy came to prominence in the mental health field in the 1960s. Its behavior change techniques are based on research with animals and humans, and utilize such established learning principles as reinforcement (positive and negative), punishment (aversive control), extinction (weakening a behavior through nonreinforcement), and counterconditioning (substituting one behavior for another). Very few MHPs are likely to be "pure" behavior therapists. Most will use behavioral techniques when the parishioner's presenting problems include specific behaviors that are either excessive (e.g., phobic reactions, compulsive behaviors, or excessive drinking) or lacking (e.g., attentiveness, social interaction, self-care), or both. Behavior therapies are quite pragmatic because they focus on the elimination of problematic behaviors and strengthening of new, more adaptive responses. In contrast to the psychodynamic therapies, behavioral approaches do not emphasize such things as the parishioner's personal history or inner conflicts. Behavior therapists use both the presentation and removal of rewards as well as aversive consequences to achieve their therapeutic goals—which are typically concrete and easy to measure.

Behavior therapists tend to use some very specific and well-researched interventions with their clients.[14] *Extinction,* one of the most common approaches to modifying behavior, involves removing whatever reinforcements are maintaining a problematic behavior. For example, a child who is acting out at school may be reinforced by the attention he or she receives from teachers and peers. The behavior therapist may work with the teacher to cease giving the child any attention when he or she acts out, focusing on children who are behaving appropriately instead. Attention will be redirected at the child only when his or her behavior has become appropriate again. One of the most common behavioral techniques, based on the principle of extinction, is *flooding.* In flooding, the client is encouraged to face his or her real-life, anxiety-arousing situation, usually with the therapist in a coaching role, and is highly encouraged not to avoid or attempt to escape the situation (the client's previous maladaptive response). Thus, the agoraphobic (see Chapter 2) client is taken to a busy mall and remains there with the therapist until his or her anxiety subsides, thereby learning a new response to the mall. An alternative to flooding is *implosive therapy,* in which the client faces his or her feared situation using only imagery. Using implosion, a man so fearful of germs that he washes his hands thirty times a day may be asked to imagine (in vivid detail) falling into the hole of an outhouse. Although intensely anxious, he is pushed to "stay with" the image until his panic subsides and is replaced by a less anxious or more relaxed response.

Systematic desensitization is another behavioral technique for modifying phobic behavior (reinforced by the relief of escaping or avoiding the feared object or situation). The client is taught to systematically relax himself or herself. After creating an "anxiety hierarchy" with the therapist (a list of feared situations from least to most fearful), the client is guided to face (in life or imagination) the least fear-inducing situation while in a state of relaxation. This continues gradually until the person can remain relaxed while imagining or actually facing the most anxiety-producing object or situation on his or her list. In effect, the behavior therapist is replacing anxiety or avoidance with relaxation.

Aversion therapy involves modification of behavior using punishment. Obviously, aversive techniques should be used only after other alternatives have been tried. In one example, an extremely self-mutilating autistic child may bang her head repeatedly against a wall—producing head injury and possibly brain damage. A brief electric shock delivered immediately after the child begins head banging may effectively eliminate the behavior permanently after only a few trials. In another example, an alcoholic man may be placed on the drug Antabuse, which will cause him to become violently ill the moment he ingests alcohol.

Behavior therapists are more inclined to use *positive reinforcement* to shape desired behavior, especially with children or clients in institutions. An adult can also be taught to effectively apply reinforcements to themselves for desirable behavior (e.g., watching a favorite television show only if he or she has exercised). *Modeling* involves teaching clients new skills by intentionally demonstrating them and then asking clients to imitate them—usually while the therapist reinforces their behavior and helps with fine-tuning. So, a parishioner fearful of talking to women (as potential dates) may learn some important social and communication skills by watching his therapist demonstrate them in the session.

Behavior therapy has the advantage of precise treatment goals (specific changes in problematic behaviors), scientifically supported treatment techniques, relative brevity, and reduced expense compared to many other therapy modalities. Behavior therapy may be especially helpful for anxiety-based problems and for children. Disorders as wide-ranging as phobias, tantrums, bed-wetting, and erection problems are all likely candidates for behavioral techniques.

Cognitive-Behavior Therapy

Cognitive-behavior therapies (CBTs) are among the most frequently employed by MHPs today. This group of therapies emphasizes both the behavioral interventions discussed previously and the powerful effects of thoughts and beliefs on behavior and emotion. Therapy in a cognitive-behavioral framework involves collaborative agreement between client and therapist on the problems to be addressed, followed by application of a range of techniques designed to change distorted or false core beliefs. These may be beliefs about events, oneself, or other people. Cognitive-behavior therapies are generally problem focused, brief, and quite effective for problems from anxiety to anger to depression. These techniques are generally well researched and frequently used by most MHPs at least some of the time.

Albert Ellis and Aaron Beck, the originators of CBT, have each developed distinct approaches to a range of psychological problems. *Rational-emotive behavior therapy* (REBT) was developed by Ellis and assumes that people are not disturbed by troubling or stressful events (A's), but by their irrational and self-defeating beliefs (B's) about the events in their lives.[2] These beliefs lead to negative and maladaptive emotional and behavioral consequences (C's). So, the parishioner who becomes angry at his wife following a disagreement is not angry and violent because of his wife's behavior, but because of what he tells himself *about* her behavior (e.g., "She is damnable for not supporting me," or "She absolutely must agree with me!" or "I can't stand it when she does that"). Irrational beliefs such as these are the target of therapy as the therapist disputes their validity, shows the client how counterproductive they are, and helps the client find helpful and rational alternatives (e.g., "I really wish she'd agree with me, but I see that sometimes she does not"). Common irrational beliefs include "I must be loved and approved of by those who are important to me" and "I must be completely successful and perfect in everything I do."

When therapists are using *cognitive therapy* as developed by Beck, they are apt to focus on the logical errors clients make in their day-to-day perception of events as well as automatic thoughts about events. Errors include the tendency for people to selectively focus on the negative in a situation while ignoring the positive, overgeneralizing in a self-defeating way (e.g., "The fact that I failed to complete one of my scheduled tasks today proves I am worthless"), magnifying the significance of undesirable events (e.g., "The fact that he ended our relationship means I'll never love again"), and engaging in absolutistic thinking (e.g., "The fact that she didn't call proves she hates me"). In contrast to the persuasive and confrontational style used in REBT, cognitive therapists focus more on having clients gather information (in the sense of an experiment) in order to demonstrate that their thinking was largely in error and that their assessments about themselves and events were erroneous.

Cognitive-behavioral therapies are quite popular with MHPs. Many practitioners to whom you refer will employ these approaches. They are generally effective with a range of emotional and behavioral problems, and have been especially useful for treating depression and anxiety disorders.

Humanistic/Client-Centered Therapies

Humanistic psychotherapists, sometimes known as *client-centered* psychotherapists, emphasize helping a client grow and self-actualize as opposed to helping him or her overcome symptoms or disorders. Humanists tend to view human beings as essentially "good" and simply in need of encouragement to fulfill innate potential. Influential humanistic psychotherapists included Carl Rogers and Abraham Maslow. Rogers is best known for his view of the importance of the *self-concept* and the importance of clients developing congruence between their "real" selves (their actual views of themselves) and their "ideal" selves (who they would like to be). Maslow is famous for the idea of *self-actualization*—the notion that when basic needs are met and people are supported and encouraged, they can achieve their full potential. Unless the typical person is excessively stressed, discounted, or otherwise blocked from doing so, he or she will generally tend to choose pathways toward personal growth and self-actualization.

In contrast to behaviorists or psychoanalysts, MHPs with a client-centered or humanistic therapy orientation will tend to be *nondirective* in the sense that they intentionally listen to clients more and intervene less often. The notion here is that with certain "necessary and sufficient conditions for change" (these include *warmth, empathy,* and *unconditional positive regard* from the therapist), clients will naturally become more self-accepting (achieve greater real-ideal self-congruence) and begin to make decisions that maximize their potential. Expect client-centered MHPs to be gentle and caring with clients but not especially focused on problems or goals. This may be an especially useful modality for parishioners whose primary struggle is with poor self-esteem or shame, guilt, or anger due to harsh self-criticism.

Eclectic Psychotherapy

The MHPs to whom you refer parishioners will rarely be rigidly or dogmatically wedded to a single therapy approach. More often, they will be at least somewhat *eclectic*—meaning they tend to use techniques from more than one school of therapy depending upon the unique client and problem. In our view, this is quite desirable for a couple of reasons. First, no single approach to therapy is likely to work with every client. Excellent psychotherapists are willing to carefully tailor their approaches based on empirical research about the best treatment for a certain disorder and based on their clinical assessments of each client. Second, eclecticism reflects a willingness to place the client's improvement before dogmatic adherence to a single treatment approach. Of course, knowing an approach to therapy well is a professional strength for an MHP. We simply recommend looking for excellent training *and* flexibility. As a pastor, you may wish to familiarize yourself with the major approaches to psychotherapy practiced today. The best text on this topic is Corsini and Wedding's *Current Psychotherapies.*[15]

MARITAL THERAPY

When parishioners approach the pastor with a personal concern or request for counseling, quite often the problem will relate directly or indirectly to marital dissatisfaction or distress. In fact, counseling for couples who are married, planning marriage, or considering termination of marriage may be one of the most frequent counseling activities for all pastors. The need for skilled treatment of distressed couples may also be one of the more common reasons for referral on the part of pastors.

Although most MHPs can practice marital or *(couples)* therapy, we highly recommend looking carefully for one or more specialists in this area. Marriage and family counselors, social workers, psychologists, and psychiatrists may all have reasonable competence and even expertise in this area; however, many will not. It is important to learn whether the practitioner has both training and considerable experience with couples. As a pastor, it is especially important that you remain attuned to recommendations and feedback from parishioners regarding which marriage therapists in the community are most respected and effective. Which MHPs seem to most consistently keep couples working together? Which therapists are known for using the couple's spiritual commitments and resources in therapy? Which ones are known for not "siding" with either spouse, but encouraging both partners to take an active role in creating change? We recommend that you find MHPs with clear expertise in marital therapy, an excellent reputation for getting good results, and a therapy model that emphasizes activity-based homework assignments (e.g., practice with communication), development of needed skills (e.g., assertiveness or active listening), and an emphasis on both accountability and forgiveness.

Not surprisingly, research has shown that couples who are happily married, or who have strong potential for remaining married, can be differentiated from couples with a poor probability of successfully staying together. For example, University of Washington psychologist John Gottman's research on hundreds of couples has shown consistently that factors such as criticism, contempt, defensiveness, and communication avoidance are strong predictors of divorce.[16] Alternatively, when couples remain calm, speak nondefensively, validate one another, and continue to work at improving their marriages, they are considerably more likely to stay together.

Marital therapy will typically address meeting each spouse's needs in the relationship; active, clear and respectful communication; forgiveness; enhanced sensitivity to the needs of one's partner; taking responsibility for one's own contribution to the marital dysfunction; frustration tolerance; and modification of unreasonable expectations. Not surprisingly, a couple's commitment to the marriage is one of the strongest predictors of treatment success. Of course, many spouses will not state (or necessarily even be aware of) their level of commitment early in the marriage, and this may surface only during therapy. Although most marital therapy sessions will involve both spouses, the therapist may at times hold individual meetings with each spouse as a means of collecting background information and allowing for safe disclosure of things such as fear of harm, level of actual commitment to the marriage, etc. Finally, structured marital separations may at times be incorporated into therapy as a reasonable way of protecting one spouse, to allow the couple to explore volatile emotions or very painful events, or as a method of building commitment to begin the relationship anew.

FAMILY THERAPY

Roughly forty years ago, some MHPs began offering approaches to treatment that involved the whole family. They recognized that family relationships and interaction patterns played a significant part in the health of individual family members. In fact, they discovered that although clients could be effectively treated in hospitals and other settings, their emotional disturbances and psychiatric problems reappeared when they were discharged and returned to their families.[17] Therefore, these MHPs began treating the entire family—involving all members of the family in therapy sessions. Family therapy may even include grandparents, noncustodial parents, stepparents, stepsiblings, and half siblings.

Family therapy is most often initiated when the family member with the "problem," often called the *identified patient,* is brought in for treatment. This is often a child or adolescent who is acting out or has become depressed. Mental health practitioners who practice family therapy are alert to the possibility that symptoms in one family member merely reflect the disturbance of the larger family system. In family therapy, the MHP "treats" the entire family and, as in the case of marital therapy, must remain impartial and committed to the health of all family members. When specific family members also require individual therapy, they are usually encouraged to see a separate MHP.

Although there are many types of family therapy, *structural family therapy* is one of the most common and most promising approaches. This approach assumes that the family "system" is a more powerful determinant of psychological disorder than individual personality styles or conflicts. Family therapists are likely to attempt "structural" change, that is, change the way the family is organized. This often involves eliminating problematic subsystems and shoring up poor boundaries. For example, a mother and her teenage son may form an unhealthy subsystem or alliance (due to the mother's poor boundaries) that harms the marital relationship, distances the father, and allows the son to behave as a mini-parent. The family therapist would move to confront this system problem, prescribe changes to the structure, and perhaps even have the family members act out day-to-day interactions for the purpose of diagnosing and correcting them.

Family therapy is often a very useful modality—particularly when a child or adolescent appears to be acting out in a way that signals a larger system problem in the home. Although many MHP types are well trained and experienced in this treatment form, marriage and family counselors, psychologists, and social workers are probably most likely to have training in this therapy modality. As in the case of marital therapy, ask colleagues and trusted MHPs about professionals in your community with expertise in family therapy. Behavioral and structural approaches to family therapy have proven most effective with a range of presenting problems.

GROUP THERAPY

Like individual therapy, group therapy is intended to help people learn skills, develop self-understanding, and reduce problematic behaviors or symptoms. First developed during World War II as a cost-effective approach to helping many people at once, group therapy has grown in popularity such that most communities currently have a range of ongoing group therapy opportunities for parishioners. Most groups have between six and twelve members and one or two leaders. Again, a range of MHPs may offer groups of various kinds. Four major types of group experiences may be helpful to your parishioners: *long-term groups, time-limited groups, focused groups,* and *self-help groups.*

Long-term therapy groups are the most traditional, yet least common approach to group therapy. Group members typically commit to attend weekly sessions for a substantial period of time (e.g., several months to several years). Members often continue in the group longer than their initial commitment, and members may come and go while the core group continues. The aim of these psychotherapy groups is typically interpersonal interaction with an emphasis on members receiving support, feedback, and, when needed, confrontation from other members. Developing a better understanding of one's own psyche and interpersonal style is usually the goal. The therapists are usually nondirective, letting the group members "work" on issues while they occasionally offer feedback and facilitate the discussion.

Long-term groups may be especially useful for more verbal parishioners with chronic relational or interpersonal problems.

Time-limited groups are similar to the traditional group format just described, with the exception that the therapist contracts to work with the group members for a more abbreviated period of time (e.g., two to six months). Group members are usually selected for the group based on their potential match with the other members and the primary problems of interest to the group. They are encouraged to stay with the group for the duration and to "terminate" (work through saying good-bye to the members) when the group ends. These groups have a distinct beginning, middle, and end. They usually do not add members once the group has begun. The length of the group will depend on the purpose of the group and the characteristics of its members. For example, a leader may create a two-month group for new managers for the purpose of providing intensive interpersonal feedback, or a six-month group for extremely introverted and low social skill clients who have never had sustained relationships.

Focused therapy groups tend to be both time-limited and directed at a specific topic or problem area. For example, MHPs may offer groups for clients with depression, those recovering from divorce, or parents of children with attention deficit hyperactivity disorder (ADHD). Groups may also focus on specific skill development. For example, it is not uncommon to find groups on anger management, assertiveness training, communication skills, stress management, and weight loss. There are groups focusing exclusively on men's issues or women's issues. Focused groups offer an excellent resource for short-term and problem-specific assistance. Clients benefit not only from the group focus and therapist's expertise, but perhaps even more so from the encouragement, support, and example of other group members who share their concern or difficulty.

Finally, pastors may consider referring parishioners to a relevant *self-help group*. Self-help groups abound in most communities and range from Alcoholics Anonymous to Parents Without Partners, to Widow to Widow (for bereaved women). Between 12 and 15 million Americans are likely to use self-help groups during their lifetimes and self-help group involvement has burgeoned during the last half-century. Self-help groups are designed for people with a symptom, disorder, situation, or experience in common who meet together to fulfill needs, overcome difficulties, or cope with a crisis.

Self-help groups are typically organized and run at the local level, and supported only by donations from participants. Information disclosed by participants remains "anonymous" or confidential. They have the benefit of informality and low cost to members. The main goal of a self-help group is to provide mutual support, education, and emphasize personal change. Although each group may have a designated leader, this person will rarely have professional mental health training, but will have experience with the problem of concern to the group members. For example, Alcoholics Anonymous (AA) is run exclusively by recovering alcoholic men and women who typically rotate leadership responsibilities.

Self-help groups are extremely diverse in makeup, focus, and effectiveness. As a pastor, it is recommended that you become acquainted with the leadership of those self-help groups of greatest interest to you as referral sources. In some communities, there will be groups or "meetings" tailored to Christians or other religious groups, and it is common for churches to sponsor their own self-help groups. These groups are ideal for parishioners with limited financial resources, those who are more needy or dependent in personality style, and those with very focused difficulties (e.g., alcoholism, drug use, grief from death of a loved one or divorce, or weight problems). The only real problem we see with self-help groups is the potential that they will be the only source of help offered to a person with a serious psychiatric (or even physical) problem. For example, a severely alcohol-dependent person should not be referred to AA until *after* he or she has been carefully evaluated by a physician and possibly hospitalized for the dangerous process of detoxification from alcohol. Similarly, referring a seriously depressed and bereaved widow or widower to a self-help group for grief may be unwise until after a mental health professional determines that risk for suicide is not significant.

PSYCHIATRIC MEDICATIONS

Fifty years ago, medication was seldom used to treat psychiatric disorders. At that time, a medication for the treatment of psychotic disorders (chlorpromazine) was introduced and radically altered the care of schizophrenic patients. Instead of simply warehousing these patients in hospitals, this antipsychotic medication radically reduced their symptoms and made it possible for thousands of patients to be released from hospitals and treated as outpatients.

Today, psychiatric medications have become an integral part of the comprehensive care of persons with psychiatric disorders. Although they are frequently used in cases of more severe disorders (e.g., severe depression, bipolar disorder, panic disorder, or schizophrenia), they may also be used to alleviate symptoms following a difficult event or to increase a parishioner's ability to function in specific circumstances. Far from magical cures, medications act by controlling symptoms. They correct or compensate for some biochemical malfunction in the body and help lessen the burden of a psychiatric disorder without necessarily curing it. Medications make it possible to treat people in less restrictive settings. In other words, they do not have to be hospitalized or bedridden, but can continue functioning in a reasonably successful way while working at overcoming their disorders. In addition, psychiatric medications often make other kinds of treatment (e.g., psychotherapy) more effective. For example, a parishioner with a severe biologically based depressive disorder may be so impaired that he or she is unable to concentrate or even find the energy to get out of bed. Antidepressant medication may allow this person enough relief from depressive symptoms to participate actively in various kinds of therapy and even continue at his or her job.

As noted in Chapter 6, only MDs may prescribe medication. Ideally, psychiatric medicine will be managed by a psychiatrist (physicians with considerable experience and training in psychiatric medications). This is particularly important when the parishioner has a serious psychiatric disorder or when his or her age, other medical problems, or other medications make prescribing more complicated. It is not uncommon for people undergoing psychiatric treatment to be placed on more than one type of medication in order to optimize therapeutic value and control side effects. It is essential that parishioners not attempt to self-medicate or alter their dosages without consulting their physicians.

The length of time a parishioner may be placed on medications depends on a range of factors including the specific disorder, symptom severity, and characteristics of the client (e.g., age, genetic predisposition to the disorder, etc.). Once placed on a psychiatric medication, a person generally stays on it for several months to several years to ensure stability. It can be quite harmful to prematurely withdraw a client from medication only to have him or her suffer a return of symptoms. Medications do not produce the same effects in all persons. Body chemistry, age, sex, size, and physical health all influence the medication's effect. Different psychiatric medications also take different amounts of time to reach maximum effectiveness. For example, antidepressant medications often require several weeks before significant reductions in problem symptoms occur, while antianxiety medications take effect quite rapidly.

In this section, we briefly describe four categories of *psychotropic* (psychiatric) medications. We cover *antidepressant, antianxiety, antimanic,* and *antipsychotic* medications. We also provide a short table of the most common medications prescribed in each category. The tables include both the trade name (most familiar to parishioners) and the generic name of each medication. These medications have been approved by the FDA as a result of research studies that demonstrate their efficacy with certain psychiatric disorders. For detailed information regarding any prescription medication, we recommend that parishioners consult the most recent edition of the *Physician's Desk Reference*.[18]

Antidepressant Medications

Antidepressant medications have become a booming business for the world's pharmaceutical companies. They will certainly be among the most commonly prescribed for parishioners. Antidepressants should generally not be prescribed unless the parishioner's depression is rather severe (in the judgment of the MHP) or unless it has persisted without improvement for some time (several weeks or more), and interferes with normal occupational and relational functioning. Although research has shown that depressed persons who receive a combination of psychotherapy and antidepressant medication improve most rapidly, some parishioners may prefer not to use antidepressants unless psychotherapy alone proves ineffective. Others may elect to try medications alone.

In most cases, antidepressants will be prescribed for major depression (see Chapter 2). A person may be experiencing some combination of the following symptoms: depressed or irritable mood, loss of interest in previously enjoyed activities, sleep disturbance, appetite change, feelings of guilt or worthlessness, loss of energy, loss of concentration, agitation or "retardation" (slowed movements), and thoughts of death or suicide. Although antidepressants will usually be used for parishioners with some of these symptoms, they are sometimes used for anxiety and phobic disorders.

Antidepressant medications will generally not begin to work immediately. Most require between one and three weeks to show significant effects (if any). Some depressive symptoms may diminish early in treatment while others require more time. In general, no improvement after five or six weeks would signal the need for the physician to try a different medication. Patients are usually started on low to moderate doses that are increased as it becomes clear the person tolerates the medicine satisfactorily. Antidepressants do not create a euphoric state, but merely stabilize mood. They will not have much effect on the mood of a normal person and do not have addictive properties. Although the majority of depressed patients show positive responses to antidepressants, some will not respond at all—even when multiple medications and dosages are tried.

There are several distinct types of antidepressant medication, and each type produces specific side effects, which parishioners should discuss carefully with their physicians. *Side effects* are any drug effects other than those intended as part of the therapeutic action of the drug. The following section describes the major types of antidepressants.

Tricyclic Antidepressants

Among the first antidepressants discovered, tricyclic antidepressants are widely used today particularly in cases of severe depression. Tricyclics work by increasing the levels of the neurotransmitters serotonin and norepinephrine in the brain. They typically require between two and four weeks to reach maximal effect. They are most often used for the treatment of major depression. Possible side effects from these medications are significant and include dry mouth, constipation, rapid heart beat, blurred vision, weight gain, fatigue, and problems with sexual functioning. However, the potential for cardiac problems is of greater concern. Tricyclics are prescribed with great caution in patients with any history of or potential for heart problems. Finally, tricyclics can be used to overdose as they are lethal in high doses. Suicidal parishioners should typically be given only a small supply at one time. It is also important for anyone taking these medications to avoid alcohol.

Monoamine Oxidase Inhibitors

Monoamine Oxidase Inhibitors (MAOIs) work by blocking enzymes that normally break down the neurotransmitters serotonin and norepinephrine in the brain. This increases the level of these neurotransmitters, which elevates the person's mood. Although MAOIs were once the primary alternative to tricyclics, they are rarely used today because of the dietary and medication restrictions required in order for them to be used safely. Patients who take MAOIs must strictly avoid certain foods and alcoholic beverages (e.g., cheese, beer, wine, foods containing MSG) and many common medications (e.g., cold and allergy medicines). If they do not, they risk a *hypertensive crisis,* which could involve a sudden increase in blood pressure, vomiting, severe headache, and possibly seizures or a stroke. In addition, MAOIs have other routine side effects—including many of those previously noted for tricyclic medications. Understandably, with these significant side effects and the dangerous risk of interaction with foods and medicines, MAOIs are used only in unusual cases of depression (e.g., depression with panic attacks) or when patients do not respond well to other antidepressants.

Selective Serotonin Reuptake Inhibitors

Today, SSRIs are undoubtedly the most popular and widely prescribed of the antidepressant medications. The most popular and well-known SSRI antidepressant is Prozac. The SSRIs act to reduce depression by blocking the brain's reuptake of *serotonin* (a common neurotransmitter in the brain thought to play a role in depression), thereby increasing the amount of available serotonin. These medications are extremely popular due to their relatively minor side effects; they are also less toxic and require less dosage adjustment. They tend to work at least as well as tricyclics without the serious side effects and physicians have fewer precautions in prescribing them to depressed patients. Similar to other antidepressants, SSRIs do not produce euphoria, but act to decrease and eliminate symptoms of depression.

Other Antidepressant Medications

Finally, three other antidepressants are chemically distinct from the categories discussed previously. *Wellbutrin* (bupropion) is unique in affecting the dopamine neurotransmitter system. *Effexor* (venlafaxine) affects both serotonin and norepinephrine. *Serzone* (nefazodone) is similar to the tricyclics and may be prescribed for anxiety associated with depression. Each of these medications has a unique profile of side effects.

Common Antidepressant Medications

Trade Name	Generic Name
Tricyclic Antidepressants	
Desyrel	Trazadone
Elavil	Amitriptyline
Norpramin	Desipramine
Sinequan	Doxepin
Tofranil	Imipramine
Pamelor	Nortriptyline
Vivactyl	Protriptyline
Surmontil	Trimipramine
Monoamine Oxidase Inhibitors (MAOIs)	
Marplan	Isocarboxazid
Nardil	Phenelzine
Parnate	Tranylcypromine
Selective Serotonin Reuptake Inhibitors (SSRIs)	
Paxil	Paroxetine
Prozac	Fluoxetine
Zoloft	Sertraline
Other Antidepressant Medications	
Effexor	Venlafaxine
Serzone	Nefazadone
Wellbutrin	Bupropion

Antianxiety Medications

Anxiety is one of the most common human experiences. Anxiety disorders are frequently a concern of parishioners who present for professional mental health care. Among these, some will have symptoms that are severe enough to merit consideration of antianxiety medications. High levels of anxiety or prolonged anxiety can become incapacitating and make the activities of daily life quite difficult. Generalized anxiety disorder, obsessive-compulsive disorder, panic disorder, and various phobias discussed in Chapter 2 all may be significant enough to warrant a trial of antianxiety medication.

Antianxiety medications help to calm and relax the anxious person and were originally called *tranquilizers* for this reason. The prevalence of anxiety disorders has made antianxiety medications the most widely prescribed psychotropic drugs. The most common among these are the *benzodiazepines*, such as Xanax (alprazolam) and Valium (diazepam). Benzodiazepines, also called *anxiolytics*, work by stimulating special receptors in the brain that enhance the effects of the neurotransmitter gamma-aminobutyric acid (GABA), which inhibits brain arousal. Benzodiazepines are relatively fast acting and most take effect within hours. They are also relatively safe medically and even large overdoses are rarely fatal. Dosage is generally started at a low level and increased until the anxiety symptoms subside. These medications have relatively few side effects; however, side effects may include drowsiness, fatigue, mental slowing, and coordination problems. They should never be mixed with alcohol and may also be harmful when mixed with other medications. Benzodiazepines have the potential to produce strong psychological and physical dependence and therefore should be carefully monitored by the physician. However, they are less addictive than barbiturates (which are no longer prescribed for anxiety). In addition, patients should never stop taking benzodiazepines suddenly since withdrawal symptoms often occur. Instead, patients must take gradually decreasing doses of the medication under their physician's supervision.

BuSpar (buspirone) has recently become a major alternative to benzodiazepines for the treatment of anxiety as it is considered free of the habit-forming properties of the other anxiolytic medications. On the downside, BuSpar cannot be taken on short notice; it must be taken continuously for a period of time before its effects are noticed. Vistaril and Atarax (hydroxyzine) are also nonaddictive alternatives to benzodiazepines. These medications do produce side effects such as trouble with coordination and low blood pressure.

Finally, sleeping pills or "hypnotic" medications are sometimes prescribed for anxiety-related problems. These are also anxiolytic drugs with strong sedative effects. Like the benzodiazepines, these medications can produce increased tolerance and the potential for addiction and withdrawal. Parishioners may also develop dependence on these medications to help them go to sleep such that discontinuing the medications makes it very hard for them to sleep. Additionally, hypnotic medications may actually deprive the person of the most important deep sleep of the night, thereby causing fatigue and poor functioning. For the most part, psychiatrists use these medications with extreme caution and generally for only a short period of time.

Common Antianxiety Medications

Trade Name	Generic Name
Benzodiazepines	
Ativan	Lorazepam
Klonopin	Clonazepam
Librium	Chlordiazepoxide
Serax	Oxazepam
Tranxene	Clorazepate
Valium	Diazepam
Xanax	Alprazolam
Other Anxiolytics	
Altarax, Vistaril	Hydroxyzine
BuSpar	Buspirone
Hypnotics (sleeping pills)	
Dalmane	Flurazepam
Halcion	Triazolam
Prosom	Estazolam
Restoril	Temazepam

Antimanic Medications

Antimanic drugs, also called *mood stabilizers,* work to help prevent wide swings in mood in either direction (toward depression or toward mania). In Chapter 2, we describe the essential features of bipolar disorder. Persons with this disorder have cycling mood changes including severe highs (mania) and lows (depression). The cycles may be predominantly manic or depressive with normal mood between cycles. At times, the mood swings may follow each other closely or may be separated by months or even years. During a manic episode, the person will have increased energy and activity, euphoric feelings, decreased need for sleep, poor judgment, extreme irritability and distractibility, and unrealistic or grandiose beliefs in his or her abilities. Manic persons also engage in reckless and potentially harmful behavior. The depressions, which follow manic episodes for bipolar persons, are typical of other depressions (see the antidepressant section in this chapter for a description, or Chapter 2).

In the 1940s, an Australian physician observed that the chemical *lithium* calmed patients suffering from mania. Today, psychiatrists routinely prescribe lithium as the primary medication intervention for bipolar patients. As a naturally occurring mineral, lithium is distinct from other psychiatric medications, which are typically manufactured compounds. Although bipolar patients do not have a lithium deficiency, this mineral helps to even out both their manic and depressive mood swings. Typically, lithium will diminish severe manic symptoms within five to fourteen days, yet it may take several months before the condition is well controlled. Although some parishioners with bipolar disorder may have only a single episode and be symptom free for years afterward, most will require continued maintenance on lithium for several years to control symptoms and prevent reoccurrences of full-blown mania.

Lithium is generally prescribed as lithium carbonate. It is essential that those taking it receive regular blood tests to ensure that the amount of the mineral in the body is within a therapeutic range. Blood level checks are also important because lithium can be potentially toxic at high levels. Signs of toxicity may include extreme fatigue, dizziness, dulling of consciousness, and severe tremors. If toxicity is not reduced, seizures, liver damage, brain damage, and cardiac problems may result. More routine side effects include increased thirst and urination, some fatigue, minor nausea, diarrhea, and a metallic taste in the mouth. Perhaps the biggest challenge in the medical treatment of bipolar patients is getting them to continue taking lithium. Because mania can be a frankly enjoyable (euphoric) state, many patients discontinue lithium shortly after they begin taking it for the first time. Of these, 50 percent relapse within four months.[19]

For some bipolar persons, lithium may not be a reasonable treatment alternative. This may be due to a medical condition (e.g., thyroid, kidney, or heart disorders) or due to nonresponsiveness to lithium. In these cases, some bipolar patients have been found to respond favorably to anticonvulsant medications typically used to treat epilepsy. The major anticonvulsants used with bipolar disorder are Tegretol (carbamazepine) and Depakote (divalproex sodium). Tegretol is widely used as an alternative to lithium and it may be especially useful for bipolar patients who cycle very rapidly between mania and depression (over a period of days or even hours). Another promising anticonvulsant is Depakote. Research shows it works about as well as lithium at controlling cycling moods. Of course, both medications also produce some side effects including gastrointestinal upset, drowsiness, dizziness, confusion, and nausea. Long-term use also raises concern about liver damage, which should be assessed by a physician.

Common Antimanic Medications

Trade Name	Generic Name
Lithium Medications	
Cibalith-S	Lithium Citrate
Eskalith	Lithium Carbonate
Lithane	Lithium Carbonate
Lithobid	Lithium Carbonate
Anticonvulsants	
Depakote	Divalproex Sodium
Tegretol	Carbamazepine

Antipsychotic Medications

In Chapter 2, we discussed the primary psychotic disorders, particularly schizophrenia, which may be the most debilitating of all the psychiatric disorders. Until the 1950s, little was available in the way of medical intervention for patients diagnosed with a psychotic disorder. These patients lost touch with reality, heard voices, and suffered from disorganized thoughts and bizarre delusions. In the 1950s, a French physician discovered Thorazine (chlorpromazine), which became the first of a class of antipsychotic drugs known as *phenothiazines,* and revolutionized the way psychotic patients were treated. Phenothiazines (also called *neuroleptic* medications) work by blocking dopamine receptor sites in the brain. They generally help clear up and control the positive symptoms of schizophrenia (hallucinations, delusions, disordered thinking, and bizarre behavior), but do little to help alleviate the negative symptoms of schizophrenia (e.g., emotional apathy and social withdrawal).

A large number of neuroleptic drugs are available for the treatment of psychotic disorders. The primary difference among them is potency (the dosage prescribed to produce therapeutic effects). For example, Thorazine is comparatively low in potency and psychiatrists may prescribe high doses (50 to 800 milligrams) for patients while Haldol is higher in potency and would be prescribed at a much lower dosage (0.5-2.0 milligrams). The difficulty with long-term use of these phenothiazine antipsychotic medications is their potential for producing serious side effects. Common side effects of these drugs include dry mouth, constipation, blurred vision, elevation in heart rate, muscle spasms, and restlessness. Unfortunately, long-term use of neuroleptic medications can cause the bizarre motor side effects that indicate *tardive dyskinesia,* a movement disorder which results directly from long-term use of these medications. Schizophrenic persons with tardive dyskinesia engage in facial grimacing, lip smacking, tongue thrusting, and flailing of the limbs, all of which are uncontrollable. Although it is generally true that schizophrenic patients are treated with antipsychotic medication for the shortest amount of time possible, schizophrenia is often a chronic disorder and long-term medication use may simply be unavoidable if there is any hope of reducing their psychosis and allowing them a somewhat normal lifestyle (outside an institution).

In 1990, Clozaril (clozapine), a new "atypical antipsychotic" medication for the treatment of psychotic disorders, was introduced. Clozaril has produced treatment outcomes equivalent to phenothiazines and it has fewer of the harmful side effects that characterize traditional antipsychotics. Many chronic schizophrenic patients who had not responded well to phenothiazines have had a very positive response to Clozaril. Clozaril is a sedating drug and is therefore started quite gradually. It may also produce some weight gain but has few other side effects. Other atypical antipsychotic medications for psychotic patients include Risperdal (risperidone) and Zyprexa (olanzapine).

Common Antipsychotic Medications

Trade Name	Generic Name
Phenothiazines	
Haldol	Haloperidol
Loxitane	Loxapine
Mellaril	Thioridazine
Moban	Milindone
Navane	Thiothixene
Prolixin	Fluphenazine
Serentil	Mesoridazine
Stelazine	Trifluoperazine
Thorazine	Chlorpromazine
Trilafon	Perphenazine
Atypical Antipsychotics	
Clozaril	Clozapine
Risperdal	Risperidone
Zyprexa	Olanzapine

INPATIENT HOSPITALIZATION

At times, a parishioner may require the most restrictive treatment setting available, the psychiatric hospital. Inpatient psychiatric facilities range from small upscale private hospitals (most expensive) to large state mental hospitals (least expensive). For the most part, a mental health professional will not be inclined to hospitalize a parishioner whom you have referred for treatment unless the person's level of impairment is so severe that he or she cannot function well enough to adequately care for himself or herself. Also, MHPs have an obligation to hospitalize clients who present a clear danger to themselves (suicidal) or others (homicidal) as a result of their psychological problem. In addition, some disorders are so acute in nature that treating them effectively may hinge on having the person in a closed environment where treatment can be comprehensive and quite intense. For example, severely alcoholic clients or adolescents with anorexia nervosa (see Chapter 2) will often improve most rapidly with intensive inpatient care.

In most states, MDs (psychiatrists) must officially admit patients to inpatient units. In some cases, psychologists may have admitting privileges, but most psychologists do not routinely admit patients to hospitals. The primary reason is that physicians must be responsible for a patient's physical exams and any psychiatric medications administered during hospitalization. Most psychiatric facilities provide a range of treatments including individual and group therapy, psychiatric medication, family therapy, recreational and occupational therapy, and *milieu* therapy. Milieu therapy is simply the utilization of the total environment as an important variable in helping the person improve. Ideally, patients become highly engaged with staff, other patients, therapy groups, and different MHPs while in the hospital.

Under ideal circumstances, hospitalization will be voluntary. The parishioner, with support from family, friends, and the church, will understand the importance of inpatient care for his or her own safety and long-term health. In other cases, parishioners may require involuntary commitment to a hospital. In this case, a physician, and later, a judge, will place a suicidal, homicidal, or obviously psychotic person on a legal "hold," which keeps the patient hospitalized until he or she can be stabilized. Inpatient mental health treatment is a critically important form of mental health care for certain parishioners in certain circumstances. Pastors should become familiar with at least one psychiatrist with admitting privileges at a local psychiatric facility. Hospitalization is an expensive form of treatment and large state hospitals are generally not known for high quality care; therefore, inpatient treatment should be reserved for very severe cases for which less restrictive alternatives are not adequate or risk the parishioner's safety.

ALCOHOL AND DRUG TREATMENT PROGRAMS

In Chapter 3, we discussed substance abuse disorders, including some of the primary forms of substance abuse treatment. However, because alcohol and drug problems are so prevalent in our culture and because they constitute such a potentially serious form of impairment, it is important for the pastor to be familiar with the range of treatment options for substance-dependent parishioners. Although we will focus primarily on treatment programs for alcoholism, there is tremendous overlap in treatment approaches for alcohol and other drug addictions. In fact, most treatment programs provide care for persons with any form of substance addiction.

Unfortunately, many substance-dependent parishioners will not admit that they have a problem until they "hit bottom." At this point, their lives have become entirely unmanageable and there may be a crisis that precipitates their willingness to finally consider treatment (e.g., a serious car accident, an arrest, severe financial problems, or a threatened marital separation). Because alcoholics often react with denial and anger when confronted with their disorder, it is best to coordinate this confrontation so that all those invested in the alcoholic or addict can be involved (e.g., spouse, children, pastor, employer, parents, etc.).

Treatment options fall into several categories and include:

1. *Inpatient treatment programs,* which require a physician's admission order and generally keep patients for one to two months. The majority of these programs emphasize medical stabilization (especially important in the case of severe physical addiction), abstinence, and lifestyle changes. Staff members are typically medical professionals and addiction counselors. During the initial phase of hospitalization, emphasis is often placed on reducing the danger of withdrawal symptoms via tranquilizing medications (e.g., Valium and Librium). The intensity of inpatient programs has been lauded by its proponents as essential to giving the seriously addicted person a new start.

2. *Residential care programs* are transitional programs that may be helpful to the most seriously impaired alcoholics and addicts. They provide a transitional "group home" environment (often following inpatient care) in which the person is expected to remain abstinent and be actively engaged in various forms of counseling, occupational training, and peer support.
3. *Outpatient treatment programs* range widely in organization and intensity, but typically involve outpatient counseling (individual and group), Alcoholics Anonymous (or Narcotics Anonymous) meetings, abstinence verification (e.g., via urinalysis), etc. The duration of these programs and the quality of the treatment and staff may vary widely.
4. *Self-help programs* include Alcoholics Anonymous (AA) and Narcotics Anonymous (NA). These programs are very popular and rely solely on the leadership and peer support by other recovering alcoholics and drug addicts. They emphasize recovery through the classic twelve-step model, which includes admission of one's illness and powerlessness to overcome it, a reliance on God or a Higher Power for direction, unrelenting honesty, and a commitment to remain involved in the program for life. Members of AA are encouraged to view their "disease" as permanent, and complete abstinence is strongly emphasized.

Although inpatient hospital treatment has long been the standard as the initial form of treatment for someone identified with a substance addiction, research has not supported the value of inpatient care in comparison to less expensive and less invasive alternatives. Mental health professionals are increasingly aware of the benefits of outpatient treatment programs and quality self-help programs such as AA. Also, outpatient therapy (specifically, group therapy or cognitive-behavioral individual therapy) conducted by MHPs with expertise in substance disorders has been shown to produce promising outcomes. Finally, Antabuse (disulfiram) can be administered to alcoholics to deter them from drinking during the time they are trying to establish abstinence. If a person ingests alcohol while taking Antabuse, he or she will become violently ill. Unfortunately, the person can simply stop taking the medication, which often occurs.

We recommend allowing the MHP with expertise in alcohol and drug-related disorders to work with the parishioner and the family in determining the most appropriate treatment match. In more severe cases (especially those involving significant danger of withdrawal), inpatient care may be an important first step. In other cases, intensive involvement in AA and outpatient psychotherapy may be appropriate. Keep in mind that relapse rates following substance disorder treatment are high (around 50 percent or higher) and that alcoholic and drug-addicted parishioners may require long-term support and more than one episode of professional treatment.

EATING DISORDER TREATMENT PROGRAMS

In Chapter 4, we detailed the range of thorny treatment issues present when parishioners suffer from eating disorders. Not only are eating disorders potentially life-threatening, they are also long-term in nature and often difficult to treat successfully. Although a range of psychotherapies have been developed for eating disorders, the pastor should be particularly attuned to inpatient programs for parishioners with anorexia. Hospitalization may be required to provide initial stabilization and intensive treatment.

When parishioners (typically adolescent or young adult females) suffer from anorexia or bulimia to the extent that they pose a danger to themselves via lack of eating (starvation) or purging (vomiting or laxative abuse), immediate hospitalization should be carefully considered by a physician. Severely underweight anorexic clients will be a serious concern due to the danger of medical complications (e.g., cardiac problems) related to starvation. Inpatient treatment for anorexic persons will involve mandatory fluid and nutrient intake (often using IVs initially), gradual increase in caloric intake, and monitoring of physical condition. Simultaneously, the patient will often be placed in a behavior-therapy setting in which all rewards (e.g., recreation, privileges) hinge on appropriate eating, involvement in individual, family, and group therapy sessions, and refraining from purging (vomiting) behaviors. The value of inpatient eating disorder programs is their intensity and their capacity to carefully control the patient's eating behavior to ensure safety while various psychotherapy approaches have time to take effect. Antidepressant medications (such as amitriptyline) may also be used during treatment to speed the recovery process—particularly when mood problems are clearly related to the eating disorder.

When hospitalization is not required, we recommend referral to a mental health professional with focused expertise in treating eating disorders. Of course, a physical examination should always be performed by a physician before a decision is made to proceed with outpatient care alone. Promising treatments for anorexia and bulimia include cognitive-behavioral, behavioral, and interpersonal psychotherapies. The parishioner will be asked to focus on self-image and self-evaluation, distorted body image, and the recognition and maintenance of appropriate weight and body fat proportions. Family therapy is also often a critical component of recovery. Treatment may focus on educating the family regarding the person's condition, identifying ways the parents inadvertently nurture a negative self-image in the child, and discerning ways the family system reinforces the eating-disordered member's behavior. Finally, group therapy is a cost-effective and extremely helpful form of treatment for eating-disordered clients. Group support, coupled with the perceptive confrontation of peers with similar behavior and thought processes, can be quite effective. An excellent MHP will typically combine multiple treatment components with eating-disordered clients.

HYPNOSIS

Hypnosis is an induced state of consciousness in which one person responds to suggestions by another person to alter perception, thinking, feelings, and behavior. Hypnosis originated in the 1700s and was initially referred to as *mesmerism* after Anton Mesmer, who first wrote about this altered state. A hypnotic state is a deeply relaxed and highly suggestible state, which can be useful for some treatment purposes. Hypnosis is typically only effective with persons who are extremely suggestible. Therapists who use this approach will assess whether a client is suggestible enough that this technique may have good effect. The MHP will use *induction techniques* to get a client into a hypnotic state characterized by heightened selective attention. Here, the client has tuned out stimuli that are not relevant and focuses solely on the therapist's suggestions. Induction techniques include progressive muscle relaxation, narrowing the client's gaze to a focused object or point, and directing the client's activities via suggestion (e.g., "You may now begin to feel very relaxed and your eyelids may become heavy").

Hypnosis may be used by MHPs for a variety of reasons. First, hypnosis has most frequently been used for creating *posthypnotic suggestions*. In this case, the therapist will suggest to the client that he or she will carry out or avoid some behavior later, while in their normal waking state. For example, a client who wishes to quit smoking may be told that he will become nauseated whenever he smells cigarette smoke and that whenever he has the urge to smoke, he will feel like chewing gum instead. Similarly, a medical patient may receive the hypnotic suggestion that she will experience very little postsurgical pain. Posthypnotic suggestions are frequently used quite successfully with a range of disorders, particularly behavioral and medical problems.

Hypnosis has also been used for recall of *repressed memories* and for *age regression*. This technique involves suggesting the client is at an earlier age and encouraging him or her to speak from that perspective to gain understanding regarding what events occurred and how he or she experienced life at that point in his or her development. Unfortunately, age regression and memory recall are plagued by unreliability and significant research has shown that memories can easily be unintentionally fabricated.[20,21] Competent MHPs who practice hypnosis would attempt these techniques with great caution.

Hypnotism depends more on the suggestibility of the subject or client than on the skill of the hypnotist or therapist. Still, MHPs who use hypnosis for clinical purposes should have had focused specialty training in this technique. There is a board that certifies professionals who use hypnosis as one approach in their clinical practices, and board certification is a strong indication of the MHP's expertise with this treatment approach. It would not be at all unusual for parishioners to receive hypnosis for the purposes of pain management, smoking cessation, weight control, performance enhancement (it is quite common among athletes), relaxation training, and anxiety management. Research has shown, however, that hypnosis is primarily effective for involuntary problems (e.g., pain, headaches, asthma, stress-related skin conditions) and not as effective for voluntary problems (e.g., smoking, weight loss, athletic performance).[22] Hypnosis would be less commonly used for routine counseling or psychotherapy issues.

ELECTROCONVULSIVE THERAPY

Severely depressed—and typically older—parishioners who have not responded to psychotherapy, medication, or any other depression treatment may be encouraged by their psychiatrist to consider *electroconvulsive therapy* (ECT) as an option in the treatment of their depression. Although ECT has been criticized in the professional literature and portrayed as barbaric in movies, research indicates that, for some very depressed patients, this is a surprisingly effective, if not well understood, treatment approach.

Electroconvulsive therapy produces its curative effect on the depressed person by essentially creating a grand mal or generalized seizure in the brain. To accomplish this, the person is put to sleep with an anesthetic and his or her muscles are paralyzed with another drug that prevents broken bones and other ill effects when the seizure occurs. Electrodes are placed at two locations on the scalp and an electric current is passed through the person's brain. The electric current lasts for only two seconds and the seizure lasts for about thirty seconds to a minute. Treatments are administered two or three times per week until the person's depression lifts or until it becomes clear the treatment is not working.[23]

Because severe biological depression in older adult clients may predict eventual suicide, ECT has a legitimate place in the psychiatrist's treatment arsenal (only psychiatrists are trained to practice this procedure). For some patients, ECT has produced dramatic results and complete remission of depressive symptoms. Research suggests that over half of those treated make substantial improvement in their depressive symptoms. Although ECT may produce good results, patients are prone to relapse and may require ECT sessions episodically. When ECT is combined with antidepressant medications, the relapse rate is lessened considerably.

It is important not to dissuade parishioners or their families from considering ECT when they suffer from severe major depression that has not been responsive to other forms of treatment. Although it is reasonable to pursue a second opinion before embarking on a trial of ECT, most psychiatrists would never consider ECT a first-order approach to handling complaints of depression.

FADS IN MENTAL HEALTH TREATMENT

Like all fallible human beings, mental health professionals occasionally fall prey to fleeting fads and bizarre trends in mental health treatment. In fact, over the years, numerous bright and well-trained MHPs have endorsed "therapeutic" approaches such as naked encounter groups, hallucinogenic drug experimentation, and "primal scream" therapy. Of course, none of these approaches were particularly useful and some were simply unethical and possibly harmful. During the past decade, MHPs have also followed diagnostic fads including multiple personality disorder (now dissociative identity disorder—see Chapter 3), which we now know to be quite rare. For a time, many MHPs believed that satanic ritual abuse was occurring in epidemic proportions and they wrongly diagnosed clients as victims of such abuse, often attempting to elicit abuse memories via age regression under hypnosis. The effect of these diagnoses and treatments on the lives of clients was harmful, to say the least.

Unfortunately, as long as there are fads and "breakthrough" treatment approaches, MHPs will be duped, and may attempt to apply these magical cures to all their clients and client problems. We recommend being wary of MHPs who use only one approach with clients or who claim to have "one of a kind" or exclusive therapeutic powers and techniques. We consider any approach to treatment that lacks careful, valid scientific research to be questionable at best and faddish at worst. Of course, most of these "rages" disappear and MHPs will recognize that author M. Scott Peck was right—"Life is hard" and there really are no therapeutic shortcuts.[24] Your troubled parishioners will get better when they work hard in therapy to understand themselves, learn new skills, and modify self-defeating beliefs, behaviors, and emotions.

Chapter 8

Self-Help Books

Reading selections of great literature has been considered therapeutic and even morally uplifting for centuries. Great scientist-philosophers such as Aristotle have written of the healing power of reading.[1] Therapists often recommend readings to their clients in order to speed the healing process and allow clients to experience both the insight and emotional connection that may occur from receiving instruction or identifying with a fictional character. If you are like many of us, you may quickly call to mind moments of powerful emotion or inspiration generated by the words of a gifted writer. Whether liberating joy, paralyzing grief, or a clearheaded sense of conviction and direction, we believe these experiences are often healing and seldom soon forgotten. When therapists use literature or self-help books with clients during counseling, they refer to the practice as *bibliotherapy*. Indeed, we are exhorted by both the Old and New Testaments to nourish and strengthen ourselves through reading God's Word: "He who gives heed to the word will prosper" (Proverbs 16:20) and "by the encouragement of the scriptures we might have hope" (Romans 15:4).

WHAT IS SELF-HELP?

In contrast to great literature or scripture, self-help books are often selected by people who, while not in any counseling relationship, hope to receive problem-specific written counsel and, hopefully, understanding or skill building in a specific area of life. We define as "self-help" any book, other than the Bible itself, which has been written to help you *improve, change, or somehow understand your personal qualities, relationships, mental health, or faith.* Authors of self-help books typically attempt to provide encouragement, information, or advice to readers who wish to "help themselves." Judging from the popular titles in Christian bookstores, self-help book consumers appear most interested in improving marriages and families, building relationship skills, understanding common emotional difficulties, finding a sense of belonging, meaning, or inspiration, and/or diligently evaluating the manner in which one is currently living life.

In case you haven't noticed, self-help is Big business (with a capital "B")! Like rabbits, self-help books seem to reproduce at amazing speed, resulting in a surging population of every variety. If your local Christian bookstore is like ours, its self-help section has been slowly (or rapidly) encroaching on other forms of Christian reading for some time. Each year, hundreds of authors clamor to help us "overcome" a myriad of difficulties, "experience" joy and happiness, or "become" something we currently are not. Self-help books are a multimillion-dollar publishing phenomenon with literally thousands of titles in print all the time.[2]

THE VALUE OF SELF-HELP BOOKS

Why are there so many self-help books (secular and Christian) to choose from? Self-help books are especially alluring for several reasons including: (1) low cost, (2) ready availability, (3) apparent relevance to everyday life concerns, (4) hopeful and optimistic tone, (5) the opportunity self-help offers for privacy in exploring highly personal concerns while avoiding the sense of shame often experienced in seeking professional help, and (6) the lack of a good alternative for many who are without a strong support network or, because of various circumstances, have no access to professional assistance. For all of these reasons, self-help books have established themselves as an important resource for thousands of Christian consumers.

Do self-help books really help? Unfortunately, research has not offered a clear picture concerning the actual changes produced by self-help books in the lives of those who read them.[3,4] We do know that among self-help readers, most report receiving significant benefits.[5] Perhaps even more interesting is the finding, from a number of well-controlled surveys, that between 60 and 95 percent of counselors and psychologists recommend self-help books to their clients.[6-12] Most licensed professionals encourage their own clients to read specific self-help books. Why? These surveys seem to suggest that psychologists believe certain self-help books really help many of their clients. Few of these professionals report negative or harmful outcomes for those who read them, and most find that good self-help books speed client progress and reduce relapse rates after counseling ends. A number of professionals have noted other advantages.[13] For instance, many people are "literature oriented" and are able to learn most effectively as they read. Some may also be visually or auditorily oriented and benefit substantially from video or audio products. Self-help books are written to be self-applied, in some cases, saving considerable health care costs for businesses and individuals. Finally, because no single professional therapist could possibly master the wide range of approaches to treating the vast variety of problems and symptoms, self-help books often allow both therapist and client a wider range of therapeutic tools from which to choose.

PROBLEMS WITH SELF-HELP BOOKS

Self-help books are not without shortcomings and a number of discerning professionals choose never to recommend most of them to their clients. In fact, many careful clinicians, who are appalled by the irresponsible advertising and poor quality of many self-help books, would prefer that these books display a consumer warning label. If we had our way, it might read something like this: "WARNING, reading this book may be dangerous to your health. This book may contain false, misleading, and ridiculous information which may prove useless or may even make your difficulties worse." Of course, no such warning exists. Instead, the covers of many Christian self-help books are adorned with alluring claims and impressive promises of curative and life-changing power. It is critical, therefore, to understand that self-help materials should only be used with caution. We hope this guide will help you to discern the most glaring problems with the self-help books you might consider recommending to parishioners.

Here are some of the major concerns with the self-help books you are apt to see on the shelves at your local Christian bookstore:

1. Only a handful of self-help books are well grounded on solid scientific evidence. This means that much of the advice given and the techniques recommended are speculative or based on the writer's be-

liefs regarding how people change or heal. In addition, not one of the books we reviewed for this guide had been tested to evaluate the extent to which those who read the book actually benefited from the techniques. As a pastor, you will often be required to evaluate, in the absence of any sound information offered by the author or publisher, whether a certain book is likely to live up to its billing and truly help. This led one reviewer of self-help books to comment: "Self-help titles, by and large, are repositories of unproven, sometimes unprovable, advice on matters of considerable importance and complexity."[12]

2. This, of course, raises another concern regarding self-help books: the tendency of many authors (often with few credentials) to grossly oversimplify very complex problems. For example, a well-intentioned author may recommend forgiveness or meditative prayer as a solution to nearly every life problem, including severe behavioral or psychiatric disorders. While we certainly acknowledge that both forgiveness and prayer are essential in the lives of healthy Christian men and women, and that they are often part of the healing process, we do not believe God is limited to two modalities when it comes to restoring lives. Further, we believe there is profound danger in oversimplifying highly complex physical and psychological symptoms. For example, a person experiencing the early stages of a thyroid condition, brain tumor, or a psychotic illness may initially present with relatively benign symptoms such as anxiety, depression, withdrawal, insomnia, or headaches. In attempting to address these symptoms merely through a self-help book, as has occurred in the past, these people run substantial risk by delaying the start of professional assistance. Unfortunately, few self-help authors encourage readers to seek professional assistance. If those parishioners to whom you recommend self-help books are experiencing the onset (especially if sudden) of unusual or disturbing physical or psychological symptoms, we believe a consultation with a physician or a knowledgeable mental health professional is critical prior to reliance on any self-help technique.

3. Self-help books, often as part of their elaborate publicity campaigns, suggest that most people in the general population somehow "need" the secret truths or techniques their covers conceal. In order to feel good, be healthy, or "maximize" something or other, you really need to purchase the book. The authors will help you to understand that, while all along you've felt just fine, you've actually been "im-

paired," "codependent" (or at least cosomething), "shamed," or, at the very least, "dysfunctional." You may also learn that your life, faith, vocation, and relationships are imperfect and in need of repair. This tendency on the part of self-help authors to portray the entire population as impaired in some way was the focus of the book, *I'm Dysfunctional, You're Dysfunctional.*[14] Becvar referred to this same tendency as the creation of "nonproblems" by self-help book authors.[15] As Christians, we believe that life in this world is difficult and that some discomfort and unhappiness are not only part of life but necessary for growth. If a self-help author suggests otherwise ("God only wants you to be happy"), as many do, *beware!*

4. Finally, we turn to an issue of grave concern with respect to self-help books—the outlandish, outrageous, and downright false claims made by many of their authors and publishers. While many critics of secular self-help books have complained about the misleading statements often made on book jackets, we believe the same complaint is relevant to those self-help books geared to Christian audiences. In our review of hundreds of self-help books (both Christian and secular) for this guide, we have encountered numerous examples of "hype" or grandiosity. Many of the books claimed to offer one-of-a-kind, revolutionary, and unique techniques that were somehow "known" to be effective. Perhaps the most humorous example of wild self-help hype we encountered was this promotional claim, made by a psychologist for a colleague's book: "_____ will shake you up, knock you down, stand you up straight, and challenge the very heart of your soul. It is a hard-hitting, eye-opening book. It is a must read for every Christian." If you are like us, you're wondering if this book comes complete with protective helmet and pads!

Like people, self-help books are often helpful but never perfect. Each of the concerns we have mentioned above are important and yet, in our opinion, do not detract from the potential value of many well-prepared and responsibly written self-help books. Using a medication metaphor, we would suggest that self-help books are "over-the-counter" healing agents whose actual curative properties vary widely. While some seem inert or inactive, others prove strikingly potent time after time and perhaps should be used with professional supervision.

BOOKS RECOMMENDED
BY CHRISTIAN PSYCHOLOGISTS

In pondering how to best determine which books to review, we decided to ask our colleagues in the field of Christian counseling.[16] We developed a self-help book survey and mailed it to all members of the Christian Association for Psychological Studies (CAPS), who listed themselves as "practitioners" (versus academics or researchers) and who held either a doctorate (451) or a master's degree (333) in counseling or psychology. Among other things, our survey asked these practitioners to list up to three self-help books in fourteen topical categories (based on the book's quality and usefulness to clients) that they would recommend and use with clients. Surveys were returned by 262 professionals. Results showed that 92 percent of these Christian professionals used self-help books with their clients at least some of the time. They also listed an average of thirteen books that they would highly recommend for self-help purposes. In the section that follows, we list the top three books recommended in each of the fourteen categories. Though not every book is explicitly Christian in authorship or content, the books listed are those most likely to be used by Christian counselors and psychologists. (Note: An asterisk indicates that the book is Christian in orientation.)

Addictions and Recovery

Codependent No More (1987). Melodie Beattie. New York: Harper and Row.
Out of the Shadows: Understanding Sexual Addiction (1992). Patrick Carnes. Minneapolis, MN: CompCare.
The Twelve Steps: A Spiritual Journey (1989). Anonymous. San Diego, CA: Recovery Publications.

Anxiety

Anxiety and Phobia Workbook (1995). Edmund Bourne. Oakland, CA: New Harbinger.
Worry-Free Living (1989). Frank Minirth and Paul Meier. Nashville, TN: Thomas Nelson.*

Hope and Help for Your Nerves (1969). Claire Weekes. New York: Hawthorne Books.

Child Development and Parenting

How to Really Love Your Child (1992). Ross Campbell. Wheaton, IL: Victor Books.

The New Dare to Discipline (1992). James Dobson. Wheaton, IL: Tyndale.*

The Strong-Willed Child (1978). James Dobson. Wheaton IL: Tyndale.*

Depression

Feeling Good: The New Mood Therapy (1981). David Burns. New York: Signet.

Happiness Is a Choice: The Symptoms, Causes, and Cures of Depression (1994). Frank Minirth and Paul Meier. Grand Rapids, MI: Baker Book House.*

Telling Yourself the Truth (1980). William Backus and Marie Chapian. Minneapolis, MN: Bethany House.*

Family

Bradshaw on the Family: A New Way of Creating Solid Self-Esteem (1996). John Bradshaw. Deerfield Beach, FL: Health Communications.

The Gift of the Blessing (1993). Gary Smalley and John Trent. Nashville, TN: Thomas Nelson.*

Secrets of Your Family Tree (1991). Dave Carder, Earl Henslin, John Townsend, Henry Cloud, and Alice Brawand. Chicago: Moody Press.*

Grief/Loss

Good Grief (1962). Granger Westberg. Philadelphia, PA: Fortress Press.*

How to Survive the Loss of a Love (1991). Melba Colgrove, Harold Bloomfield, and Peter McWilliams. Los Angeles: Prelude Press.*

A Grief Observed (1961). C. S. Lewis. New York: Seabury Press.*

Interpersonal Skills

Boundaries: When to Say Yes When to Say No to Take Control of Your Life (1992). Henry Cloud and John Townsend. Grand Rapids, MI: Zondervan.*

Your Perfect Right: A Guide to Assertive Living (1990). Robert Alberti and Michael Emmons. San Louis Obispo, CA: Impact.

Men Are from Mars, Women Are from Venus (1992). John Gray. New York: HarperCollins.

Marriage

Getting the Love You Want: The Guide for Couples (1990). Harville Hendrix. New York: Harper Perennial.

Men Are from Mars, Women Are from Venus (1992). John Gray. New York: HarperCollins.

His Needs, Her Needs (1994). Willard Harley. Grand Rapids, MI: Revell.*

Gender Issues

Men Are from Mars, Women Are from Venus (1992). John Gray. New York: HarperCollins.

The Dance of Anger (1985). Harriet Lerner. New York: Harper and Row.

His Needs, Her Needs (1994). Willard Harley. Grand Rapids, MI: Revell.*

Personal Adjustment/Improvement

The Search for Significance (1990). Robert McGee. Houston, TX: Rapha.*

The Road Less Traveled (1978). M. Scott Peck. New York: Simon and Schuster.*

Healing for Damaged Emotions (1981). David Seamands. Wheaton, IL: Victor Books.

Relationships

Boundaries: When to Say Yes When to Say No to Take Control of Your Life (1992). Henry Cloud and John Townsend. Grand Rapids, MI: Zondervan.*

The Friendship Factor (1979). Allan McGinnis. Minneapolis, MN: Augsburg.

Codependent No More (1987). Melodie Beattie. New York: Harper and Row.

Sexuality

The Gift of Sex (1981). Clifford Penner and Joyce Penner. Waco, TX: Word.*

Intended for Pleasure (1977). Ed Wheat. Old Tappan, NJ: Revell.*

The Act of Marriage: The Beauty of Sexual Love (1976). Tim La Haye and Beverly LaHaye. Grand Rapids, MI: Zondervan.*

Spirituality

The Search for Significance (1990). Robert McGee. Houston, TX: Rapha.*

The Road Less Traveled (1978). M. Scott Peck. New York: Simon and Schuster.*

Disappointment with God (1988). Phillip Yancy. Grand Rapids, MI: Zondervan.

Top Classics

Boundaries: When to Say Yes When to Say No to Take Control of Your Life (1992). Henry Cloud and John Townsend. Grand Rapids, MI: Zondervan.*

The Road Less Traveled (1978). M. Scott Peck. New York: Simon and Schuster.*

Feeling Good: The New Mood Therapy (1981). David Burns. New York: Signet.

SUMMARIES OF TOP-RATED SELF-HELP BOOKS

In the next section, we have listed the top ten most frequently recommended self-help books overall. Again, about half the books are clearly Christian oriented, as indicated by an asterisk. We also offer short reviews of the top self-help books recommended in each category as well as each book in the top ten list. Keep in mind that these reviews represent our opinions about each book's quality and usefulness. We review the books in alphabetical order.

TOP 10 SELF-HELP BOOKS RECOMMENDED OVERALL

1. *Boundaries: When to Say Yes When to Say No to Take Control of Your Life* (1992). Henry Cloud and John Townsend.
2. *Feeling Good: The New Mood Therapy* (1981). David Burns.
3. *The Search for Significance* (1990). Robert McGee.
4. *Men Are from Mars, Women Are from Venus* (1992). John Gray.
5. *Getting the Love You Want: The Guide for Couples* (1990). Harville Hendrix.
6. *Codependent No More* (1987). Melodie Beattie.
7. *The Road Less Traveled* (1978). M. Scott Peck.
8. *Happiness Is a Choice: The Symptoms, Causes, and Cures of Depression* (1994). Frank Minirth and Paul Meier.
9. *Love Is a Choice* (1989). R. Hemfelt, F. Minirth, and P. Meier.
10. *His Needs, Her Needs* (1994). Willard Harley.

Bradshaw on the Family: A New Way of Creating Solid Self-Esteem **(John Bradshaw)**

Based on the PBS television series of the same name, this book attempts to explain how the rules and attitudes learned while growing up become encoded within each family member. Unhealthy family rules are transmitted between generations; this book helps the reader understand how this occurs and how to address it. Bradshaw studied for the Catholic priesthood and holds a degree in counseling. Nonetheless, this book is clearly secular in its overall presentation.

We think the grandiosity of the book's title speaks for itself. Bradshaw suggests that 96 percent of all families are to some degree emotionally impaired and we would like to know where he gets his figures! The book is based on Bradshaw's own thinking, not any scientific evidence, and of the thirty-one references used, twenty-six are other self-help books. Bradshaw does attempt to present steps for change, but most of these are based on the AA twelve-step model. Most alarming is Bradshaw's heavy use of psychobabble (e.g., "inner child," "codependence," "family trance," and "hole in the soul").

Boundaries: When to Say Yes When to Say No to Take Control of Your Life (Henry Cloud and John Townsend)

If "codependence" was the buzzword of the 1980s, "boundaries" was surely the buzzword of the 1990s, due in large part to the popularity of this book. It was the number one–rated book by our sample of Christian therapists. The authors define a boundary as one's personal property line and delineate those things for which an individual should and should not feel responsible. The book's essential premise is that a number of psychological, spiritual, and relationship problems have boundary violations at their core. The solution lies in knowing when to say yes and when to say no, thereby taking greater control of one's life.

The authors, both Christian clinical psychologists, offer a book on relationships with strong biblical support. The writing contains extensive reference to scripture and the book is generally well written and free of jargon. Problematically, the scope of the book is quite broad and the only supporting references are to the Bible and other self-help books. Given the high ranking of this book among Christian practitioners, it must have proven helpful to many readers.

Getting the Love You Want: The Guide for Couples (Harville Hendrix)

The author presents what he calls "Imagio Relationship Therapy" for use by couples. The book describes how unresolved childhood conflicts and experiences form the basis for selecting our mates. This results in what Hendrix calls the "unconscious marriage." The goal is to move from the unconscious to the conscious marriage, and sixteen exercises are presented to help couples accomplish this transition.

This appears to be a very well-written and potentially helpful book. The author holds a PhD in pastoral counseling and has extensive experience in work with couples. He avoids psychobabble and offers very specific and easy-to-follow steps for couples to apply in their own work together. The author supports his claims with substantial research, and gives credit to other authors and theorists when appropriate. We were impressed.

Good Grief (Granger Westberg)

The thirty-fifth anniversary edition of this top-rated grief and loss book was published in 1997. At seventy-nine pages, this is more a booklet than a book and there are no references. The author indicates that grief may be "good" in the sense of allowing those who successfully cope with loss to emerge from the experience at a higher level of emotional and spiritual maturity. They may also be better equipped to help others address grief problems. Nine stages are described in the grief recovery process, beginning with struggling with shock and ending with the affirmation of reality.

Though the author's credentials are not provided, the book jacket indicates that he held academic positions in medicine and religion at the University of Chicago and in preventive medicine at the University of Illinois College of Medicine. The book does not refer to research or theory in the field of grief; the ideas are presented in the manner of sage advice from a wise and experienced man. Although the book does not contain many of the characteristics of a good self-help book, it has sold nearly 2 million copies and has obviously been helpful to many people coping with loss and grief.

Happiness Is a Choice: The Symptoms, Causes, and Cures of Depression (Frank Minirth and Paul Meier)

The authors are both psychiatrists and cofounders of the Minirth-Meier Clinic. This book offers an in-depth look at the causes and cures of depression from medical, psychological, and Christian perspectives. Important questions addressed in the book include: What is depression? What causes it? Why would a Christian commit suicide? Is depression genetic? Does depression indicate a spiritual problem? When should antidepressants be used? What hope is there for recovery? What medical or psychological resources are available? Finally, the book offers a number of helpful practical recommendations for dealing with depression.

This is an excellent book. The authors' credentials clearly qualify them to write in this area and the book is strongly reinforced by solid research from scientific journals and books. Although the authors sometimes offer the reader technical information, it is presented clearly and helpfully. The authors are careful to discuss the multiple causes of depression and the entire book is very Christian oriented. This is a solid self-help book and one of the best we have seen.

His Needs, Her Needs (Willard Harley)

This book asks, "Is your marriage affair proof?" It suggests that most marriages will experience the pain of infidelity (though no studies are cited) and then boldly suggests that it will offer measures to "ensure faithfulness in your marriage." Harley begins with the premise that each spouse has a "love bank" that needs to maintain a positive balance in order for the marriage not to be vulnerable to an affair. Pleasant interactions result in deposits while painful interactions result in withdrawals. The book identifies ten needs (five for women and five for men) that must be met in order for each spouse's love bank to remain in the black. The author includes many case histories to illustrate points and discusses concrete methods for communicating love for one's spouse. The appendix contains questionnaires for each spouse to use to analyze his or her individual needs.

The author is a clinical psychologist with twenty years of experience as a marriage counselor. Although his emphasis is on preserving marriage and the book claims to be written from a Christian perspective, there are no references to scripture. The book's only references are to other self-help books, and no research is cited to support the author's list of "needs." The book is very readable and minimal jargon is used. Our primary concern with this book is the author's rather audacious and frankly ridiculous claim that one can "affair proof" a marriage. Not only is this unsupported by any evidence we know of, it is also out of keeping with the scriptural admonition to "submit yourselves one to another out of reverence for Christ."

How to Really Love Your Child (Ross Campbell)

Even though it was published twenty years ago, our sample of Christian therapists rated this book "tops" in the parenting category. At present, it has been translated into twenty languages. Written from a distinctly Christian point of view, this book purports to teach parents how to actually convey love to their children. Topics include how to establish a loving and nurturing climate and bond with children based on a foundation of unconditional love (1 Corinthians 13), the components of love (e.g., eye contact, physical contact, and focused attention), discipline, and spiritual development. The author's notable enthusiasm for behavior modification reflects the book's era.

The author is a psychiatrist from Tennessee. He has worked in a psychiatry clinic, served as a faculty member at the University of Tennessee, and has been a medical missionary in Bolivia. It is unclear what his background in child development might be. The book is clearly Christian oriented and scriptures are frequently used to augment principles throughout. No scientific support is offered for any of the book's major points, though it would be easy to find. In fact, the book contains no references. It is well written and easy to understand. Technical jargon has been avoided and its popularity suggests many practitioners have found it useful for clients.

Men Are from Mars, Women Are from Venus (John Gray)

This mega best-seller begins with the metaphor that Martians and Venusians met, fell in love, and had happy relationships together because they respected and accepted their differences. When they came to earth, amnesia set in, and they forgot they were from different planets. Throughout this book, this metaphor is used to explain the conflicts that commonly occur between men and women. Chapters discuss gender differences in values, coping mechanisms, motivation, communication styles, intimacy needs, love cycles, love needs, and conflict resolution styles. Later chapters offer techniques for improving relationships.

This book has no Christian orientation whatsoever, yet Gray is an outstanding and clear writer and avoids psychobabble. It is easy to see why this book sells and why many find it useful. Gray has questionable academic credentials, and it is difficult to evaluate his competence to write on this topic. Gray has made big business from his book including frequent seminar and television appearances. His ideas are void of research support, and all ideas are presented as though they were exclusively his own. Our primary concern with this book is the stereotyped notions it promotes of men and women as static creatures and innate opposites. The book tends to simplify very complex relational issues.

The Anxiety and Phobia Workbook (Edmund Bourne)

The Anxiety and Phobia Workbook is a set of easy self-help exercises and guidelines for dealing with the full range of anxiety disorders from agoraphobia to panic. Early chapters define the different disorders, discuss their causes from a number of perspectives, and present comprehensive, multimodal approaches to treatment. Later chapters present specific treatments from biomedical, behavioral, cognitive, and spiritual perspectives. The book is replete with questionnaires, exercises, and charts to be used by the reader.

Bourne is a psychologist from the University of Chicago with a lengthy career as a teacher and researcher. His work has garnered national recognition and his experience relevant to the book includes directorship of the Anxiety Treatment Center in Santa Rosa, California. This book is secular and exclusively focused on treatment of anxiety. The author provides excellent research-based information and techniques and supports them with references to research and theory. The book avoids psychological jargon and, in our experience, this is by far the finest self-help book available on the topic of anxiety.

The Gift of Sex (Clifford Penner and Joyce Penner)

The authors have prepared this book for any couple interested in learning all they can about using the God-given gift of sexuality to enhance their relationship. This book begins with a biblical perspective on sexuality and then proceeds to consider the physical dimension of sex, the components of a sexual experience, techniques for overcoming sexual barriers, common sexual difficulties, and treatment for sexual difficulties. The book also contains eighteen sexual enhancement exercises, an annotated bibliography, and extensive scriptural references.

The authors are husband and wife; he is a clinical psychologist and she is a nurse with a master's degree. They have extensive experience conducting workshops on sexuality and appear very well qualified to write on the topic. This book is exceptionally well written. Terminology is technical when necessary (e.g., the arousal cycle), but not at all daunting. An annotated bibliography comprises other self-help books on sex, and the enhancement techniques are research-based and easy to apply. This book is clearly Christian and each chapter is replete with scriptural references. "Hot topics" for Christians such as masturbation and oral sex are handled with great sensitivity, but with a clear biblical and scientific base.

The Search for Significance (Robert McGee)

The author indicates that his purpose for writing this book is to convince Christians to build their self-worth (significance) on the love and forgiveness of Christ, and not on the ability to please others. The first 187 pages of this 479-page book is text, while the remainder is an extensive workbook with specially designed Bible studies and applications. Topics covered include the biblical basis of one's self-worth, problems with seeking approval, blame, shame, guilt, and other obstacles to growth.

McGee presents a reasonable guide to self-esteem from a biblical perspective and offers some helpful exercises and recommendations. There are very few references and, beyond biblical exegesis, the book is not well supported. The book is strongly Christian oriented and extensive scriptures relevant to self and significance are offered throughout. The author appears to be a professional counselor of some kind, but no credentials are offered.

Love Is a Choice (Robert Hemfelt, Frank Minirth, and Paul Meier)

The authors, a psychologist (Hemfelt) and two psychiatrists (Minirth and Meier), attempt to convince us that one in four Americans is "codependent," which they define as "an addiction to people, things, or behaviors." They also suggest that, if you are not codependent, you more than likely know or love someone who is. The authors offer ten steps toward "recovery" from this malady, the most important of which is seeing God's unconditional love as the answer to our "love hunger."

It is difficult to believe that Minirth and Meier (the authors of a much better book, *Happiness Is a Choice*) have jumped so thoroughly on the "I'm dysfunctional, you're dysfunctional" bandwagon, but with this book they certainly do. The book is utterly unsupported by any credible evidence and contains only three references, all of which are other self-help books. We find that the authors have defined codependence so broadly that it becomes basically meaningless and the book ends up as an exercise in psychobabble.

GUIDELINES FOR EVALUATING SELF-HELP BOOKS

Though our survey should help you select some helpful books to use with counselees, the self-help book market is ever expanding. Many titles not covered in this guide will certainly find their way into bookstores and the hands of your flock. It is important that pastors have a set of guidelines for use in determining which self-help books (Christian or not) should be used in counseling and recommended to Christians in need.[17] The following guidelines may be useful in that regard.

1. *Credentials.* Is the author qualified by virtue of education, clinical training, and/or experience in the area in which he or she writes? Although academic degrees and credentials do not guarantee the quality or usefulness of the contribution, in our experience, inspirational writing and anecdotal storytelling are poor substitutes for sound training.

2. *Knowledge of discipline.* Does the author appear to have expertise in the specific topic addressed by the book? Does the author reject professional standards or research-supported principles of behavior in favor of fringe or grossly speculative ideas and approaches? Does the author present spiritual wisdom and biblical truth as contradictory to science-based principles? If so, we recommend extreme caution in using the book.

3. *Knowledge of scripture.* Does the author promote ideas and recommend interventions that are congruent with Christian beliefs and values? If references to scripture are used, are they responsibly invoked and used in a manner appropriate to their context?

4. *Academic honesty.* Does the author give credit to those other professionals and authors whose ideas he or she has utilized in preparing his or her self-help book?

5. *Nature of claims.* Are the claims made by the book realistic or exaggerated? Does the cover of the book promote false or highly misleading claims?

6. *Scope.* Is the scope or breadth of the book realistic? Does the author clearly address, with adequate specificity, those problems for which the book is intended? Does the author inform readers of the reasonable boundaries regarding the book's application or usefulness? Books that claim to help with nearly any problem should be greeted with some skepticism.

7. *Clarity of language.* Is the book written in clear, common language that can be easily understood by persons with no specialized education? Does it use popular psychobabble, which conveys very little useful information, such as "inner child" or "toxic parents?"

8. *Problem complexity.* Does the book acknowledge that most psychological problems have multiple causes (e.g., biochemical problems, irrational thinking patterns, traumatic situations, bad habits, and poor spiritual health) or does the author attempt to oversimplify difficult issues? Unfortunately, most consumers are often attracted to promises of simple solutions.

9. *Self-diagnosis.* Does the book responsibly and clearly instruct readers regarding how to determine whether they may have a particular problem, thereby helping the reader determine whether the book may be a good match for them?

10. *Specific steps for change.* Are the directions for change written with sufficient clarity and specificity that most readers can understand and apply them with relative ease?

11. *Research basis.* If the book recommends an approach to overcoming or coping with a recognized disorder or common symp-

tom, is the approach based on treatment outcome research? Have the techniques themselves been validated in any way? We are always most impressed with authors who go beyond anecdotes and testimonials from "cured" clients and give attention to available research on the topic.

Chapter 9

Ethical Guidelines:
What to Expect from Professionals

What should I expect from the mental health professionals to whom I refer parishioners? Should they tell me anything I want to know about the case? Is it normal for a professional to insist that he or she can treat any mental health problem with 100 percent success? Should I be concerned to hear that a parishioner has been seeing her therapist "socially"? Is it okay for a counselor to recommend that his or her clients use Benadryl to help them sleep at night? Each of these questions raises important issues regarding professional behavior and adherence to ethical principles. As a pastor who refers parishioners to mental health professionals, you have a vested interest in ensuring that the MHPs with whom you do business are personally healthy and adhere to the highest standards of their profession—including the code of ethics relevant to their professional group. Although it is also ideal to find a practitioner who is theologically competent and spiritually mature, this may not be feasible in many small communities.

In this chapter, we briefly outline the major ethical guidelines common to all major mental health practitioner groups. These groups include psychiatrists, psychologists, social workers, counselors, and pastoral counselors, and each of them adheres to a clearly articulated set of ethical guidelines or standards.[1-5] We first discuss the basics of ethics and differentiate moral from ethical standards. We then describe six essential ethical standards, which you should be aware of when your parishioners are referred to a mental health professional.

For each standard, we give both an unethical and ethical version of the same case example. We then describe the standards and discuss indicators that an MHP is not practicing within the ethical standard. Finally, we recommend an approach you may use in responding to concerns of unethical conduct on the part of MHPs. Although it is hoped this will be a rare occurrence, we provide contact information for the ethics boards of all the major MHP organizations, should it become necessary for you or a parishioner to file an ethics complaint.

AN ETHICS PRIMER

Most pastors will not, and some would say *should* not, devote a great deal of their time to pastoral counseling.[6] Unless counseling is the pastor's specific church assignment and the pastor has specific professional training in mental health and counseling skills, most pastors would be wise to set firm limits on the frequency and intensity of formal counseling relationships with parishioners—particularly those with indications of serious psychiatric symptoms (see Chapters 2 through 5). Most pastors will want to refer their parishioners to MHPs who can provide specialized and effective treatments and who will (we hope) collaborate effectively with clergy. In Chapter 6, we suggested that pastors should be accountable for referring their troubled parishioners to other professionals and be knowledgeable about when, and to whom, a parishioner should be referred. This requires some effort on the part of the pastor or pastoral staff to become familiar with local MHPs and assess the extent to which these professionals appear competent, caring, respectful of parishioners' faith concerns, and willing to work in tandem with the pastor, particularly when this is the parishioner's wish.

Once a referral to an MHP has been made, the pastor will usually be able to assume that the practitioner will care for the parishioner competently and ethically. However, MHPs, like other human beings, will make errors or simply not be competent to provide the needed service. In this section, we briefly describe the notion of professional ethical codes and why they exist. This provides the foundation for our discussion of the major ethical principles shared by all mental health professions.

Ethics codes for MHPs exist for one primary reason—to protect the welfare of the clients these practitioners serve. When it appears that a parishioner has been harmed by a mental health practitioner, it is reasonable to ask the question, "Was the professional's decision or behavior really in the parishioner's best interest?" Ethics codes are rooted in moral principles and adapted by groups as rules for right or "correct" conduct. While moral principles provide a broader standard or context than ethics, they are often hard to translate to specific situations or professional dilemmas.

Most ethical codes have several fundamental moral principles. Kitchener identified four essential moral principles, which she believes provide the backdrop for nearly all ethics codes and a reasonable starting place in making ethical/moral decisions about how best to care for clients.[7] These principles include: (1) *autonomy*—the promotion of self-determination or the freedom of clients to choose their own direction, (2) *beneficence*—promoting the good of others, (3) *nonmaleficence*—avoiding doing harm, including refraining from actions that risk hurting clients, and (4) *justice*—fairness, or providing equal treatment to all people. These attitudes are fundamental to appropriate and sound ethical decisions in clinical practice.

It is reasonable to think of ethics codes as *necessary, but not sufficient* guidelines for ethical practice, for the reason that ethical codes are not explicit enough to deal with every situation the practitioner might face. Further, it is often difficult to interpret ethical codes, and people differ over how to apply them in specific cases.[8] For example, psychiatrists and psychologists in the state of Oregon are currently struggling with how to ethically respond to the Death With Dignity Act passed by Oregon voters in 1994, that requires mental health evaluations of terminally ill patients who legally elect to terminate their own lives. As you might expect, there is tremendous disagreement among professionals regarding the "most" ethical and moral response to this new law.

Although ethical standards are clearly needed, they are also often reactive—responding to violations that have occurred instead of seeking to prevent or anticipate future difficulties. Also, ethical standards may at times conflict with legal requirements or other regulations. For example, mental health professionals working with military personnel may be required to violate the client's confidentiality if the commanding officer believes there is a "need to know" about the service member's treatment.

Even though the better training programs carefully screen those who graduate at both the application and training stages, many other programs do very little screening—resulting in a steady stream of poorly suited or personally troubled practitioners into the marketplace. Also, some MHPs may have excellent intentions and strong moral convictions, yet at times might be exhausted, burned out, or poorly suited for clinical work. Mental health professionals may themselves lead unhealthy lives, have very disturbed relationships, and have no intention of following the very advice they deliver daily to their clients. Others may become burned out or overwhelmed as a direct result of their work. If they do not have the self-awareness needed to address these problems, the problems may worsen and negatively impact their professionalism. For all of these reasons, it is essential that the pastor get to know the practitioners to whom he or she refers parishioners. What are their reputations? What have other parishioners and clergy said about their professional and personal conduct? Are they involved in continuing education, consultation, and professional organizations, or are they isolated, burned out, and incongruent in their own lives? We raise these concerns to alert pastors to the fact that practitioners are human, and that there is often a wide range of competence and professional conduct among MHPs.

It is important for the pastor to keep in mind that the vast majority of MHPs to whom he or she might refer parishioners will be highly responsible and ethical. When ethical violations do occur, it is often because the specific situation was novel or unexpected, because of competing demands between ethical guidelines and other requirements, or because of a simple lack of awareness or experience on the part of the practitioner. Yet even if the root of the problem is benign or innocent, these practitioners are still responsible for the outcome of their services and the extent to which their behavior is in the best interest of their clients. Thankfully, malignant and irresponsible MHPs are clearly the small minority.

ETHICAL STANDARDS

Dual Relationships (Boundaries)

Unethical. Helen is a forty-nine-year-old parishioner who has become increasingly depressed and "aimless" over the past several months. Aware of her depressive symptoms, you refer her to a psychiatrist who begins seeing her in weekly therapy sessions. Three months later, Helen reports back to you that she is "not sure what to do about her psychiatrist." You learn that they are now meeting twice a week and that the majority of each session is devoted to "sharing our problems with each other." She describes in great detail her psychiatrist's struggles with his own midlife depression, his job, and even his marriage. Although there is no physical side to their relationship, it is clear Helen has been placed in the role of a therapist, or at least friend, to her therapist. Although she likes him, she is worried she "can't really help him."

Ethical. Dr. Jensen has been struggling with some symptoms of depression and some midlife concerns for about a year. Aware of these developments, he has been careful to monitor his feelings about clients and his standard of practice, particularly with clients he finds especially warm and nurturing. When he begins seeing Helen, he quickly becomes aware that she is bright, kind, and even "mothering" in some ways. He is tempted to disclose more to her than would be typical of his practice in general. He therefore consults with a colleague and describes the problem in detail. He decides he will be most helpful to Helen if he continues to monitor her antidepressant medication every other week while referring her to an excellent social worker colleague for ongoing counseling. He carefully explains to Helen that he believes this will be most helpful for her.

What to Expect

Good therapists have good boundaries. Specifically, they place careful boundaries around their professional roles with clients, recognizing that this is ultimately best for their clients. Ethics boards are asked to investigate countless cases of negative outcomes related to MHPs allowing their professional roles with clients to become blurred or mixed with social or business roles. The problem with engaging in more than one kind of relationship (role) with a client is that the client (and MHP) can become confused about the nature of the relationship, and the primary focus on helping the client with a specific problem almost always gets blurred. In general, MHPs know to avoid combining roles (e.g., therapist/teacher, therapist/relative, therapist/social acquaintance, therapist/romantic partner, therapist/business partner). Imagine the potential damage to the client, and the therapy relationship, when he or she feels exploited by a therapist in a sexual or business relationship, or when a grade in a course taught by the therapist seems either too high or too low. In general, MHPs should avoid entering into any kind of relationship with a client, other than the therapy relationship.

Mental health professionals who attend the same church as the parishioner are at risk for unintended multiple relationships that can potentially harm the client. Although it may be impossible to avoid all multiple roles with clients, especially in small communities, keep in mind that parishioners usually feel most "safe" and that their concerns are most "confidential" when they have no contact with their therapists outside of the therapy hour. In the church, there is danger of inadvertent violation of the parishioner's confidence or of being placed in a situation (committee or social gathering) with a parishioner that makes him or her uncomfortable. Therefore, we almost always recommend that pastors have a list of good MHPs who do not attend their churches.

It is important to offer a few words about sexual involvement with clients. It is always wrong. In no case will sexual involvement with a client ever be acceptable professional behavior, and such relationships nearly always lead to harmful outcomes for clients (e.g., depression, substance abuse, and other forms of emotional disturbance). Sexual relationships with therapy clients are the leading cause of malpractice suits against MHPs, and most insurance companies now limit the coverage for this class of ethical violation. In addition to malpractice suits, therapists engaging in these relationships are likely to lose their professional licenses, their jobs, their insurance coverage, and in some states, they may be convicted of a felony.

Although sexual involvement with clients is always wrong, sexual attraction to clients is likely to occur at times. Good MHPs are aware of their responses to clients and are careful to guard against becoming romantically and sexually involved. They seek consultation from peers in the field and refer clients to other providers when this appears wise. Good MHPs also avoid even subtle forms of sexual harassment or exploitation. For example, they do not request or encourage disclosure of material in therapy that is not directly related to the problem at hand.

As a pastor, you should be alert to reports from parishioners of blurred boundaries and inappropriate roles with their mental health professionals. Although a client may occasionally hug his or her therapist, especially during a final session, physical contact should not be a frequent component of a therapy relationship. Social and business relationships are nearly always wrong. In general, be suspicious of any MHP who attempts to engage the parishioner in anything but a professional relationship focused on the parishioner's primary symptom or complaint.

Competence

> *Unethical.* You learn that a member of your congregation, Tim, has been having considerable back pain lately (probably due to his construction job). He says he has already been to a doctor and that he has only been given "pain killers." You decide to refer Tim to a local psychologist who may be able to help with pain management. Six months later, Tim is dead as a result of a large tumor on his spine (the source of his pain). Unfortunately, the psychologist had very little experience or training in pain management and had attempted to treat the pain symptoms without recognizing the potential signs of a tumor. He had not ensured that Tim had a complete physical exam. It turns out that Tim had never seen his physician, but had received some prescriptions over the phone.

> *Ethical.* Dr. Phillips receives a "pain management" referral from a local pastor. He recognizes immediately that he has not had either the training or practice experience necessary to treat pain patients without supervision. He informs the pastor that he would prefer to have the parishioner see a colleague of his with expertise in pain management and whom he trusts to do excellent work. Dr. Phillips provides the referral information to the pastor and then calls his colleague and explains the nature of the referral—emphasizing that the parishioner is devout in his faith and may find treatments that integrate his faith with pain-reduction techniques to be especially useful.

What to Expect

State boards and professional organizations offer licensure and certification of mental health practitioners. This assures the public that practitioners have completed the minimum number of hours of supervised training and have gone through evaluation or screening to ensure minimum competence.[8] However, these bodies do not ensure that MHPs will competently *do* what their credentials permit them to do.

Pastors typically refer parishioners to various MHPs precisely because they recognize the boundaries of their own competence to treat mental disorders. In a similar fashion, they will want to refer to MHPs who also recognize the limits of their competence and are also ready to refer if they lack the expertise to help particular parishioners or those with specific kinds of problems. Ideally, MHPs *only* provide the services and use techniques for which they are qualified by training and experience. Not only are they cognizant of their limitations, but they pursue additional education, experience, professional consultation, and spiritual growth in order to improve their effectiveness in serving people in need.[9]

As a pastor, we recommend that you look for MHPs who sometimes respond to your referrals by saying, "I'm not prepared to treat that sort of problem, but let me give you a couple of names of people I'd recommend." Truly competent professionals only accept client populations and problem types for which they are qualified. Before practicing in a new treatment area, they seek additional training and experience. Competent MHPs do not imply that they have qualifications, experiences, or capabilities which they do not. When it seems to you that a professional suggests that he or she is equally "expert" in treating a wide variety of problems, be very suspicious. Finally, competent MHPs routinely seek peer support and peer review. This means that they have a strong professional network (much like wise pastors who network and seek support from their colleagues); they are willing to remain accountable and seek consultation from other experts when this is indicated.

Confidentiality

Unethical. Concerned that Stuart, a parishioner whom you referred to a pastoral counselor, is looking increasingly sad and withdrawn, you call the counselor to report this change and ask if there is anything else you could do to help. The counselor thanks you for calling and then immediately begins telling you that Stuart has good reason to be "down" as he has been dealing with concerns about his sexual orientation in his counseling sessions. The counselor notes that she thinks Stuart may in fact be gay, but that she needs more time to discern this. You feel startled that this information was disclosed by the counselor so quickly, given that Stuart is a very private person. It is unlikely that Stuart would have signed a release allowing his therapist to discuss his case with you.

Ethical. Nina Brown, a certified pastoral counselor, receives a phone call from the pastor who recently referred a new client to her. He notes that the client has appeared more depressed lately and he is concerned. Ms. Brown thanks the pastor for calling and for referring Stuart to her. She acknowledges that ongoing support from the pastor is likely to be very helpful to Stuart. She kindly thanks him for the referral, but also informs the pastor she is unable to discuss Stuart unless Stuart is willing to sign a formal release of information allowing her to legally and ethically do so. She promises to mention this to Stuart when he comes to see her and reminds the pastor that he can also discuss this with Stuart.

What to Expect

Client *confidentiality* may be the closest thing to "sacred" among all types of MHPs. Confidentiality refers to an ethical—and usually legal—responsibility of MHPs to safeguard clients from unauthorized disclosure of information given in the therapy relationship. With a few exceptions (discussed later), information revealed by clients in the context of treatment must not be disclosed. In general, there will rarely be cause for the MHP working with one of your parishioners to violate the principle of confidentiality and disclose private information. If an MHP does violate a client's confidence (and the reason is not one of those covered below), you should avoid referring your parishioners to that person in the future.

Confidentiality is closely linked to two additional terms that are distinct, but related.[8] *Privileged communication* is a legal concept referring to a client's right to withhold legal testimony (on the part of the MHP) in court proceedings. Most state statutes clearly identify communication between a therapist and client as privileged, and this communication is therefore protected from disclosure in legal settings. *Privacy* is a basic freedom (constitutionally protected) that allows clients to decide when and where they wish to have their beliefs, behavior, and opinions shared or withheld from others. In general, MHPs should work hard to protect the privacy of their clients by making sure that their privileged communication and the ethical mandate for confidentiality are both honored. In addition, MHPs protect privacy by eliciting only that information from the client which is germane to the problem and by documenting only that information which is relevant to treatment. For example, disclosures made by a client about his or her love life should probably not be included in the client record unless they are directly related to the client's disorder and treatment.

When may an MHP violate a client's confidentiality? Ethical guidelines and state laws usually require all MHPs to violate a client's confidence by disclosing information obtained during treatment under the following circumstances:

1. When the client is a clear risk to himself or herself (acutely suicidal) or clearly a risk to others (homicidal)
2. When the client is so disturbed that he or she cannot care for himself or herself—such as in the case of psychosis or head injury
3. When the client has abused a child or elderly person, or if a client or elderly client has been abused
4. When the client takes legal or ethical action against the therapist, the record may be disclosed as part of the therapist's defense
5. When a legitimate court order compels the MHP to release the record.

All exceptions to confidentiality must be fully disclosed to clients before they begin treatment. This is known as *informed consent* and will be discussed in the next section. Keep in mind that these circumstances are relatively rare and that in the vast majority of cases, an MHP would only violate a client's confidence in order to keep him or her alive or to protect the immediate well-being and safety of others who could be harmed by the client.

We highly recommend that you seek out MHPs who are extremely cautious when it comes to protecting the confidentiality of their clients. If an MHP discusses a client before obtaining a signed release from the client, or faxes you copies of the client's evaluations or record, you have reason to be concerned. Although it is admittedly difficult to maintain confidentiality in small communities, including churches, we believe confidentiality is the cornerstone of good mental health treatment. It is true that the pastor can often serve as an important part of the overall treatment plan for parishioners undergoing therapy; however, it is not appropriate for a pastor to hound his or her clients into signing releases to speak with MHPs. We recommend simply letting parishioners know, preferably at the time of referral, that you will be available to assist in any way—including talking with parishioners' therapists if they feel that would be useful. Parishioners can then decide whether or not to involve the pastor in this way.

Informed Consent

Unethical. A twenty-five-year-old parishioner whom you have referred to a psychiatrist for assistance with severe anxiety symptoms approaches you following Sunday services with a bewildered and concerned look on her face. She notes that she was only able to see the psychiatrist for fifteen minutes due to his busy schedule. She pulls a bottle of antianxiety medication from her purse and states that the pills have helped her feel less anxious, but that they make her very drowsy and she is alarmed by some physical sensations that have occurred since starting the medicine. She is not even sure what the medicine is, how it works, or what the side effects are. When you ask what else the treatment might entail, how long it might last, or whether she can contact her psychiatrist on an emergency basis to report the side effects, she is unsure and states that none of these things were addressed in the short first session.

Ethical. Dr. Reed Smith has a busy psychiatry practice and particularly enjoys consulting with clergy. He receives a call from a woman who has been referred for assistance with worsening anxiety symptoms. Given that he has only a fifteen-minute time slot available in the next two days, he offers to refer her to another provider. She insists she is "okay" waiting and schedules a regular ninety-minute intake appointment for three days from now. During the initial session, Dr. Smith does a careful assessment of her physical and psychological functioning. He also provides her with an informed consent form that lists all the parameters of treatment, emergency procedures, limits on confidentiality, and financial information. He discusses each of these issues with her and then describes the treatment options available for her anxiety disorder, including medication. He describes the pros and cons of talking therapy and medication, and the client agrees to try both. He recommends an antianxiety medication and carefully reviews all of the possible side effects with her.

What to Expect

Informed consent refers to a client's right to be informed about the therapy that he or she is to receive and to make independent decisions about it. In order to become active participants in their own mental health treatments, it is critical that parishioners are treated by competent professionals who recognize and honor clients' needs for information about therapy and therapy options. At the most basic level, clients have a right to decide whether to even enter treatment. To make this decision, they must be clearly informed about the treatment options including risks and benefits. When MHPs fail to adequately inform clients about the services they provide, there are two possible legal complications: (1) breach of contract and (2) negligence or malpractice.

When a pastor refers a parishioner to an MHP, it is reasonable to expect that the parishioner will come away from the very first session with a basic understanding of the following:

1. Treatment alternatives for his or her specific problem or disorder
2. Risks and benefits associated with each of the treatment options

3. The MHP's qualifications
4. Financial issues (including billing, bill collection agencies, and fees)
5. Emergency procedures and treatment interruptions
6. Limits on confidentiality
7. What services the MHP will provide and what is expected of the client
8. The anticipated length of treatment
9. Willingness of the MHP to collaborate with clergy if this is requested by the client.

Informed consent is a critical component of competent mental health treatment. Look for MHPs who are careful about providing parishioners with all the information they need to make good decisions about their own treatments without overwhelming them with irrelevant details. It is imperative that parishioners have the capacity to fully understand what MHPs are conveying to them about treatments. In cases where the client is a child or an adult who is psychotic, a legal guardian is often able to provide the informed consent required for mental health care. In the same way that one would want to carefully understand an elective surgery, a parishioner is often most comfortable (and successful) in mental health treatment when he or she actively participates in making decisions about the type and direction of treatment.

Advertising

> *Unethical.* You receive a flyer from Todd Noonan, a new social worker in town. The flyer is a large multicolored advertisement for this man's private practice which states in emphatic tones that Mr. Noonan has a specialty in treating codependence. In fact, he has developed a biblically based "anti-codependence therapy," which he claims is guaranteed to help the 50 to 75 percent of American people who are codependent. His brochure offers several testimonials from actual clients (one of whom attends your church) who claim their lives were radically changed for the better thanks to therapy with Mr. Noonan. The flyer also hints that failing to have this therapy is all but certain to lead to suffering and discontent compared to the "abundant happiness"

available after anti-codependence therapy. Mr. Noonan phones you later in the week and asks if he can announce his new services from the pulpit the following Sunday.

Ethical. A new social worker in the community contacts you to let you know that he is beginning a practice and that he prefers to work with Christian clients when possible. He is interested in meeting with you sometime to discuss his background, special interests, and to explore any specific needs the church might have that he might be able to address. He notes having a special interest in working with dependent clients and clarifies that he means those stuck in unhealthy relational patterns.

What to Expect

Good MHPs are careful to avoid any public statement or advertisement that contains false or deceptive statements. They are very concerned about not misleading or misinforming their clients or the public. Any advertisement or promotion of their practice is tasteful and appropriate. It may include brief information about their credentials, training backgrounds, institutional affiliations, and the kinds of services they are competent to render. They may describe the kinds of clients or disorders with which they have particular expertise. Appropriate and professional advertising is not flashy or otherwise outlandish.

When you see evidence of the following in the promotional materials of MHPs, we recommend that you be very cautious about referring parishioners to them:

1. Promises of marked, though unsubstantiated, positive personal change
2. Suggestions of "one of a kind" or unique therapeutic techniques or abilities
3. Personal aggrandizement
4. Overdiagnosis of problems (e.g., "Nearly everyone is at least a little codependent")
5. Creating fear as a way of generating business (e.g., "If you care about your adolescent, you'll call us today")
6. Use of client testimonials.

All of these techniques involve some misrepresentation or exploitation, and they raise concerns about the integrity and competence of the provider. Finally, we recommend that you watch out for MHPs who attempt to solicit potential clients in person. This is unethical according to most professional organizations[4] and, again, is a possible indicator that these MHPs are attempting to exploit vulnerable populations. In our experience, excellent MHPs are often the most subdued and cautious in their efforts to promote their practices. They do not claim unique abilities and they are clear about the limits of their competence.

Respect for Differences

> *Unethical.* You have met with a couple regarding some marital problems. The husband, Daniel, is Jewish and occasionally attends services at a local synagogue while his Christian spouse attends your church. During their meeting with you, Daniel acknowledges a considerable history of pornography use and compulsive sexual activity which, at times, interferes with his job and responsiveness to his wife. You refer him to a Christian psychologist who happens to specialize in sexual disorders. Two weeks later, Daniel comes to see you in a state of anger. He reports being very offended by the psychologist who, in the first session, insisted on praying with him and attempted to "convert" him to Christianity instead of focusing on his sexual problem. Daniel notes, "He read scriptures from the New Testament and suggested that placing myself under Christ's rule was probably 'just the medicine I needed.' "

> *Ethical.* Dr. Hugh Lucas receives a referral from a local pastor. Dr. Lucas determines in the initial session that the client's primary objective is to curtail and eliminate his use of pornography as well as to reduce his masturbatory activity. Dr. Lucas is a Christian and sensitive to the manner in which the client's religious background and belief may both contribute to his problem and serve as a potential aid to treatment. He asks the client to help him understand sexual concerns of this kind from the perspective

of the Jewish faith and whether the rabbi or others connected with the synagogue might offer support. When the client expresses hesitancy to explore this further, Dr. Lucas reminds him that religious resources are simply one source of support. He moves on to outline a cognitive-behavioral approach to reducing the undesirable sexual behaviors and is careful to secure the client's full consent before proceeding.

What to Expect

Every MHP to whom you may refer parishioners will hold important personal values. Most professional organizations now recognize that it is neither possible nor desirable for MHPs to be "neutral" with respect to values. Instead, therapists should be aware of and clear about their own values and how these values influence their work with clients. Practitioners should be honest about their own value positions without attempting to coerce clients into modifying their own perspectives.

Although it would be ideal for pastors to find a range of MHPs who hold religious and moral values similar to their own and those of the majority of parishioners, this may be difficult in some communities with limited numbers of MHPs. When the pastor cannot find Christian practitioners in his or her community, we recommend looking for MHPs who are congruent and honest about what they believe, who evidence sincere respect for clients' religious values, and who express concern about minimizing the influence of their own values on clients. Excellent MHPs, whether religious or not, are interested in using the client's own values and beliefs to enhance the counseling process and strengthen the client's faith.

When an MHP holds moral or religious values that differ from a client's, he or she should be willing to refer when the value differences lead to any of the following conditions: (1) the MHP is uncomfortable working with the client, (2) the boundaries of the MHP's competence are reached in addressing moral/religious issues, (3) the MHP is unable to remain objective, or (4) the MHP has grave concerns about imposing his or her values on the client.[10] In a nutshell, competent MHPs need not have experienced everything their clients have experienced, or believe or value all that the client does. It is essential, however, that MHPs be cognizant of their own values, sensitive to the differences between themselves and their clients, and willing to refer them to MHPs with more congruent values when this appears likely to be helpful.

A STRATEGY FOR RESPONDING TO UNETHICAL BEHAVIOR

As a pastor, you may be among the first to learn of problematic or clearly unethical behavior on the part of an MHP in the community. We recommend two distinct strategies for responding to this information—depending on how you become aware of it. Unethical MHP behavior described to you by a parishioner/client calls for a very different response than unethical behavior that comes to your attention via other avenues, including your direct experience with the MHP.

Most commonly, a pastor will hear directly from a parishioner that he or she has concerns or questions about a particular MHP's professionalism or conduct. The pastor must remember that respecting the parishioner's right to privacy and confidentiality are paramount concerns and that, in these cases, it is critical to explore the parishioner's concerns while refraining from taking any action independent of the parishioner. In most cases, licensing boards and ethics committees refuse to pursue complaints regarding client care that are not filed directly by the client. When a parishioner discloses ethical concerns about an MHP to you, we recommend the following strategy for responding:

1. Assure the parishioner that you will not violate his or her confidence.
2. Listen carefully to the concerns or questions about the MHP's behavior.
3. Inform the parishioner of your concerns and the nature of any apparent ethical violations. For example, "It sounds like your therapist has had trouble keeping your relationship strictly professional and that she has allowed a dual relationship to develop. Let me tell you why dual relationships are a concern . . ."

4. Describe the range of possible responses available to the parishioner. These include no response, discussion of the concerns with the MHP, termination of the relationship, and, in more serious cases, making a formal complaint to a licensing or ethics board.
5. Provide support and any necessary assistance as the parishioner pursues one or more of these options. This may include providing organizational contact information listed in the table on page 222.
6. If you have good reason to believe that the concerns expressed are valid, you may elect to cease referring parishioners to this MHP. In cases where the parishioner gives you permission to do so, you may also explain to the MHP directly that you have reservations about making additional referrals. This seems to us to be the most Christlike response to the MHP.

For those cases in which you, the pastor, become aware of dubious or troubling MHP behavior without any disclosure by a parishioner or client of the MHP, we recommend a somewhat different approach. Essentially, the pastor has at least three options in such cases and they are not mutually exclusive because one or all of these options may be appropriate in a specific situation. First, the pastor may simply elect to discontinue making referrals to the MHP. For example, a pastor may learn from a colleague that a certain MHP tries to talk clients out of their religious beliefs. In such cases, it may simply be prudent not to make any referrals to this person. Second, the pastor may elect to inform the MHP of his or her concerns in hopes of correcting or clarifying the initial impression or information regarding the MHP's behavior. In this case, the MHP may provide information that allays the pastor's concerns or may appear genuinely surprised by and concerned about his or her oversight or error, and express a clear willingness to correct it at once. Finally, there may be cases in which a pastor elects to file a complaint against an MHP directly. In these cases, the pastor may have attempted to discuss the issue collaboratively with the MHP with no receptivity on his or her part, or the nature of the unethical behavior may be so severe that the pastor feels the MHP's clients may be at significant risk. For example, when a pastor becomes aware that a local MHP routinely requires clients to stop attending church and describes all pastors as "psychotic," or when an MHP refuses to cease outlandish and unethical advertising to Christian clients in the community, the pastor may elect to file a formal ethics complaint with the MHP's state licensing board or primary professional organization.

The addresses and contact numbers in the table on page 222 correspond to each of the major professional organizations covering the majority of MHPs. Although each of these organizations will have a formal ethics panel that reviews and investigates complaints, contacting the state licensing board may be more expeditious. Although we do not have space to list the various licensing boards for each state, these are generally available from the state's professional licensing division. In cases where the state does not license a certain kind of MHP (e.g., many states do not license master's level counselors), then referring the complaint directly to the national organization is recommended. If a state or national board takes action against an MHP, this information will be shared with other professional boards and licensing agencies— meaning that the pastor need not worry about making complaints to multiple bodies.

Contact Information for National Professional Organizations

American Association for Marriage and Family Therapy
    1100 17th St. NW, 10th floor, Washington, DC 20036
    (202) 452-0109

American Association of Pastoral Counselors
    9504-A Lee Highway, Fairfax, VA 22031-2303
    (703) 385-6967

American Counseling Association
    5999 Stevenson Ave. Alexandria, VA 22304-3300
    (703) 823-9800

American Psychiatric Association
    1400 K St. NW, Washington, DC 20005
    (202) 682-6000

American Psychological Association
    750 First St. NE, Washington, DC 20002-4242
    (202) 336-5500

National Association of Social Workers
    750 First St. NE, Suite 700, Washington, DC 20002-4241
    (202) 408-8600

National Board of Certified Counselors
    3-D Terrace Way, Greensboro, NC 27403
    (910) 547-0607

Notes

Chapter 1

1. Benner, D. (1992). *Strategic pastoral counseling: A short-term structural model.* Grand Rapids, MI: Baker Book House.

Chapter 2

1. American Psychiatric Association (1994). *Diagnostic and statistical manual of mental disorders,* Fourth edition. Washington, DC: Author.

2. Robins, L. N. and Regier, D. A. (Eds.) (1991). *Psychiatric disorders in America.* New York: Free Press.

3. Benner, D. (1992). *Strategic pastoral counseling: A short-term structural model.* Grand Rapids, MI: Baker Book House.

4. Kessler, R. C., McGonagle, K. A., Ahzo, S., Nelson, C. H., Hughes, M., Eshleman, S., Wittchen, H., and Kendler, K. S. (1994). Lifetime and 12-month prevalence of DSM-III-R psychiatric disorders in the United States: Results from the National Comorbidity Study. *Archives of General Psychiatry, 51,* 8-19.

5. Beck, A. T. and Emory, G. (1985). *Anxiety disorders and phobias: A cognitive perspective.* New York: Basic Books.

6. Bowlby, J. (1980). *Attachment and loss, III: Loss, sadness, and depression.* New York: Basic Books.

7. Ciarrocchi, J. W. (1993). *A minister's handbook of mental disorders.* New York: Paulist Press.

8. Roukema, R. W. (1997). *The soul in distress.* Binghamton, NY: The Haworth Press.

9. Reiger, D. A., Narrow, W. E., Rae, D. S., Manderscheid, R. W., Locke, B. Z., and Goodwin, F. K. (1993). The de facto U.S. mental and addictive disorders service system: Epidemiologic catchment area prospective 1-year prevalence rates of disorders and services. *Archives of General Psychiatry, 50,* 85-94.

10. Swanson, D. W., Bohnert, P. J., and Smith, J. A. (1970). *The paranoid.* Boston: Little, Brown.

11. Fisher, J. E. and Carstensen, L. L. (1990). Behavior management for the dementias. *Clinical Psychology Review, 10,* 611-630.

12. Luckasson, R., Coulter, D. L., Polloway, E. A., Reiss, S., Schalock, R. L., Snell, M. E., Spitalnik, D. M., and Stark, J. A. (1992). *Mental retardation: Definition, classification, and systems of supports,* Ninth edition. Washington, DC: American Association on Mental Retardation.

Chapter 3

1. Kessler, R. C., McGonagle, K. A., Ahzo, S., Nelson, C. H., Hughes, M., Eshleman, S., Wittchen, H., and Kendler, K. S. (1994). Lifetime and 12-month prevalence of DSM-III-R psychiatric disorders in the United States: Results from the National Comorbidity Study. *Archives of General Psychiatry, 51,* 8-19.
2. Robins, L. N. and Regier, D. A. (Eds.) (1991). *Psychiatric disorders in America.* New York: Free Press.
3. American Psychiatric Association. (1994). *Diagnostic and statistical manual of mental disorders,* Fourth edition. Washington, DC: Author.
4. Toufexis, A. (1990). Drowsy America. *Time,* December 17, pp. 78-85.
5. Roth, T. (1995). An overview of the report of the commission on sleep disorders research. *European Psychiatry, 10,* 109-113.
6. Masters, W. H. and Johnson, V. E. (1966). *Human sexual response.* Boston: Little, Brown.
7. Diokno, A. C., Brown, M. B., and Herzog, A. R. (1990). Sexual function in the elderly. *Archives of Internal Medicine, 150,* 197-200.

Chapter 4

1. American Psychiatric Association (1994). *Diagnostic and statistical manual of mental disorders,* Fourth edition. Washington, DC: Author.
2. Vaughan, R. P. (1994). *Pastoral counseling and personality disorders.* Kansas City, MO: Sheed and Ward.
3. Fong, M. L. (1995). Assessment and DSM-IV diagnosis of personality disorders: A primer for counselors. *Journal of Counseling and Development, 73,* 635-639.
4. Weismann, M. M. (1993). The epidemiology of personality disorders: A 1990 update. *Journal of Personality Disorders, 7, Supplement,* 44-62.
5. Lively, W. J., Jang, K. L., Jackson, D. N., and Vernon, P. A. (1993). Genetic and environmental contributions to dimensions of personality disorders. *American Journal of Psychiatry, 150,* 1826-1831.
6. Millon, T. (1996). *Disorders of personality: DSM-IV and beyond.* New York: Wiley.

Chapter 5

1. Zill, N. and Schoenborn, G. A. (1990). Developmental, learning, and emotional problems: Health of our nation's children. *Advanced data: National Center for Health Statistics.* Hyattsville, MD (Number 190).
2. Institute of Medicine (1989). *Research on children and adolescents with mental, behavioral, and developmental disorders.* Washington, DC: National Academy Press.
3. Verhulst, F. C. and Koot, H. M. (1992). *Child psychiatric epidemiology: Concepts, methods, and findings.* Beverly Hills, CA: Sage.

4. American Psychiatric Association (1994). *Diagnostic and statistical manual of mental disorders,* Fourth edition. Washington, DC: Author.

5. House of Representatives (1990). *No place to call home: Discarded children in America. A report of the select committee on children, youth, and families.* Washington, DC: U.S. Government Printing Office.

6. Straus, M. A. and Gelles, R. J. (1990). *Physical violence in American families: Risk factors and adaptations to violence in 8,145 families.* New Brunswick, NJ: Transaction Publishers.

7. American Academy of Child and Adolescent Psychiatry (1991). Practice parameters for the assessment and treatment of attention deficit hyperactivity disorder. *Journal of the American Academy of Child and Adolescent Psychiatry, 30,* 1-111.

8. Quay, H. C. and Hegan, A. E. (1999). *Handbook of disruptive behavior disorders.* New York: Kluwer Academic publishers.

9. Wells, K. C. and Egan, J. (1988). Social learning and systems family therapy for childhood oppositional disorder: Comparative treatment outcome. *Comprehensive Psychiatry, 29,* 138-146.

10. National Clearinghouse on Child Abuse and Neglect (1999). *Definitions of Child Abuse and Neglect.* Washington, DC: Author.

11. U.S. Department of Health and Human Services (1988). *Child maltreatment 1996: Reports from the states to the National Child Abuse and Neglect Data System.* Washington, DC: U.S. Government Printing Office.

12. Belsky, J. (1993). Etiology of child maltreatment: A developmental-ecological analysis. *Psychological Bulletin, 114,* 427.

13. Holtzworth-Munroe, A. (1995). Marital violence. *The Harvard Mental Health Letter,* August.

Chapter 7

1. Carson, R. C., Butcher, J. N., and Mineka, S. (1996). *Abnormal psychology and modern life,* Tenth edition. New York: HarperCollins.

2. Ellis, A. (1970). *Reason and emotion in psychotherapy.* New York: Lyle Stuart.

3. Garfield, S. L. (1994). Research on client variables in psychotherapy. In A. E. Bergin and S. L. Garfield (Eds.), *Handbook of psychotherapy and behavior change,* Fourth edition (pp. 190-228). New York: Wiley.

4. Lambert, M. J. and Bergin, A. E. (1994). The effectiveness of psychotherapy. In A. E. Bergin and S. L. Garfield (Eds.), *Handbook of psychotherapy and behavior change,* Fourth edition (pp. 143-189). New York: Wiley.

5. Smith, M. L., Glass, G. V., and Miller, T. I. (1980). *The benefits of psychotherapy.* Baltimore: Johns Hopkins University Press.

6. *Consumer Reports* (1995). Mental health: Does therapy help? November, 734-739.

7. Jones, S. L. and Butman, R. E. (1991). *Modern psychotherapies: A comprehensive Christian appraisal.* Downers Grove, IL: InterVarsity Press.

8. Johnson W. B. and Johnson, W. L. (1997). Can counseling be Christian? *Christian Counseling Today, 5* (15), 52-53.

9. American Psychiatric Association (1994). *Diagnostic and statistical manual of mental disorders,* Fourth edition. Washington, DC: Author.

10. Anastasi, A. (1988). *Psychological testing,* Sixth edition. New York: Macmillan.

11. Buros Institute for Mental Measurement (1994). *Tests in print,* Fourth edition. Lincoln, NE: Author.

12. Buros Institute for Mental Measurement (1998). *Mental measurement yearbook,* Thirteenth edition. Lincoln, NE: author.

13. Maris, R. W., Berman, A. L., Maltsberger, J. T., and Yufit, R. I. (1992). *Assessment and prediction of suicide.* New York: Guilford Press.

14. Wolpe, J. (1990). *Behavior therapy,* Fourth edition. New York: Pergamon.

15. Corsini, R. J. and Wedding, D. (1995). *Current psychotherapies,* Fifth edition. Itasca, IL: Peacock.

16. Gottman, J. (1994). *Why marriages succeed or fail.* New York: Simon and Schuster.

17. Haley, J. (1962). Whither family therapy. *Family Process, 1,* 69-100.

18. Medical Economics Data Production Company (1999). *Physician's desk reference,* Fifty-third edition. Montvale, NJ: Author.

19. Baker, J. P. (1994). Outcome of lithium discontinuation: A metal-analysis. *Lithium, 5,* 187-192.

20. Crasilneck, H. B. and Hall, J. A. (1985). *Clinical hypnosis: Principles and applications,* Second edition. New York: Grune and Stratton.

21. McKonkey, K. M. (1995). Hypnosis, memory, and the ethics of uncertainty. *Australian Psychologist, 30,* 1-10.

22. Bowers, K. S. and Le Baron, S. (1986). Hypnosis and hypnotizability: Implications for clinical intervention. *Hospital and Community Psychiatry, 37,* 457-467.

23. Morris, F. (1982). *ECT: A clinical guide.* New York: Wiley.

24. Peck, M. S. (1977). *The road less traveled.* New York: Simon and Schuster.

Chapter 8

1. Stevens, M. J. and Pfost, K. S. (1982). Bibliotherapy: Medicine for the soul? *Psychology: A Quarterly Journal of Human Behavior, 19,* 21-29.

2. Shapiro, L. (1987). Advice givers strike gold. *Newsweek,* June, 64-65.

3. Glasgow, R. E. and Rosen, G. M. (1978). Behavioral bibliotherapy: A review of self-help behavior therapy manuals. *Psychological Bulletin, 85,* 1-23.

4. Pardeck, J. T. (1991). Using books in clinical practice. *Psychotherapy in Private Practice, 9,* 105-119.

5. Halliday, G. (1991). Psychological self-help books—How dangerous are they? *Psychotherapy, 28,* 678-680.

6. Giblin, P. (1989). Use of reading assignments in clinical practice. *American Journal of Family Therapy, 17,* 219-228.

7. Marx, J. A., Gyorky, Z. K., Royalty, G. M., and Stern, T. E. (1992). Use of self-help books in psychotherapy. *Professional Psychology: Research and Practice, 23,* 300-305.

8. Santrock, J. W., Minnett, A. M., and Campbell, B. D. (1994). *The authoritative guide to self-help books.* New York: Guilford.

9. Smith, D. and Burkhalter, J. K. (1987). The use of bibliotherapy in clinical practice. *Journal of Mental Health Counseling, 9,* 184-190.

10. Starker, S. (1986). Promises and prescriptions: Self-help books in mental health and medicine. *American Journal of Health Promotion, 1,* 19-24.

11. Starker, S. (1988). Do-it-yourself therapy: The prescription of self-help books by psychologists. *Psychotherapy, 25,* 142-146.

12. Starker, S. (1988). Psychologists and self-help books: Attitudes and prescriptive practices of clinicians. *American Journal of Psychotherapy, 42,* 448-455.

13. Ellis, A. (1993). The advantages and disadvantages of self-help therapy materials. *Professional Psychology: Research and Practice, 24,* 335-359.

14. Kaminer, W. (1993). *I'm dysfunctional, you're dysfunctional: The recovery movement and other self-help fashions.* New York: Vintage Books.

15. Becvar, R. J. (1978). Self-help books: Some ethical questions. *Personnel and Guidance Journal, 57,* 160-162.

16. Johnson, W. B. and Johnson, W. L. (1998). Self-help books used by religious practitioners. *Journal of Counseling and Development, 76,* 459-466.

17. Johnson, W. B., Johnson, W. L., and Hillman, C. (1997). Toward guidelines for the development, evaluation, and utilization of Christian self-help materials. *Journal of Psychology and Theology, 25,* 341-353.

Chapter 9

1. American Association for Counseling and Development (1988). *Ethical standards,* Revised edition. Alexandria, VA: Author.

2. American Association for Marriage and Family Therapy (1991). *AAMFT code of ethics.* Washington DC: Author.

3. American Association of Pastoral Counselors (1994). *Code of ethics.* Fairfax, VA: Author.

4. American Psychological Association (1992). Ethical principles of psychologists and code of conduct. *American Psychologist, 47,* 1597-1611.

5. National Association of Social Workers (1990). *Code of ethics.* Washington, DC: Author.

6. Blackburn, B. (1997). Pastors who counsel. In R. K. Sanders (Ed.), *Christian counseling ethics: A handbook for therapists, pastors and counselors* (pp. 75-85). Downers Grove, IL: InterVarsity Press.

7. Kitchener, K. S. (1984). Intuition, critical evaluation and ethical principles: The foundation for ethical decisions in counseling psychology. *The Counseling Psychologist, 12,* 43-55.

8. Corey, G., Corey, M. S., and Callanan, P. (1993). *Issues and ethics in the helping professions,* Fourth edition. Pacific Grove, CA: Brooks/Cole.

9. Christian Association for Psychological Studies (1992). *Ethical Guidelines.* New Braunfels, TX: Author.

10. Tjeltveit, A. C. (1986). The ethics of value conversion in psychotherapy: Appropriate and inappropriate therapist influence on client values. *Clinical Psychology Review, 6,* 515-537.

Index

Abandonment, 91, 116-119
Abdominal pain, 12
Abuse, 48, 124-129, 212
Academic performance, 109-110, 115
Accidents, 34-35, 42
Acrophobia, 11
Addictions, 49-50. *See also*
    Codependency; Food;
    Substances
ADHD (attention deficit
    hyperactivity disorder),
    108-111, 162
Adjustment disorders, 20-21
Admiration, need for, 87
Adolescents, 107-108, 112, 119-124
Adopted children, 115
Adultery, 195
Affect, 18
Age factors
    and conduct disorder, 114-115
    and mood disorders, 19, 181
    and organic brain damage, 34, 36
    and personality disorders, 94
    and psychotic disorders, 25, 27, 28
    and separation anxiety, 118
    and sexual disorders, 67-68, 72
    and sleep disorders, 62-63
    and substance use, 55
    and suicide, 150, 181
    and traumatic event, 46
Aggression, 15, 112, 115
Agitation, 14, 22, 27
Agoraphobia, 13-14
Alcohol
    abuse, 53
    community support, 56-57
    gender factors, 19

Alcohol *(continued)*
    and PTSD, 43
    and sleep, 60
    treatment programs, 176-178
Alcoholics Anonymous, 162-163, 177
Aloofness, 75, 80, 97
Alprazolam, 169
Alters, 46-47
Alzheimer's disease, 36-37
Amitriptyline, 178
Amnesia, 35, 43, 45
    dissociative, 46
Amphetamines, 54
Anger, 78-79, 91, 115, 127
Anger management, 162
Animals, 115
Anorexia nervosa, 120-121, 178-179
Anticonvulsants, 172
Antisocial personality disorder, 75, 93-96
Anxiety
    definition, 16
    and head injury, 35
    and maladaptive persons, 82
    and personality types, 75-76
    recommended reading, 188-189, 197
    and sexual performance, 67
    and sleep, 59-60, 64
    social, 97
    and substance use, 55
    therapy, 168, 169-170, 180
    and traumatic event, 43, 45
Anxiety disorders. *See also*
    Separation anxiety disorder
    agoraphobia, 13-14
    and behavioral therapy, 154-155

Anxiety disorders *(continued)*
  in children, 116-119
  and eating disorders, 122
  guidelines, 16-17
  panic disorders, 12-13, 118
  phobias, 10-12
  presenting complaints, 8
  symptoms, 8-10
Anxiolytics, 169
Apathy, 34, 80
Approval-seeking, 100
Arousal, 45, 48, 61. *See also* Sexual
    disorders
Arrogance, 89-90
Assertiveness, 162
Assertiveness training, 162
Assessment, 144-146, 149-150. *See
    also* Testing
Athletes, 180
Attention deficit hyperactivity
    disorder, 108-111, 162
Attention span, 109-110
Attention-seeking, 85
Authority, 95, 112
Aversion therapy, 155
Avoidance, 9, 10
  post-traumatic, 43, 44, 45
  of sex, 66, 67, 69
Avoidant personality disorder, 75-76,
    96-99

Barbiturates, 54-55, 60
Beck, Aaron, 156
Bed-wetting, 155
Behavior
  addictive, 49-50
  attention-seeking, 85
  childlike, 36
  clinging, 99, 117, 127
  dangerous, 55
  irresponsible, 23, 50-51, 54, 94
  of maladaptive persons, 82-83
  manipulative, 75, 86, 94, 96, 115
  in organic brain disorder, 34

Behavior *(continued)*
  in psychotic disorders, 28-29, 32
  submissive, 117
  unethical, 219-221
Behavior therapy, 153-155, 156, 178
Behavioral therapy, 16, 114
Beliefs, 156
Belligerence, 94
Benzodiazepines, 169
Bereavement, 21, 31, 119, 162
  recommended reading, 189
Binging, 91, 121
Bipolar disorder, 18, 19, 23-24, 25,
    171-172
Books
  Christian-oriented, 188-191
  evaluating, 190-201
  self-help, 184-187, 192-201
Borderline personality disorder, 75,
    90-93
Boundaries, 193, 206-209
Bourne, Edmund, 197
Bradshaw, John, 192-193
Bragging, 88
Brain, 58
Brain injury, 34
Brain tumor, 35, 64
Breathing, 9, 64
Bridges, 13
Brief psychotic disorder, 31-32
Bulimia nervosa, 121-124, 178-179
Bupropion, 168
Buspirone, 169-170

Caffeine, 60
Campbell, Ross, 195-196
Carbamazepine, 172
Caretakers, 39
Celebrities, 30
Change, 36, 103, 157. *See also*
    Adjustment disorders
Chest pain, 12
Child abuse, 125-127, 212
  history of, 48

Children. *See also* Pedophilia
   ADHD, 108-111
   adopted, 115
   and behavioral therapy, 155
   conduct disorder, 94, 111,
      112-113, 114-116
   ODD, 111-114
   recommended reading, 189
   separation anxiety disorder, 116-119
Chills, 9, 12
Chlorpromazine, 173
Christian counseling, 188-196, 199,
   217-219
Claustrophobia, 11
Client-centered psychotherapy, 157
Cloud, Henry, 193
Clozapine, 174
Cocaine, 54
Codependency, 198-199
Cognitive therapy, 12, 14, 156-157
Cognitive-behavioral therapy, 16-17,
   155-157, 177
Combat, 42, 43, 46
Communication
   between pastoral staff, 96
   and organic brain disorder, 34
   and personality disorders, 81, 82
   and psychotic disorders, 28
   skill acquisition, 162
Community support
   abuse awareness, 127, 129
   for retarded persons, 39
   for schizophrenic persons, 32
   self-help groups, 163
   and social workers, 133
   for substance users, 56
Comprehension, 54. *See also*
   Rational processes
Compulsions, 15. *See also*
   Paraphilias
Concentration
   and anxiety, 14
   and mood disorders, 20, 22, 23
   and substance use, 51
   and trauma, 35, 44

Conduct disorder, 94, 111, 112-113,
   114-116
Confidentiality, 211-213, 219
Conflict, 91, 113. *See also*
   Disagreement
Conscience, 95
Consent, 212-215
Control
   and boundaries, 193
   of emotions, 35, 36
   fear of losing, 12, 14
   of impulses, 53
   of muscles, 36
   and personality disorders, 103
   resistance to, 78
   self-, 56
Coping techniques, 73
Corsini, R. J., 158
Counseling. *See* Christian
   counseling; Psychotherapy
Counselors, 133-134, 142
Counting, 15
Couples therapy, 158-160
Criminal activity, 54, 94
Cross-dressing, 71
Crowds, 13
Cruelty, 115

Danger
   and confidentiality, 212
   feelings of, 9, 15, 42
   and hospitalization, 175, 178
   of maladaptive persons, 80
   and psychedelic drugs, 55
   of schizophrenics, 28
Darkness, 11, 117
Daydreaming, 28
Dazed feeling, 45
Death, 9, 12, 21-22, 119. *See also*
   Bereavement; Grief;
   Post-traumatic stress
   disorder; Suicide
Deceitfulness, 93, 112
Decision-making, 22, 99

Defiance, 112
Delegation, 103
Delusional disorder, 29-31, 78
Delusions, 22, 28
Dementia, 34, 36-37
Dependent personality disorder,
     75-76, 99-102
Depersonalization disorder, 46
Depression. *See also* Mood disorders
     in children, 107-108, 127
     and eating disorders, 122
     major, 21-23
     mild, 19-21
     and personality disorders, 90
     recommended reading, 189,
          194-195
     and sleep, 59, 60
     and substance use, 51, 54, 56
     and suicide, 150
     testing for, 149
     therapy, 162, 165-168, 181
Desensitization, 154-155
Destructiveness, 115
Detachment
     in children, 127
     and panic disorder, 12
     and personality types, 75, 79-84
     and psychotics, 26-27
     as religious experience, 32
     and traumatic event, 45
Details, 8, 103
Developmental disabilities. *See*
     Mental retardation
Diagnosis, 144-146, 182. *See also*
     Testing
Diazepam, 169
DID (dissociative identity disorder),
     46-48, 182
Diet pills, 122
Disagreement, 100
Disasters, 42, 46
Discipline, 125
Disclosure, 208-209
Disorganized schizophrenia, 28-29
Disruptiveness, 23-24

Dissociative fugue, 46
Dissociative identity disorder, 46-48,
     182
Disulfiram, 177
Divalproex sodium, 172
Divorce, 159, 162
Dizziness, 9, 35, 54
Dogmatism, 78-79, 103
Domestic violence, 125-129
Downers, 54
Dramatization, 86
Dread, 9
Dreams, 44, 152. *See also*
     Nightmares
Driving, 91
Drugs, 31-32, 43. *See also*
     Medication; Substances
Dry mouth, 9
DSM-IV, 7, 59, 73
Dyspareunia, 69-70
Dyssomnias, 59-61
Dysthymia, 19-20

Eating, 11, 20, 22, 51. *See also* Food;
     Weight
Eating disorders, 119-124, 178-179
Eccentricity, 75, 82
Eclectic psychotherapy, 158
ECT (electroconvulsive therapy), 25,
     181
Egocentrism, 88
Elation, 18
Electroconvulsive therapy, 25, 181
Ellis, Albert, 141, 156
Embarrassment, 13, 24, 97
Emotional abuse, 125
Emotions
     and brain damage, 35, 36
     and mood disorders, 18
     and personality disorder, 80, 85,
          90
     and psychotic disorders, 27-29
     recommended reading, 190
     and traumatic event, 45

Empathy, 87, 88
Encounter groups, 182
Endocrine abnormality, 60, 64
Entitlement, sense of, 88
Envy, 88
Erectile dysfunction, 67-68, 155
Erotomania, 30
Euphoria, 23, 54, 56, 90
Exaggeration, 86
Exercise, excessive, 122
Exhibitionism, 71
Exploitativeness, 94
Extinction, 154
Eysenck, Hans, 141-142

Fads, 182
Faintness, 12
Family. *See also* Children
    abuse, 48, 124-129, 212
    of ADHD children, 111, 162
    of dementia patients, 37
    and eating disorders, 123
    of maladaptive persons, 90
    of mentally retarded children, 39
    of ODD children, 113
    of psychotic persons, 32
    recommended reading, 189,
        192-193
    referrals by, 22
    of substance users, 52, 56
Family therapy, 160-161, 179
Fantasy, 28, 82, 88
Fasting, 122
Fatigue
    and anxiety, 14
    and head injury, 35
    and mood disorders, 20, 22
    and sleep, 60
    and substance use, 51
Fear. *See also* Phobias
    of abandonment, 91, 116-119
    in advertising, 216
    of being alone, 100
    of darkness, 117

Fear *(continued)*
    of death, 9, 12
    distress about, 10
    of embarrassment, 9, 11, 13
    of evaluation, 98
    of impending danger, 9, 15
    of losing control, 12, 14
    of nightmares, 61
    of panic attacks, 12-13
    and personality types, 75-76
    post-traumatic, 42
    of rejection, 14, 97
    of sinning, 104
    and sleep disorders, 61, 62
Fetishism, 71
Fickleness, 90-91
Fires, 115
Flashbacks, 45, 55
Floating sensation, 56
Flooding, 154
Focused therapy groups, 162
Food, 50, 120, 121
Forgetfulness, 34
Forgiveness, 79
Free association, 152
Freud, Sigmund, 151-152
Frigidity, 67-68
Frotteurism, 71
Fugue, 46

GAD (generalized anxiety disorder),
    14
Gambling, 91
Gender factors. *See also* Men;
        Women
    and abuse, 126
    and childhood disorders, 107, 112,
        114
    and mood disorders, 18-19
    recommended reading, 190
    and suicide, 150
Generalized anxiety disorder, 14
Germs, 11, 15, 154
Giggling, 28

Goal-directed activity, 23, 28. *See also* Motivation
Gottman, John, 159
Grandiosity, 30, 87-89
Gray, John, 196-197
Grief, 194. *See also* Bereavement
Grimacing, 173
Group therapy, 161-163, 177, 179
Grudges, 78-79
Guilt
    and depression, 22
    of family, 32, 111
    therapy for, 157
    and trauma history, 44

Hallucinations, 28, 54
Hallucinogens, 55
Hand washing, 15
Harley, Willard, 195
Head injuries, 34-36, 60
Headaches, 35, 54
Healing powers, 83
Heart rate, 9, 12, 61, 62
Heights, 11
Helplessness, 42
Hemfelt, Robert, 198-199
Hendrix, Harville, 193-194
Heroin, 53
Histrionic personality disorder, 75, 84-86, 88
Holy Spirit, 144
Hopelessness, 20, 150
Horror, 42
Hospitalization, 174-176, 178-179
Hostility, 112
Hot flashes, 9, 12
House, inability to leave. *See* Agoraphobia
Household items, saving, 103
Humanistic psychotherapy, 157
Humiliation, 9, 11, 97. *See also* Embarrassment; Paraphilias
Hydroxyzine, 170
Hygiene, personal, 26, 36, 80

Hyperactivity, 108-111
Hypersensitivity, 78
Hypnosis, 47, 179-180
Hypnotics, 170

Identity, 46, 91, 107
Illness, 22, 30
Imagery, 154
Impartiality, 159, 160
Implosive therapy, 154
Impulsivity, 53, 75, 91, 94, 150. *See also* Attention deficit hyperactivity disorder; Conduct disorder
Inadequacy, 97
Independence, 77-78
Individual psychotherapy
    description, 139-141
    effectiveness, 141-143
    individual, 151-158
Informed consent, 212-215
Initiative, 34, 100
Insomnia, 59-60
Instability, 90-91
Intelligence tests, 147-148
Intenseness, 90
Interpersonal interaction, 73, 190. *See also* Group therapy; Relationships
Introverts, 162
Irresponsible behavior, 23, 50-51, 54, 94
Irritability, 14, 23, 35, 44

Jealousy, 29-30
Judgment, 34, 35, 36, 53

Language impairment, 34
Laxatives, 122
Learning difficulty, 34, 36, 115. *See also* Attention deficit hyperactivity disorder

Legal issues
  and mental health professionals,
      212, 214
  and paraphilias, 71
  and personality types, 75
  and substance use, 54
Licensing, 132, 210, 219, 222
Lines, 13
Lithium, 25, 171-172
Loners, 80, 97
Long-term groups, 161-162
LSD, 55

Magical thinking, 83
Maladaptive persons. *See* Personality
      disorders
Mania, 17, 18, 23, 171-172
Manipulativeness, 75, 86, 94, 96, 115
Mannerisms, 29
MAOIs, 167
Marijuana, 55-56
Marital therapy, 158-160
Marriage
  affairs, 195
  divorce predictors, 158
  recommended reading, 190,
      193-194
  and sexual disorders, 72
  and substance use, 50, 54
Maslow, Abraham, 157
Masochism, 71
McGee, Robert, 198
Medication
  for ADHD, 111
  for alcoholics, 177
  antidepressant, 16, 165-168, 178
  antipsychotic, 29, 32, 173-174
  for anxiety, 16, 168, 169-170
  background, 163-165
  for DID, 47
  for mood disorders, 19, 24-25, 72,
      171-172
  and psychiatrists, 133
  for PTSD, 44

Medication *(continued)*
  sexual effects, 72
  and suicide, 166-167
Meier, Paul, 194-195, 198-199
Memory. *See also* Dissociative
      identity disorder
  and hypnosis, 180
  and organic brain damage, 34, 35,
      36
  and PTSD, 44
  and substance use, 54, 56
Men
  personality disorders, 95, 101
  sexual disorders, 67-69, 70-71
  uniqueness, 195, 196-197
  wife beater profile, 128
Mental abuse, 125
Mental health professionals
  advertising, 215-217
  competence, 209-210
  complaints, 219-221
  confidentiality, 211-213, 219
  dual relationships, 206-209
  ethics, 204-206
  feedback about, 158-159, 219
  and hypnosis, 180
  informed consent, 212-25
  organizations, 222
  religious orientation, 143-144,
      217-219
  and suicide risk, 150
  types, 134-137
  and values, 217-219
Mental retardation, 34, 37-39
Milieu therapy, 175
Minirth, Frank, 194-195, 198-199
Miserliness, 104
Modeling, 98, 150, 155
Monoamine oxidase inhibitors, 167
Mood disorders. *See also* Depression
  adjustment disorders, 20-21
  bipolar, 18, 19, 23-24, 25, 171-172
  and borderline personality, 92
  dysthymia, 19-20
  guidelines, 24-25

Mood disorders *(continued)*
  and head injury, 35
  presenting complaints, 17-18
  and sleep, 59
  and substance use, 51, 54, 55, 56
  symptoms, 18-19
Moodiness, 90
Morphine, 53
Motivation, 36
Motor functioning, 27, 37, 54, 173
Movement disorders, 14, 179
Multiple personalities. *See*
      Dissociative identity disorder
Muscles, 14, 36
Mysophobia, 11

Narcissistic personality disorder, 75,
      87-90
Narcotics, 53
Narcotics Anonymous, 177
Natural disasters, 42
Nausea, 9
Neediness, 99-100
Nefazadone, 168
Neglect, 125
Neuroleptics, 173
Neurotransmitters, 19, 24, 27
Nightmares, 45, 61
Numbness, 12, 43, 45
Nyctophobia, 11

Obsessions, 15
Obsessive-compulsive disorders,
      15-16
Obsessive-compulsive personality
      disorder, 75-76, 102-105
OCD (obsessive-compulsive
      disorders), 15-16
ODD (oppositional defiant disorder),
      111-114
Oppositional defiant disorder,
      111-114

Order, preoccupation with, 15
Organic brain damage. *See*
      Dementia; Head injuries;
      Mental retardation

Pacing, 9
Pain, 53, 180
Palpitations, 12, 61
Panic, 9, 10, 11
  definition, 16
Panic disorder, 12-13, 118
Paranoid disorder. *See* Delusional
      disorder
Paranoid personality disorder, 75,
      77-79
Paranoid schizophrenia, 28, 78
Paraphilias, 66, 70-71
Parasomnias, 59, 61-63
Parenting. *See also* Child abuse
  and childhood disorders, 113-114,
      116, 118-119
  group support, 162
  recommended reading, 189,
      195-196
Passivity, 76, 80
Pedophilia, 71
Penner, Clifford, 197-198
Penner, Joyce, 197-198
Perception, 34, 82-83, 121
Perfectionists, 102-105
Performance enhancement, 180
Persecution, 30
Personal development, 190
Personality, 72, 73
Personality disorders
  antisocial, 75, 93-96
  avoidant, 75-76, 96-99
  borderline, 75, 90-93
  definition, 73-74
  dependent, 75-76, 99-102
  and eating disorders, 122
  histrionic, 75, 84-86, 88
  narcissistic, 75, 87-90
  obsessive-compulsive, 75-76,
      102-105

Personality disorders *(continued)*
  paranoid, 75, 77-79
  schizoid, 75, 79-81
  schizotypal, 75, 81-84
  symptoms, 74
Personality tests, 148
Phenothiazines, 173
Phobias. *See also* Agoraphobia
  and behavioral therapy, 155
  social, 11-12, 97
  specific, 10-11
Physical abuse, 91, 125
Planning ability, 37
Pleasurable activities, 21, 23
Positive reinforcement, 155
Postpartum psychotic disorder, 31
Post-traumatic stress disorder, 43-44,
  62
Powers, religious, 83
Praying, 15-16
Premature ejaculation, 68
Primal scream therapy, 182
Pro bono work, 137
Problem solving, 36
Professional organizations, 222
Promiscuity, 95, 122
Psychedelic drugs, 55
Psychiatrists, 132-133, 175-176
Psychic powers, 83
Psychoanalysis, 151-152
Psychodynamic therapy, 152-153
Psychological assessment, 144-146
Psychologists, 132, 137
Psychosis, 26, 55
Psychotherapy
  family, 160-161
  group, 161-163
  individual, 139-143, 151-158
  marital, 158-160
Psychotic disorders
  brief, 31-32
  delusional disorder, 29-31
  presenting complaints, 25-26
  schizophrenia, 27-29
  symptoms, 26-27
  therapy, 173-174

PTSD (post-traumatic stress
  disorder), 43-44, 62
Punishment, 22, 125, 155

Rage, 23
Rape, 42
Rational processes, 53. *See also*
  Comprehension
Rational-emotive behavior therapy,
  156
Reality, 26, 82, 86. *See also*
  Unreality
Recklessness, 91
Recognition, 37, 88
Referrals. *See also* Mental health
  professionals
  for DID, 47
  to emergency room, 84
  by family, 22
  and feedback, 158-159
  to parishioners, 208
  to physicians, 13-14, 16, 24, 35,
    39, 64, 70, 72
  to psychiatrists, 84, 111, 175-176
  for sexual disorders, 72
  for social services, 37, 39
  tactful, 76, 98-99
Reinforcement, 154
Rejection, fear of, 14, 97
Relationship problems, 153, 162
Relationships. *See also* Interpersonal
  interaction
  of maladaptive persons, 79, 80-81,
    83-84, 85-86, 90-91, 95, 97,
    100
  with mental health professional,
    206-209
  recommended reading, 190-191
  and social phobia, 97
Repetition, 15
Resistance, 152
Restlessness, 14, 51, 54
Rigidity, 103

Rogers, Carl, 157
Romantic involvement, 208
Runaways, 115

Sadism, 71
Satanic rituals, 182
Schizoid personality disorder, 75,
     79-81
Schizophrenia, 27-29, 173
Schizotypal personality disorder, 75,
     81-84
School performance, 109-110, 115
Scripture, 144, 198, 199
Seductiveness, 85, 86
Selective serotonin reuptake
     inhibitors, 24, 167
Self-actualization, 157, 190
Self-aggrandizement, 88
Self-care, 28
Self-control, 53, 56
Self-criticism, 157
Self-disclosure, 98
Self-esteem, 22, 97, 127, 157. *See
     also* Bradshaw, John;
     Grandiosity; McGee, Robert
Self-help
   books, 184-187, 192-201
   description, 183-184
   evaluation, 199-201
   groups, 162-163, 177
Self-image, 90, 91
Self-importance, 87
Self-mutilation, 91
Self-righteousness, 79
Sensory perception, 55
Separation anxiety disorder, 116-119
Sexual abuse, 125
Sexual acting out, 127
Sexual activity, forced, 115
Sexual behavior, 23, 50, 56, 80, 91
Sexual disorders
   aberrant behavior (paraphilias),
        66, 70-71
   arousal disorders, 67-68
   desire disorders, 66-67

Sexual disorders *(continued)*
   dysfunction, 65-66, 72, 155
   guidelines, 66
   orgasmic disorders, 68-69, 72
   painful intercourse, 69-70
   presenting complaints, 64-65
   response cycle, 65-66
Sexual harassment, 208
Sexual promiscuity, 95, 122
Sexuality, 15-16, 191, 197-198
Shame, 157
Shopping sprees, 23, 122
Sin, 104
Skin conditions, stress-related, 180
Sleep cycle, 58
Sleep disorders
   nightmare disorder, 61
   parasomnias versus dyssomnias, 59
   presenting complaints, 57-58
   primary hypersomnia, 60-61
   primary insomnia, 59-60
   sleep terror disorder, 62
   sleepwalking, 62-63
   symptoms, 58-59
Sleep disturbances. *See also*
     Nightmares
   and anxiety, 14, 17
   and head injury, 35
   and mood disorders, 20, 22
   and substance use, 51, 55
   and trauma, 44
Sleeping pills, 170
Sleepwalking, 62-63
Sluggishness, 54
Smoking, 180
Social phobia, 11-12, 97
Social situations, 11
Social skills, 162
Social workers, 133
Spatial perception, 34
Speaking in tongues, 32
Speech
   disorganized, 28
   fear of public, 8, 11-12
   and head injury, 35

Speech *(continued)*
impressionistic, 86
loud, 9
persuasive or threatening, 75
rambling, 17, 23, 84
sexual content, 127
slow, 54
speed, 9, 23
"we" versus "I," 47
Spirituality, 191
Spouse abuse, 127-129, 212
SSRIs, 24, 167
Stalking, 30
Startle response, 44, 127
Stealing, 115
Stimulants, 54
Stress. *See also* Trauma-related
disorders
and abuse, 126
and agoraphobia, 13
and eating disorders, 120, 122
and hypnosis, 180
and mood disorders, 18, 20-21
and psychotic disorders, 31
and sleep, 59
and substances, 59, 60
and suicide, 150
Structural family therapy, 160
Submissiveness, 99-100
Substances
abuse, 48-51, 53, 91, 115, 122
caffeine, 60
compulsive use, 51-52, 54
dependence, 49-50, 51-52, 53-55,
169-170
and pastoral role, 56-57
recommended reading, 188
and sexual disorders, 72
and sleep, 59, 60
and suicide, 150
symptoms of pathology, 49-51
tolerance, 51, 54
treatment programs, 176-178
types, 52-56
withdrawal, 51

Suicide
and confidentiality, 212
and maladaptive persons, 90-91
and medication, 166-167
predictors, 22, 149-150
Suspiciousness, 29-30, 77-78, 83
Swallowing, 9
Sweating, 9, 12, 51
during sleep, 61, 62

Tardive dyskinesia, 173
Tension, 9, 14
Testing, 146-149
Thinking
all-or-nothing, 92
disturbed, 14, 23, 36, 82
suicidal, 150
Threats, 75
Time, 56, 103
Time-limited groups, 162
Townsend, John, 193
Tranquilizers, 169
Transference, 152
Transvestic fetishism, 71
Trauma-related disorders. *See also*
Head injuries; Separation
anxiety disorder
abuse-related, 126
acute stress disorder, 45-46
DID, 46-48
guidelines, 48
presenting complaints, 41-42
PTSD, 43-44, 62
and sleep, 62
symptoms, 42-43
Travel, 13
Trembling, 9
Tremors, 51
Tricyclic antidepressants, 166-167

Unipolar disorder, 18
Unreality, 9, 12
Uppers, 54

Vaginismus, 69
Values, 134-135, 217-219
Venlafaxine, 168
Verbal abuse, 125
Vigilance, 44, 77
Violence, 95, 125, 127-129
Visions, 32
Visual-spatial perception, 34
Voices, 26, 47
Vomiting, 117, 121
Voyeurism, 71

Weakness, 14
Weapons, 115
Wedding, D., 158

Weight, 22, 119-120, 180
Westberg, Granger, 194
Withdrawal, 28, 53, 75-76, 178. *See
    also* Substances
Witnesses, 44
Women
    eating disorders, 120, 122
    personality disorders, 95, 101
    phobias, 9-10
    psychotic disorders, 31
    sexual disorders, 67, 68, 69-70
    uniqueness, 195, 196-197
Workaholics, 103
Worry, 9, 14, 60
Writing, in public, 11

Order Your Own Copy of
This Important Book for Your Personal Library!

THE PASTOR'S GUIDE TO PSYCHOLOGICAL DISORDERS AND TREATMENTS

_____ in hardbound at $49.95 (ISBN: 0-7890-0712-6)

_____ in softbound at $24.95 (ISBN: 0-7890-1111-5)

COST OF BOOKS _____

OUTSIDE USA/CANADA/
MEXICO: ADD 20% _____

POSTAGE & HANDLING _____
*(US: $3.00 for first book & $1.25
for each additional book)*
*Outside US: $4.75 for first book
& $1.75 for each additional book)*

SUBTOTAL _____

IN CANADA: ADD 7% GST _____

STATE TAX _____
*(NY, OH & MN residents, please
add appropriate local sales tax)*

FINAL TOTAL _____
*(If paying in Canadian funds,
convert using the current
exchange rate. UNESCO
coupons welcome.)*

☐ **BILL ME LATER:** ($5 service charge will be added)
(Bill-me option is good on US/Canada/Mexico orders only;
not good to jobbers, wholesalers, or subscription agencies.)

☐ Check here if billing address is different from
shipping address and attach purchase order and
billing address information.

Signature _____

☐ **PAYMENT ENCLOSED:** $ _____

☐ **PLEASE CHARGE TO MY CREDIT CARD.**

☐ Visa   ☐ MasterCard   ☐ AmEx   ☐ Discover
☐ Diner's Club

Account # _____

Exp. Date _____

Signature _____

Prices in US dollars and subject to change without notice.

NAME _____

INSTITUTION _____

ADDRESS _____

CITY _____

STATE/ZIP _____

COUNTRY _____ COUNTY (NY residents only) _____

TEL _____ FAX _____

E-MAIL _____

May we use your e-mail address for confirmations and other types of information? ☐ Yes   ☐ No

Order From Your Local Bookstore or Directly From
The Haworth Press, Inc.
10 Alice Street, Binghamton, New York 13904-1580 • USA
TELEPHONE: 1-800-HAWORTH (1-800-429-6784) / Outside US/Canada: (607) 722-5857
FAX: 1-800-895-0582 / Outside US/Canada: (607) 772-6362
E-mail: getinfo@haworthpressinc.com
PLEASE PHOTOCOPY THIS FORM FOR YOUR PERSONAL USE.

BOF96